THE MULTICAMPUS SYSTEM

THE
MULTICAMPUS
SYSTEM

Perspectives on Practice and Prospects

Edited by *Gerald H. Gaither*

WITH AN INTRODUCTION BY
Frank Bowen and Eugene C. Lee

STERLING, VIRGINIA

STYLUS PUBLISHING, LLC.

COPYRIGHT © 1999 STYLUS PUBLISHING

Published by STYLUS PUBLISHING, LLC.
22883 Quicksilver Drive
Sterling, VA 20166-2012

Distributed outside USA and Canada by:
Kogan Page
120 Pentonville Road
London N1 9JN
United Kingdom

Stylus is a registered trademark of Stylus Publishing, LLC.

Library of Congress Cataloging-in-Publication Data
The multicampus system: perspectives on practice and
   prospects/ edited by Gerald Gaither: with an introduction by
   Eugene C. Lee and Frank Bowen.—1st ed.
       p.   cm.
   Includes bibliographical references and index.
   ISBN 1-57922-016-9 (alk. paper)
     1. Public universities and colleges—United States—
Administration. 2. Education, Higher—United States. 3.
Educational change—United States. I. Gaither, Gerald H.
   LB2341.M77   1999
   378.73—dc21

                                                    98-40753
                                                    CIP

ISBN: 1-57922-016-9 (cloth)

Printed in USA on acid free paper.

CONTENTS

PART ONE: ROLE, SCOPE, MISSION, AND PURPOSE OF MULTICAMPUS SYSTEMS

PART FOUR: CHALLENGES TO FUTURE DEVELOPMENT:
FUTURE TRENDS AND IMPEDIMENTS

INTRODUCTION

Eugene C. Lee
Frank Bowen

*The internal organization of multicampus
systems closely resembles that described thirty
years ago, but the next three decades may see
dramatic change caused by demographic
shifts in age and ethnicity, technological
advance, problematic state fiscal support, and
increasing enrollments.*

Thirty years ago, we were invited to study the organization of multicampus universities. At that time, we noted that, although multicampus systems, generally, had a long history, the multicampus university, as we defined it, was a fairly recent development. A search of the literature in 1968 revealed almost no information about the internal governance of multicampus universities "despite their unquestioned and increasing importance on the educational scene" (*Multicampus University* 12). Our study was an attempt to fill that void.

Today, multicampus institutions have become the most prominent organizational form in American public higher education. A rich and growing literature on multicampus systems is starting to emerge, some written by contributors to this volume. There is even a National Association of System Heads. As a result, comparisons can begin to be drawn about the impact of political and social forces upon educational institutions, about the internal dynamics of campus-system relationships, and about a host of other factors. The essays in this collection address major problems and challenges now confronting these systems.

We appreciate the opportunity to revisit "multicampus universities" after an absence of nearly three decades. Since that time—aside from a short sequel in 1975 (*Managing Multicampus Universities*)—our interest has been largely sporadic and personal, rather than sustained and professional. We have had the opportunity to serve as consultants to several university systems, most interestingly, perhaps, the University of London, a complex congeries of schools, colleges, and institutes (*The University of London*). And to speak about multicampus systems at the University of Bologna, which has recently found itself a multicampus university after nearly 1,000 years! But we have not had the chance systematically to update our 1971 study. Nor do we do so here. Instead, we reflect briefly on how the systems described in this collection of essays contrast to, and compare with, the multicampus snapshot we reported in 1971.

The first of these essays, that by D. Bruce Johnstone, sets the stage with an excellent review of the contemporary scene of multicampus organizational form. The concluding, thought-provoking essay by Donald Langenberg looks into the twenty-first century and attempts to forecast some of the changes that will impact the higher education scene. Within these two "bookends," the other authors discuss particular programs and systems. We are pleased to contribute to this dialogue by venturing our perceptions of the continuity and change over the past thirty years. What has remained constant? What has changed?

Continuities

The world is a different place than it was thirty years ago. But have multicampus systems changed as much as the world around them? We doubt that they have. *Plus ça change, plus c'est la même chose.* As significant as are the changes discussed in the essays, much remains the same. There are similarities in the issues raised and conclusions drawn to those reported in *The Multicampus University* nearly thirty years ago. This comes not as a surprise but as a reminder of the enduring nature of the university. Clark Kerr reminds us that "Universities are among the oldest continuing institutions in Europe and the Americas" (*12 Systems* 158). In this historical context, a span of three decades is but an instant.

To underscore this point, the fundamental rationale for the multicampus university in 1999 remains the same as earlier reported: "to promote specialization, diversity, and cooperation— a division of labor and alternative approaches to education in a coordinated, intercampus context" (*Multicampus University*, 8–9). This rationale is implicitly repeated in virtually all of the essays, as the authors assess the effectiveness of the multicampus structure that has come to dominate public higher education.

The conclusion to be drawn from the essays is that much has been accomplished, but that the full potential of the multicampus system is far from being realized. In 1971, for example, we reported that "differential plans and programs have been nurtured and sustained in the multicampus framework . . . [these were] contained within a relatively narrow and traditional spectrum . . . few multicampus innovations exist" (*Multicampus University* 390). Burke, in his examination of twelve systems facing resource constraints in the early 1990s, sounds a similar note. He highlights important examples of effective systemwide activity, but finds that many decisions were left to the campuses, "which encourages institutional interests over collective needs." He concludes that the period "represented something less than the finest hour for university systems . . . few tried to enhance, much less transform, performance of their campuses through coordinated effort" (Burke, Ch. 3).

With respect to the division of labor of authority and responsibility between the campus and the system, the goal of achieving "creative tension" between the whole and its parts remains a continuing challenge. In 1971, we suggested that conditioning factors included the origins of the system (flagship or consolidated), its organization (segmental or comprehensive), and size (measured by the number of campuses). These continue to be critical in understanding the internal dynamics of the multicampus systems. To our restricted definition of a multicampus *university*, Johnstone (Ch. 1) adds further detail and breadth, for this collection of essays includes all multicampus *systems*, not just the nine we described. He states that, to the above factors, one must add "the great geographic, demographic, and economic variations in the several states . . . the differing levels and roles of private higher education and . . . the absence of any strong unifying federal role in American higher education."

University-state relations, as one would expect, remain a key theme in virtually all of the essays. In 1971, we noted that "the state government is inextricably involved in the governance of higher education . . . the governor is everywhere a key element in the multicampus university" (*Multicampus University* 384). Although, as we note below, state appropriations constitute a smaller share of total budgets in 1998 than they did earlier, the importance of the state is undiminished. As Boatright concludes: "Systems have political, rather than educational, roots, and their continued existence is a political balancing act" (Ch. 2). Pickens' (Ch. 8) description of "The California Experience" clearly illustrates this generalization: the state's segmented approach—writ large in constitution and statute—dominates any discussion of higher education, leading to an "iron grip of 'segmental thinking' on the minds of Californians." The state's importance may actually be increasing. Johnstone (Ch. 1) touches on the reason in mentioning a state-asserted "need for greater efficiency." In many states, higher education policy has recently tilted toward market concepts of competition and efficiency. These have led to structural change and intervention, especially in large systems—Illinois and New York, in particular.

Other essays highlight the continuing impact of legislative and gubernatorial influence on a state's colleges and universities. The importance of the multicampus system administration in this context is well-described by Boatright (Ch. 2) in his discussion of the external relations role of the systemwide administration, ideally "the conductor of a choir . . . someone who can provide for the system what no single campus would ever be permitted to provide: a sense of balance among competing colleges."

Change

Although much of multicampus system organization and practice has remained constant over the past thirty years, important changes have occurred. For the most part, these changes are the result of forces external to the systems, largely forces less overt than the crude, political intervention that makes headlines. Johnstone (Ch. 1) and Langenberg (Ch. 12) identify how demographic, technological and economic factors have shaped multicampus systems in the past. Donald Langenberg states that multicampus higher education systems are only one of many open systems in society, that they adapt to each other and to their more inclusive societal environment, and that they will continue to so adapt in the future. The emerging recognition of this need to adapt may well be the major change we found in reading the essays in this collection.

ORGANIZATIONAL ADAPTATION TO AN UNCERTAIN FUTURE

Thirty years ago, at the time of our original study, planning was, for the most part, driven by demographics. More students would knock on higher education's gates; and the multicampus systems were building new campuses so that gates would be open to receive them. A few of these new campuses were planned to be distinctive and "innovative"—Old Westbury in New York, Santa Cruz in California, perhaps Chicago Circle in Illinois—but most were not. In 1970, the tacit assumption was that the future would be much like the past, only more of it. In the late 1990s, by contrast, there appears to be little expectation among the writers of these essays that multicampus systems in 2030 will be simply a straight line extrapolation of today's. Several quote Aims McGuinness to the effect that multicampus systems will survive as instruments of state policy (e.g., Langenberg, Ch. 12). But most expect that significant change will be compelled largely by the logic of technological advance and uninspiring budgetary prospects. Burke (Ch. 3) quotes Michael Hooker, present chancellor of the University of North Carolina at Chapel Hill:

> We cannot continue simply to "muddle through," engage in "wishful thinking"; or assume a bigger state appropriation is a "divine right." We live in an era of fundamental social and economic restructuring in which all institutions must change in order to survive and compete.

Undoubtedly not all multicampus administrators are as concerned about the future as the authors of these essays. But some clearly are.

HEIGHTENED CONCERN ABOUT FINANCES

The essays reflect considerably greater anxiety over the financial future of higher education than we encountered earlier. Thirty years ago and now, annual system and campus budgets were and are high on priority lists. But the essays suggest a longer-term anxiety about finances than in 1970. Two fairly recent developments suggest the reasons for this anxiety. *First,* a breakdown of consensus on who is responsible for financing higher education is most evident in the dramatic increases in tuition in many states (Burke, Ch. 3). And equally evident is the extent of reliance on student debt financing, a policy shift that took place with little discussion or debate, and is not emphasized in the essays. *Second,* the competition for state funds has become more intense. Burke notes that for the six systems in his study, higher education's share of tax revenue fell by a minimum of 13 to a high of 36 percent. Layzell and Caruthers chart a national decline of 15 percent in state funds as a percentage of the operating revenues of public colleges and universities (Ch. 6). And others have expressed similar concern: "Like the federal government, state and local governments are increasingly allotting greater shares of their budgets to health and welfare programs" (*Commission on National Investment* 12). Health and welfare are only two of the major state services that have increasingly competed with higher education for state dollars. The public schools require support to meet the "baby boom echo" (Riley). And, because of "three strikes" legislation, corrections is becoming a strong competitor in many states. To compound the problem, several states have established constitutional limitations on state tax revenues, expenditures, or both, to place a ceiling on the pie to be divided among state agencies.

Admittedly, this somewhat free-floating concern is not specific to multicampus systems, but financial stringency has at least two specific implications for systems that it does not have for free-standing institutions. *First,* governors and legislatures are usually happy in good times to rely on systems to handle many managerial tasks, personnel matters, construction, and, particularly, allocation of funds to campuses. But when fiscal times are bad, systems are often seen as just another costly layer of administrative overhead, one that duplicates activities of state agencies and the individual campuses. At least in part for cited reasons of duplication and economy, multicampus systems in New Jersey and Illinois were abolished in recent years. In contrast to free-standing campuses, multicampus systems are particularly vulnerable because they are simply offices—there are no students, alumni, faculty, football teams, or ivied walls. *Second*, multicampus systems have a theoretical advantage over free-standing institutions in responding to fiscal stringency: They can moderate its programmatic impact on the system mission by selectively spreading fiscal pain across several campuses. In practice, however, and as we have noted above, Burke (Ch. 3) was unimpressed by the use that multicampus systems have made of their advantage.

TECHNOLOGY

In 1970, a hand-held calculator was a major purchase. Today, such a calculator could be a gift in a cereal box. Technology has already revolutionized research, and has had a major impact on college and university administration. Several of the essays make it clear that it is now having an emerging impact on instruction. Langenberg (Ch. 12) believes that multicampus systems will shortly feel the impact of new technology; geographic turf will be undercut; new competitors will appear, and already are appearing; and traditional, input measures of quality will be replaced. His concern is voiced by others who suggest that faculty now opposing instructional use of technology "may find themselves blindsided down the road by a much greater force that simply eliminates their institution altogether" (*Technology and Restructuring Roundtable* 12).

MISSING PIECE I: NEW CAMPUSES AND QUALITY CONTROL

There is little we observed thirty years ago that is not mentioned in the chapters to follow—budgeting, planning, government relations, governing boards, the administration, faculty, students. However, like Sherlock Holmes' dog that did not bark in the night, one topic of unquestioned importance is almost totally absent from the essays. In *The Multicampus University*, we described "the major achievement of the multicampus university [to be] the establishment of new campuses and the transformation of old ones" (416). In particular, we heard much about the role of the "flagship" campus in assuring quality control over faculty and academic programs at the new institutions.

In the present collection of essays, new campuses are rarely mentioned. Quality control is considered in discussions about the difficulty of assessing performance of students whose education has multiple sources, especially in distance learning (Langenberg, Ch. 12). And it seems implicit in discussions of performance budgeting (Norris, Ch. 5) and the descriptions of reorganizations in the Maricopa and Miami-Dade community college districts (Lukenbill, Ch. 10; Thor, Schober, and Helminski, Ch. 11). But quality control as an explicit, high priority concern of the multicampus systems seems to have faded as the emphasis on new campuses has declined.

MISSING PIECE II: COORDINATING AGENCIES

In 1970, multicampus systems saw themselves threatened by coordinating agencies—now the state higher education agencies—that states were interposing between the systems and state government. There was, we found, lack of "any clear understanding of the roles of the multicampus system and the coordinating agency or recognition of their unique relationships" (*Multicampus University* 384). Although Burke (Ch. 3) notes tensions between multicampus systems and campuses, relationships between the system and the state higher education agency are not discussed. Nothing in the other essays suggests that state higher education agencies are of great concern to the writers.

"PERFORMANCE BUDGETING" AND "STRATEGIC PLANNING"

In 1970, most multicampus systems were writing "master plans" and "five-year plans," and some were struggling with state-imposed Planning, Programming and Budgeting systems (PPB or PPBS). Since then, the words have changed. The authors of the planning and budgeting essays in the present collection use terms that are new since our earlier venture (Szutz, Ch. 4; Layzell and Caruthers, Ch. 6). Szutz writes that "Strategic planning . . . has been in vogue in higher education, at least as the term of choice, since the early 1980s." Layzell and Caruthers date performance budgeting from Tennessee's initiation of it in 1978. They note that what is new in the 1990s is the comprehensiveness of current state initiatives and the seriousness with which these are taken. The jury is still out on the South Carolina approach that would use performance measures for 100 percent of institutional budgets (Trombley).

Then—and now—we are skeptical about management fads, except as these encourage specific, relatively narrow actions (see Lukenbill, Ch. 10; and Thor, Schober, and Helminski, Ch. 11). The health and future of multicampus systems will be found in the broader context of state higher education policy. It is state policy that answers fundamental policy questions about which students will be educated, and where and what that education will be. Regardless of multicampus planning and budgeting procedures, these answers will still be found in state budgets, which "are policy declarations, explicit in the figures regardless of the words" (*Multicampus University* 248). We are skeptical about new "terms of choice" that are "in vogue." The giants of our day—Clark Kerr, William Friday, and David Henry, to name but three—lacked the advantages of today's sophisticated technological tools. But they were assuredly concerned about performance—about the effectiveness and efficiency of the multicampus systems under their stewardship. And they routinely "scanned the environment" in making system plans without suggesting that this was an innovation.

There is an important exception to our skepticism about new management fads—about whether different words have made any practical difference. The essays make it clear that the concept of assessment of outcomes is explicit in "performance budgeting" (Szutz, Ch. 4), and necessarily implicit in "strategic planning" (Norris, Ch. 5). The earlier "term of choice," PPB (or PPBS), probably faded because of both the inability (or unwillingness) of states and academic professionals to define outcomes and their inability to measure the extent to which outcomes were achieved. The wonders of technological advance may help in measurement, but the definitional problem is still with us (Johnstone, Ch. 1). The recent emphasis on "performance budgeting" seems a fair indication that states want to know what public money is buying, and that these persistent definitional and measurement problems will not go away. Almost uniquely, major multicampus systems have the intellectual resources to probe and possibly resolve these troublesome "outcome" problems.

Closing Thoughts

As we wrote in 1971, "the *organization* of higher education will not determine the place or future of the university in society . . . Indeed, our inability to understand the political and social context of organizational form has beclouded our understanding of the dynamics of university governance. . . . The organization of higher education is critical *in combination* with its environment" (*Multicampus University* 421–422). Our reading of the essays that follow is that changes in the environment—economic, demographic, political, and technological—over the past thirty years have been greater than changes within the systems themselves. But this will not continue. In many states, the intersection of increased competition for state funds with rising enrollments will require fundamental adaptation by multicampus systems. And systems in all states will face the challenges of rapidly changing technology.

Change there will be. But the public interest will also be served by continuity, the preservation of what is best in American higher education. The charge to the multicampus institution in the twenty-first century is to continue to seek the balance between these two forces of continuity and change. To return to our earlier theme:

> Organizational form affects the goals and values that control the life of the universities and colleges—singly and collectively—and will determine to a significant degree the response of these institutions to the more fundamental forces shaping higher education. (*Multicampus University*, 421–22).

A multicampus institution can be highly effective in addressing these "fundamental forces." Its underlying concept has been established—a system of governance one step removed from the politics of both state government and—let's admit it—its constituent campuses. Such a system is open to pressures for change from state government and the marketplace, and subject to countervailing forces to maintain the status quo from its campuses. In the twenty-first century, multicampus systems will, as they have in the past, be required to balance these forces. But over the next thirty years, they will be tested in a quite different societal and economic crucible than in the past. They will change, perhaps radically, but they will survive and prosper, for they are unique in both their intellectual resources and their capacity to be more than the sum of their parts.

PREFACE

Gerald H. Gaither

The modern American multicampus system of higher education came of age in the years following World War II. While such systems predated the war, they were rooted in the postwar premises of growth—burgeoning enrollments, increased resources, and more campuses, among others—which largely transformed the American higher education system. Before the World War II, for example, only 10 percent of Americans attended college, but this number jumped to 51 percent after the war. Before the war there were only twenty-five Carnegie I Research universities in the United States, but by 1956 when the G.I. Bill ended, there were 125 such institutions. The growth in faculty research efforts was aided by the creation of the National Science Foundation in 1950. The success of Russia's Sputnik space program, which launched the first artificial satellite of the earth in late 1957, also dramatized the nation's need for more and better university research and scientific graduates to meet the Russian challenge. This event is of particular interest here because, around the twin themes of the space race and/or the threat of an external adversary (e.g. Russia, and later Japan), coalesced many of the great postwar political forces and factors that stimulated the growth of modern higher education systems.

Appreciable sums of state and federal dollars began to find their way to college campuses. The states' share of higher education expenditures peaked at 57 percent in 1974. Formula funding began to emerge as a more equitable means to distribute such funds and resist the growing political clout of flagship and multicampus systems at the expense of smaller, less well organized and non-system affiliated institutions. Out of this amazing amalgam of enrollment growth, support for education, and desire for opportunity, the multicampus system model found fertile ground, if for no other reason than the need for a central governing authority to better coordinate these expanding pressures and needs.

By the time Eugene Lee and Frank Bowen published their initial work on *The Multicampus University* (1971), 40 percent of all students were attending institutions that were part of multicampus systems. Over one-fifth of all campuses were now part of these educational behemoths (xi). Four years later (1975), when Lee and Bowen issued their second volume, they found 25 percent of all students in public four-year colleges and universities in the United States in only nine multicampus systems (*Managing Multicampus Systems* 3).

While enrollments ebbed and flowed over the next two decades, the market share of students served by the multicampus model continued to expand. By 1993, Gade found that multicampus systems enrolled "well over half of America's college and university students" (*Four Multicampus Systems* viii). By 1997, The National Association of System Heads (NASH) reported a total of 50 public higher education systems in 38 states, enrolling "approximately three quarters" of all students found in public colleges and universities (NASH n.p.). The State and Land Grant Universities and community colleges—the so-called "people's colleges"—serve as the flagship or backbone for many of these public higher education systems. Within these institutions alone, a full 70 percent of our undergraduates receive their baccalaureate degree, according to the National Association of State Universities and Land Grant colleges (Foster 1).

Recent years have brought other far-reaching changes to higher education systems. The expanded growth and role of community colleges have helped transform the mission, role, and scope of American higher education systems. The California Community College System now enrolls over one million, two hundred-thousand students (1997), and the Maricopa Community College District serves over 200,000 students in its credit and noncredit programs. (Both systems are discussed later in these pages.) Other large community college systems throughout the United States have undergone far-reaching changes and have expanded their role as an alternative to the traditional multicampus model of senior-level institutions.

During the last half-century, then, multicampus systems have become the dominant model of public higher education in the United States. According to this author's calculations, approximately 80 percent of the students currently enrolled in two—and four—year public colleges and universities attend institutions that are part of a multicampus system. Yet, there is a dearth of publications on the subject while the multicampus structure threatens to consume all of public higher education. These systems and their leaders are being subjected to intense accountability pressures with high expectations of performance, but with little published information to guide them in their search for enlightened practices and policies. Because of the sheer size and visibility of these systems, and because they consume so many resources, systems and their heads are under constant scrutiny and criticism from external as well as internal constituencies. Consider the observations of Joseph Kauffman:

> I believe the system presidency [chancellor] is the least stable of higher education presidencies and often the least satisfying chief executive position. System presidents get caught between the often-ambiguous expectations of system boards and the tendency of the respective campuses to blame all ills on the system's administration. The board presses the system to take charge, while the campus chancellors [presidents] are pushed to defend maximum campus autonomy. Flagship campuses worry about having their institution's special missions and prestige compromised by loss of revenue and recognition, while other campuses demand equity and fairness in teaching loads and salary levels. Given the political nature of seeking legislative appropriations, system leaders are often disparaged as politicians rather than respected as educators. ("Supporting and Assessing the Presidency" 128).

[For purposes of clarity, it should be noted that the National Association of System Heads (NASH) reports that, of the 50 public higher education systems in 38 American states, system heads have the title "chancellor" in 25 systems, the title "president" in 16 systems, the title "executive director" in 6 systems, and the title "commissioner" in 3 systems.]

Peter Flawn, former president of the University of Texas at Austin (1979–1985), indicated that leading a major system or public university "may be the hardest job in the world." On a day-to-day basis, "you have to put up with 'jackass' regents, win-at-all-cost football coaches, and [a] fickle faculty" who "complains of weak leadership" but "does not want to be led"—all the while, managing an institution which may have an annual operating budget in excess of $500 million (Houston *Chronicle* 1990). Clearly, any chancellor or president who does not effectively shape and influence the actions of others in such a hostile environment will soon be mastered by it. Even so, it is difficult for anyone to stay in that kind of atmosphere for too long a time. It takes something out of the soul of even the most exemplary leader. It is a Faustian bargain: you really are giving up a lot to direct the actions of others under circumstances, conditions, and situations over which the senior executive often has little control but complete accountability for both failed and successful endeavors.

A challenge to higher education systems in the twenty-first century will be to ensure that such pressures do not discourage our best and brightest from assuming or retaining such leadership positions. The extended tenure (20 years) and leadership of a chancellor like Dr. Paul Elsner, described by Dr. Linda Thor and her coauthors, will be an unlikely feature of tomorrow's multicampus system. This volume, by author practitioners, several of whom have or have had tenure as chancellors/presidents, can serve as a valuable resource of practical information, ideas, advice, and policy options for such senior executives who daily face these pressures.

No comprehensive examination of multicampus systems has been conducted since the efforts of Eugene Lee and Frank Bowen in the early 1970s. Marian Gade and Terrence MacTaggart's contributions in the nineties are the most current efforts but neither author focuses in a pointed, extended way on the territory covered by this volume (*Four Systems; Restructuring*). Consequently, this monograph helps to fill a void in the existing literature. Furthermore, the challenges confronting multicampus systems today are not the same as those of three decades ago when first examined by Lee and Bowen. Both national and state commitments to higher education, which helped the multicampus model bloom in the aftermath of World War II, have eroded. The state's share of higher education expenditures, for example, had fallen to 45 percent in 1994, having peaked at 57 percent in 1974. The federal contribution—mostly in student work, grants, and loans—was at 12 percent in 1982 and is now lower than 9 percent. Similarly, federal research dollars have declined sharply in recent years. Congress authorized $763 million in FY 1993 for research funding; $651 million in FY 1994; $600 million in FY 1995; and $299 million for FY 1997.

And as Layzell and Caruthers point out in the pages that follow, state funds as a percentage of all operating revenues in public colleges and universities have, in general, declined since 1980, falling to 40 percent in FY 1995. Such erosion in state support brings a whole new meaning to the idea of "privatizing" higher education. All this is at a time when such public institutions face escalating demands from bypassed groups who now seek the same opportunities in future years that higher education systems have provided other Americans in the past. If today's participation rates are maintained, expected enrollments in 2015 are projected to be over 13 million students—some 3 million more than today. (Benjamin, "Looming Deficits" 16). And they will be quite different from today's students in terms of age, ethnicity, and goals. Poor and immigrant groups who dominate the population in states like Texas, Florida, California, and New York seem most likely to be adversely affected. The postwar promise and opportunity that began largely with the G.I. Bill and federal research funding, and found early fulfillment in these large public systems, has been challenged and eroded in recent decades by new agendas such as crime and prisons, the aged, and child and health care. More claimants on society's resources have shaped and influenced the notion of public higher education as a good for all of society.

Increases in tuition and fees seem inevitable, but any such increases challenge the very philosophy of the public benefit resulting from the broad access to higher education which characterized the organizational system model that flourished following World War II. The dimensions of the fiscal problem were further brought home recently by a report from the Commission on National Investment in Higher Education, which projected a funding shortfall of about $38 billion (in 1995 dollars) by 2015 for the higher education sector (Benjamin, "Looming Deficits" 16). Against this backdrop it must be asked if America's multiuniversity model will be able to meet the growing demands of the future, as it did in the postwar years. So, at the brink of the new millennium, multicampus systems stand embattled—and all of higher education does as well. How such systems are coping—and will cope—with today's problems and priorities requires a whole new response to the management of higher education and deserves renewed scrutiny about how these organizations can, and do, deal with their problems through system management practices.

Overview and Scope of the Monograph

This monograph is divided into four parts. Part I initially describes the functions of multicampus systems of higher education in the United States; considers their role, scope, mission, and purpose; identifies their common concerns and notes differences; and presents ideas for addressing their concerns, both at present and in the future. In addition it discusses how systems help manage external relationships such as legislative relations and fund raising, and budget and policy matters.

Part II of the monograph provides background discussion on major operational issues that will surface in individual situations discussed in the case studies that follow. How can the leaders and managers of multicampus systems cope with some of the operational challenges that confront them, now and in the years ahead? How should they respond to the increasingly uncertain and interconnected environments in which their organizations operate? How should, or have, these leaders responded to dwindling or unpredictable resources as well as new public expectations or formal mandates for account-ability and productivity? What should their organizations' missions be? How can they build on organizational strengths and take advantage of opportunities while minimizing organizational weaknesses and overcoming threats to their existence? How can they formulate desirable strategies and implement them effectively? These are the types of questions this section of the monograph addresses. Said differently, in this section there is an emphasis on strategic thinking and action. Strategic planning, budgeting, and productivity systems are useful only if they improve strategic thought and action.

Part III provides more detailed information, using case studies, about some distinct types of multicampus systems (segmented, urban, and two community college systems). This task is essential to recognizing and developing good ideas which are adaptable to comparable types of systems. We should emphasize here what it is we hope to gain from such case studies. In the study of large organiza-tions such as multicampus systems, as in the study of individual personalities and culture, the intensive investigation of a single case (or type of system, in this situ-ation) remains the best means for revealing the wholeness of the system in action. The case studies presented in Part III permit us to see how particular compo-nents—history, culture, mission, coordination, demographics, personalities, prob-lems, and opportunities—all participate in the character of the whole system, and how that distinctive character of the whole consists in the patterns of interrelations among the components. Generalized knowledge of these inner dynamics and of their relations to outside forces will help to eventually form the core of a science of multicampus functioning and the basis for planned change in comparable types of systems and situations. More than this, such case studies can immediately help to lift the discussion of higher education systems to a higher level of realism and sophistication, and thus make public policy planning more effective.

How are systems affected by competition or cooperation among campus-es? How do certain types of structures influence what is done at the campus level and the system level? How does the culture of the system, and the state, influence the system's operations? Do centralized systems work better than decentralized ones? In what areas of operation? These issues are at the heart of these case studies, and understanding them is necessary to strengthen the effectiveness of other multicampus structures.

The final section of the monograph—let it be confessed—demands a cer-tain amount of prescience. The aim of this section is to present an outlook about the future role of multicampus systems, and thus give a future context in which the problems and processes treated in earlier chapters may be viewed. Donald Langenberg, the Chancellor of the University of Maryland System, and the current President of the National Association of System Heads (NASH), provides an eloquent and visionary chapter about the future for this organizational model. Further, the general conceptions that have guided the organization of this volume will allow the reader to extrapolate a picture of multicampus systems, emphasizing the extent to which the great differences among, and complexities within, our multicampus systems depend upon forces in our larger society and culture.

Nearly thirty years ago Clark Kerr referred to the multicampus system as a "quasi-public utility" (*Multicampus University* xvi). As multicampus systems ostensibly become more like corporations and more bureaucratized, with more decisions made by non-campus based elements and with less faculty responsibility for decisions, the individuals who live and work in multicampus systems must be able to predict, or at least to explain, what will happen and plan to cope with it.

It has been our hope that we might contribute to the general advancement and knowledge of multicampus systems. Indeed, the principal purpose of this monograph is to update our understanding of the role, scope, mission, and purpose of multicampus systems in modern day academic life. Secondarily, with the current widespread calls for more accountability and "reinventing government," the differential impact of multicampus systems and their management—since they are so highly visible and generally large—may also offer guideposts to future approaches to managing other large public, nonprofit organizations which are also under attack. To achieve these purposes the authorship is somewhat unique. The chapter authors are persons who, in addition to their reputation as scholars, have *extensive experience* in managing or working with multicampus systems. They have, in this sense, distilled collective wisdom and experience about that which they write. The intended result is a volume of thorough examination and application of findings, which can be used by anyone with a serious interest in, and responsibility for, managing multicampus systems. It assumes, with due regard for the uniqueness of dispassionate scholarly examination, that management experience is important, that there is a general body of knowledge gained from experience that can be applied to such institutions and systems, and that enhanced skills and strategies can be learned from and communicated by such practitioners.

Concluding Observations

As Eugene Lee and Frank Bowen observe in their Introduction, the postwar college and university system—despite consolidation, greater market share, the emergence of the community college system, greater coordination and control, and hierarchical restructuring—has changed less than the world around it.

The central systems in research universities seem more frozen in time than is the case for comprehensive universities or community colleges. In the future, though, it will be critical for all college and university systems of whatever stripe to change, to restructure more rapidly to the world outside and to the bur-geoning technology and information revolution, particularly in our current shift from a capital or labor intensive economy to a knowledge economy. The col-lege and university system of the third millennium must adapt at the speed of demand, rather than respond to the largely invisible reflexes of the marketplace. Indeed, this seems to be the greatest challenge for the system model—to make such changes with only a modest increase in resources.

Such rapid change is a major challenge to system leadership who, like politicians, seem of necessity to be spending more of their time raising and protecting diminishing resources, as Joe Burke notes in his contribution, rather than providing vision, innovation, and academic leadership. Lee and Bowen have, at least indirectly, acknowledged the inherent conservatism and multiple constituencies of large, cumbersome, bureaucratic systems that seem unwill-ing to abandon anything, to restructure, and to reeducate themselves or seek more clarity of mission and purpose. The key to such system reforms may be to institute government financial incentives, which are what really influence system behavior and encourage priorities in new directions. It seems likely that the most successful future systems will be leaner and more agile, fueled by the information revolution and nurtured by alliances. This will require a commit-ment to collaboration, to inter-connectiveness—among campuses, students, and even, sometimes, competitors—and will change the system's shape and structure over and over again.

As Peter Drucker has astutely observed, the creation of wealth in the twen-ty first century will depend on leveraging knowledge. The key to success in that future is producing smarter, more educated people, a role that the early postwar university system, in conjunction with the G.I. Bill, fulfilled very well. Drucker suggests that the current university model—and by extension, the current sys-tem model—is doomed unless it changes and restructures more rapidly to adopt to the new knowledge economy. "In the next fifty years," he concluded recently, "schools will change more and more drastically than they have since they assumed their present form more than 300 years ago as they organized themselves around the printed book."

In the chapters that follow, contributors such as Bruce Johnstone, Donald Norris, and Donald Langenberg emphasize the importance and pervasiveness of change and the need for such restructuring, and they suggest that the system model of the future will have to adapt or anticipate at the speed of demand—

while perhaps being leaner. With approximately three-fourths of higher education enrollments now consolidated under the system model, it must become a producer of new and different strategies and structures if it wishes to both retain its integral and central role in our society as well as maintain market share. Current central system office concerns over such parochial issues as campus service areas and in-state vs. out-of-state tuition rates seem destined to become minor issues as both geographical and technological issues dissipate in the face of change. Reacting to the invisible reflexes of the marketplace will be too slow in a more rapidly changing world.

What are some of the challenges facing the college and university system model? It will need to educate and elevate the historically bypassed of all races in our emerging society—as the postwar system did so successfully through the vehicle of the G.I. Bill. The opportunity cost of not attending college in a knowledge society has never been greater. The creation of new wealth depends on a society leveraging such educated persons. A 5 percent annual increase in college graduates over five years , for example, will produce $26 billion dollars for the State of Texas, according to the State Comptroller's Office Texas, N.P. Another challenge is to produce enough of, and the right kind of, graduates needed in the growing information age. For example, American universities

are currently graduating only about 25,000 computer science majors each year—40 percent fewer than 10 years ago, and not enough to replace, much less feed, the growing demands of the information age. Such challenges are leading rapidly to redefining the tasks to be done and redefining the enterprises that perform those tasks. Is the system model up to such challenges, and will the enterprise be redefined from what it is to what it should be?

This new model will require risk taking strategies and different questions and responses, reminiscent of the system model's finest hours. For example, the G.I. Bill, mass higher education, and the expansion of the system and land grant model, in combination, helped democratize postwar higher education and develop an economy, based in part on the contribution of graduates of these systems, in which knowledge rather than labor become the crucial resource in our current society. As in the postwar period, the functional system in the third millennium will require great innovation, a new clarity of vision and mission, determination, perseverance, and a rededication to old-fashioned service goals. The following contributions should galvanize rather than dishearten the reader, not by suggesting ways to ameliorate these heady challenges, but by suggesting some ways to navigate through them.

ACKNOWLEDGEMENTS

Any book requires a great deal of effort and cooperation. I would like to thank the chapter authors for the contributions they made. All of the authors are busy professionals who are actively involved on a daily basis with the topics they discuss. As noted earlier, our intention was to select authors who are not only scholars but also experienced practitioners who have helped shape American higher education and have influenced our thinking about multicampus systems. These leaders have already left their mark on the academic landscape about which they write. This valuable experience has proved to be a double-edged sword. Such duties provide the insight lacking in nonpractitioners, but requires busy professionals to overextend themselves in many cases and challenges them to remain civil about the many interruptions and short deadlines imposed. However, I believe this volume can make a greater contribution to the profession because of these frontline experiences, and I hope it proves useful in the ongoing discussion about multicampus systems.

The idea for this book was originally conceived through several projects funded by the Fund for the Improvement of Postsecondary Education (FIPSE). The chapter on instructional productivity by Michael Middaugh was also supported indirectly by a FIPSE grant. I am particularly indebted to Drs. Frank Frankfort and Charles H. (Buddy) Karelis (the Director of FIPSE) for their support and resources used in the preparation of this monograph. The opinions expressed by this author and his colleagues are not necessarily those of FIPSE and no endorsement should be inferred. I would also like to acknowledge the contributions of John von Knorring, the publisher of Stylus Publishing, and his staff for their critical comments which made this a better volume. Also, two members of my staff, Iris Sawyer and Ginger Philips, made numerous sacrifices to help prepare this manuscript. Finally, this volume is dedicated to our colleagues Frank Bowen and Eugene Lee who graciously agreed to write the Introduction to this volume. All efforts on the topic of multicampus systems must begin with their scholarship on the subject. To all these people and agencies, I extend my heartfelt thanks.

Gerald H. Gaither
Editor

PART ONE

ROLE, SCOPE, MISSION, AND PURPOSE OF MULTICAMPUS SYSTEMS

As Kerr and Gade have observed, the trend in public higher education during the past forty years has been "toward consolidation and toward control" (*The Guardians* 115–118). The multicampus system has, in one sense, been the beneficiary of this trend toward consolidation in higher education, but constant friction arises over the demarcation concerning control: between campuses and the system; between internal and external constituencies; over freedom and control, liberty and license, and rights and responsibilities of the involved parties.

The multicampus system is constantly challenged, both externally and internally, by conflicting values and ideologies such that managing this enterprise is a constant balancing act.

As Lee and Bowen point out in their Introduction, more change has occurred external to the multicampus system than internal. However, any greater disconnect between traditional internal campus participatory processes and central offices, as a result of more centralization of authority (control), endangers the traditional balance between consensual and hierarchical management. A not so subtle long-term impact of the postwar centralized multicampus management model, then, could be a deterioration of the traditional sense of purpose and academic community that has characterized American higher education.

Any projected future actions concerning more consolidation and control raise a number of questions about growing faculty resistance to systems, lower campus morale, and ultimately lower productivity. Yet, as Joe Burke points out rather paradoxically, at a time when systems were being challenged internally, if not invited, through budget constraints to promote more coordination, control, and leadership, there was a decentralization of authority from central systems offices. Systems and campuses did not seriously examine or change their priorities or missions in the face of such fiscal austerity, tending to use across-the-board cuts instead. Other cases of the failure to provide leadership challenge one of the very purposes for such system models. But when decisions must be made quickly, as state governments assume greater control, traditional participatory processes at the campus level have not infrequently become, of necessity, causalities to haste and the hierarchical management style attributed to many central offices—the "consolidation" and "control" features outlined by Kerr and Gade.

Part One is devoted to helping the reader better understand these challenges in governance and other conflicting values and ideologies. Its three chapters focus on the disturbances caused by these conflicts over mission, money, serving multiple masters, and purpose; on maintaining a healthy tension between the striving factions; and on the various monopolists of truth and excellence that create these head-on struggles. Bruce Johnstone, Kevin Boatright, and Joe Burke, in their respective chapters, provide the reader a meaty examination of these issues and offer intelligent discussion about the trends.

I

MANAGEMENT AND LEADERSHIP CHALLENGES OF MULTICAMPUS SYSTEMS

D. Bruce Johnstone

This chapter describes the origins, variations, and functions of public multicampus systems, and suggests the future challenges for system heads and their governing boards.

Public multicampus systems, for the purpose of this chapter, are defined as groups of public institutions, each with its own mission, academic and other programs, internal governing policies and procedures, and chief executive officer (either "president" or "chancellor"), but governed by a single board with a systemwide chief executive officer, generally called "chancellor" or "president"—whichever term is not used for the campus heads. The system governing board selects the system head, sets broad system policies, allocates public resources among the constituent institutions (within whatever latitude is allowed by the state), appoints the campus heads (generally with the advice of the faculty, and sometimes of a separate campus lay board or council), and establishes, reaffirms, or alters the missions and programs of the constituent institutions.

The Origin and Variations of Multicampus Systems

Multicampus systems evolved according to several patterns, shaped by the different histories of public higher education in different states. Some systems (University of California) or parts of systems (University of Wisconsin) emerged from the states' original doctoral and/or land grant universities and the branches that were created by (or forced upon) them as state needs grew and population centers changed. Other systems or parts of systems (California State

University, the State System of Higher Education in Pennsylvania) were created from the states' former teachers colleges, now comprehensive colleges and universities, some of them doctoral-granting, that were once governed directly by state departments of education. Others, such as the University of Houston, the City University of New York, or the former regional systems of Illinois, emerged as distinctly regional or metropolitan systems.

These differing histories, compounded by (or in part a function of) the great geographic, demographic, and economic variations in the states, and further compounded by the differing levels and roles of private higher education and by the absence of any strong unifying federal role in American higher education, have led to great diversity in the form and structure of multicampus systems. Creswell, Graham, and more recently the *State Postsecondary Education Structures Handbook* by McGuinness, Epper, and Arredondo have attempted, with only some success, to construct simplifying typologies to describe these variations. Among the critical dimensions of these variations are the following:

COMPREHENSIVENESS

"Comprehensiveness" refers to the degree to which the system incorporates all of the state's public postsecondary institutions, as among:

1. the research university or universities (one—and sometimes more—of which may claim to be their state's "flagship") which award the Ph.D. and advanced professional degrees and carry out the Land Grant mission;

2. the so-called comprehensive colleges and universities, many of which are former teachers colleges that typically award baccalaureate and masters degrees;

3. various other public four-year colleges and universities that may have special professional missions or special histories, such as the historically or traditionally black colleges and universities;

4. community colleges, often with origins in local school districts or local county governments, that award various kinds of two-year associate degrees and that may also award postsecondary certificates and provide other industry- and firm-specific training; and

5. local and regional postsecondary, but noncollegiate, technical institutes, separate from the community colleges, that award certificates and diplomas of two or fewer years duration, with few if any of the credits being transferable to four-year degrees.

Comprehensiveness is most usefully descriptive as a position along a continuum. The most comprehensive systems, as in Wisconsin or Georgia, incorporate all of the state's colleges and universities, although usually still exclude the public noncollegiate technical institutes. The natural impetus toward comprehensiveness stems from the simple fact that some publicly accountable authority must allocate state tax resources, hire and fire system and campus heads, and determine, reinforce, or alter the system and the separate institutional missions. Multiple public systems and independently governed public institutions thus require some other, presumably "higher," body to allocate resources and determine missions among the systems or units of the state. In the absence of such authority vested in a lay governing or coordinating body, coordination and resource allocation authority will almost assuredly gravitate even more strongly either to the governor (perhaps via the state budget office) or to the legislature (principally to the legislative appropriations committees).

At the same time, parts of the public higher education enterprise of any state resist incorporation within a system. Many historic state flagships resist system governance out of a concern that their special status, national prestige, or special claim on state resources might be eroded. This may be true even when some of their branches (e.g. of the Universities of Michigan or Minnesota) clearly carry out a predominantly baccalaureate mission indistinguishable from that of their state's comprehensive colleges and universities (and sometimes, as with Penn State's two-year branches, very much like community colleges). In many cases, these flagships have had sufficient political clout in their state legislatures, often buttressed by state constitutional status, to resist incorporation into any larger multicampus system.

Community colleges, for different reasons, also often resist incorporation into a statewide system. They are inherently "local" in a way that even regional four-year colleges are not, extending frequently to local origin and local ownership. They may be legally required to take all applicants, making their enrollments and budgets especially volatile and subject to very local demographic and economic perturbations. And even when nominally incorporated into a larger multicampus system, the community colleges may (as in The State University of New York) have a vastly different—and far more autonomous—legal and budgetary status than the four-year institutions in the same system.

Finally, separate vocational-technical systems, where they exist, may resist being incorporated into a larger multicampus system, in part for the reason that any local unit resists being "taken over," but more specifically because of the very real fear of job loss and/or closure due to the mission overlap with local community colleges. In Georgia and Wisconsin, for example, the otherwise comprehensive multicampus university systems do not incorporate the technical institutes. Minnesota, by contrast, in 1996 combined three hitherto separate systems (four-year colleges, community colleges, and vocational-technical institutes) into the single State University System of Minnesota (but still excluded the flagship University of Minnesota and its branches).

Thus, some states have single comprehensive governing boards for all public higher education, including community colleges. Others, still quite comprehensive, may include all four-year college and university campuses, but not the community colleges. Still others may include all of the state's four-year campuses with the exception of the flagship research university. The less comprehensive systems may include states with regional systems, or sector systems—or, as in Michigan or Ohio, only a coordinating agency and no true system at all.

BRANCH AND MULTI-SITE CAMPUSES   — UAA

Campuses with branches or multiple sites can resemble "systems" in their governance by a single board, but they lack the separate-but-equal institutional heads and faculty governance bodies characteristic of a multicampus system in the meaning of this chapter. Campuses with multiple sites or branches generally have a single head who is also the head of the largest, or principal, campus, and generally also have a single faculty governance body that speak= for all of the faculty on matters of curriculum, academic policies, and faculty membership. Campuses with branches or multiple sites are characteristic of large flagship universities that formed these branches in response to demands for regional coverage and for strictly teaching (as opposed to research) institutions—often before the full flourishing of their states' comprehensive college and university systems. Multi-site institutions are also characteristic of large urban community colleges that have enrollments and geographic catchment areas that are too large, or political districts that are too disparate, to be served by a single site. In such cases, it is possible to have "system like" multi-site campuses within true multicampus systems.

SECTOR VARIATION OR HOMOGENEITY

Related to comprehensiveness is the degree to which the constituent institutions are limited to a single higher education sector—i.e., research universities, as in the University of California, or comprehensive colleges and universities, as in the Pennsylvania State College and University System—or embrace several sectors—research universities, comprehensive colleges, and sometimes two-year colleges, as in New York, Wisconsin, or Georgia. McGuinness ("Perspectives" 4) calls these variations "segmental" and "consolidated."

THE PRESENCE OR ABSENCE OF SEPARATE COORDINATING BOARDS *Texas*

In all but the comprehensive states (as described above, and even including some of them), there are usually separate boards, consisting of lay persons and sometimes state officials *ex officio*, that do not govern the public colleges and universities—that is, do not appoint chief executive officers, approve budgets, or make policy—but that coordinate the several public institutions or systems (and sometimes the private colleges and universities) through budgetary recommendations and academic program approval authority. The somewhat overlapping jurisdictions between coordinating and governing boards may confuse the outsider and sometimes the insider, and even some members of the boards themselves.

THE PRESENCE OR ABSENCE OF LOCAL, LIMITED-AUTHORITY *UNT* LAY BOARDS

Particularly in large systems, or in systems composed of campuses that once had their own governing boards, there may continue to be local campus boards with limited jurisdiction, such as searching for and recommending presidential candidates, dealing with property or physical plans, or simply maintaining liaison with the local business, civic, and political establishments. Clearly a potential exists for conflict between the jurisdictions of the local boards or councils and the true governing boards at the system level.

DEGREE OF SYSTEM AUTONOMY FROM STATE GOVERNMENT

This dimension of variation has to do with the degree to which state government (not the governing board or the central system administration) reaches into the operations of the institutions. The three principal arenas of potential intrusion are:

1. Fiscal. Highly intrusive, or controlling, states require extensive pre-audit approval before expenditures, constrain the movement of funds among expenditure purposes, and discourage or forbid the disposition of assets or the incurring of debt. More autonomous systems are more likely to be permitted to execute contracts and incur debt, and to be granted a single line of expenditure authority to be allocated among the campuses, with each campus in turn allocating funds among its several schools or faculties and other major spending units.

2. Personnel. Highly intrusive or controlling states retain employment and collective bargaining authority for all faculty and staff. More autonomous systems, through the authority of the governing boards, are their own employers and must assume all financial obligations and legal liabilities resulting therefrom.

3. Programmatic. Highly controlling states require approval of a separate coordinating board, and perhaps even of the governor (as in New York state) before a new degree program may be added, with such approval contingent upon demonstrations of demand, capacity, and sometimes the approval of other institutions or sectors. More autonomous systems require only the approval of the governing board for new academic programs.

DEGREE OF INSTITUTIONAL OR CAMPUS AUTONOMY FROM THE GOVERNING BOARD AND/OR CENTRAL SYSTEM ADMINISTRATION

To the individual campus, intrusion may be intrusion, and its origin—i.e., from the system governing board or the state budget office—may make little difference. Also, intrusion originating in state law or with the governor's office may take the form of demands placed upon the board or system head, only seeming to the campus to have originated with the board or system chancellor. It is also the case that institutional autonomy, while an abstraction that can seem to be an unqualified good to the campuses, may be quite qualified in application, depending on the observer and the kinds of decisions over which the campus may or may not have autonomy. For example, campus presidents may use "the system" as an excuse or a foil when decisions may be quite within their authority, but liable to be unpopular. (Indeed, a system head will often invite such obfuscation, or displacement to the central system office, of unpopular campus decisions.) Faculty, while wanting individual and generally departmental autonomy, frequently fear their own dean or president more than the more distant chancellor or governing board. Thus, faculty may perceive the authority of the system head—or even of the governor or legislature—as safer, particularly in matters having to do with job security, than the authority of their dean, provost, or president, and may thus resist any further devolution of authority from system to campus.

Nevertheless, there can be considerable variation in the degree to which a governing board and/or system head takes seriously the principles of decentralization and devolution of authority to the individual campus, particularly in matters of curriculum, appointments, and resource allocation. In general, conventional good management principles favor the maximum decentralization of decision-making authority consistent with overarching system goals and policies. The generally more conservative, business-oriented political climate of the late 1990s favors such devolution of authority from governing boards and system administrations to constituent campuses. At the same time, this political conservatism is also associated with considerable mistrust of the academy. As a consequence, governing boards and central system staff can easily go the other way: micro management, excessive demands for accountability, and other intrusions into the kinds of academic and curricular matters that ought to be left to campus authorities.

Public Higher Education Governance: The Principal Parties to, and Objects of, Authority

Another way of viewing and analyzing public multicampus systems is as the interplay of: (a) parties, whether individuals or corporate-like bodies, with different degrees of authority and/or influence; and (b) the objects of such decision-making authority or influence, all involving public higher education. Within this construct, the key parties are:

1. the multicampus governing board (or boards);
2. the multicampus system head (generally a chancellor or president);
3. the individual institutional, or campus, heads (presidents or chancellors);
4. the State Higher Education Executive Officer, or SHEEO—who may be a multicampus system head, but is more often the officer of the state coordinating board;
5. the governor and the key executive appointees (e.g., director of the budget);
6. key legislative leaders (may be heads of the respective bodies, such as speaker of the state house or senate, or the heads of the legislative higher education committees);
7. the systemwide elected faculty body and leader;
8. institutional or campus faculty bodies and leaders; or
9. the heads or chairs of individual campus boards or councils (if any).

These parties, often in combination, need to make the following critical decisions, all of which ultimately impact on the individual campuses and their academic programs:

1. What are the missions of the individual campuses—to be created or altered, or reaffirmed?

2. What are the academic programs and the organized research that will carry out these missions?

3. What are the curricula—i.e., what students are to know and be able to do—for these programs?

4. Who is to be appointed membership—both temporary and tenured—in the faculty?

5. Who is to be appointed to the position of system head and to other positions of system leadership?

6. Who is to be appointed to the positions of institutional or campus head and to other positions of campus leadership?

7. Who is to establish standards for the admission and graduation of students?

8. What students are to be admitted to study, by what criteria, and in what numbers?

Considered in this way, it should be clear that most of the decisions of everyday importance to the higher education enterprise are not made by system governing boards or system administrators, nor are they made even by campus heads. Rather, many decisions are made, or are at least influenced very substantially, by the faculty. This faculty influence and authority can be exercised through the formal institution-wide faculty senate. But considerably more influence is exercised over more of the core operations of the university by the "faculty" of separate schools (as in schools or faculties of arts and sciences, medicine, or law), departments, and programs, and by individual faculty in their largely autonomous professional capacities deciding what and how to teach and research.

The decisions that are generally the most contested and that have the most powerful impact are those dealing with curriculum, standards, and the allocation and reallocation of resources, and with the appointment, promotion, and granting of tenure to the faculty. From such decisions emerge the priorities of the institution and the ownership of academic judgments: who shall teach what and how, what shall be researched and how, and who is to establish the standards by which both students and scholars are to be judged? It is significant that, in this day of heightened suspicion and increased contestation generally, the stated goal of most state governments is to decentralize: to devolve decision-making to the campuses. At the same time—and in clear tension with the aforementioned principles of decentralization, delegation, and devolution—

many state governments, sometimes through state governing or coordinating boards, are demanding more institutional accountability, a greater say in matters of curriculum and academic standards, and a greater responsiveness by their faculties to the needs of business and industry. It is to this question—which decisions most properly belong to the system as opposed to the campus or to state government—that we now turn.

Functions of Public Multicampus Systems ⟨9⟩

Using principles set forth by Johnstone writing in 1992 and 1993 as president of the National Association of System Heads, the essential decisions of public multicampus systems—indeed their essential functions—are the following nine, in approximate order of the degree to which they belong to the system as opposed to the campuses or to the state government.

1. *To determine, reaffirm, and occasionally alter the missions of the system and of its constituent campuses.*

By "system mission" is meant something that should be greater than the sum of the missions of its constituent campuses. By "campus mission" is meant whether the campus will have, for example, a predominately research or teaching mission, and the kinds of resources, degree programs, and faculty expectations so called for. The system board cannot by declaration alone make a research university out of a comprehensive college. Ultimately, such a determination would usually take legislative and gubernatorial support, as well as the even more critical affirmation of the larger scholarly community. But it is the system board and the system head that must convey to the constituent campuses, particularly those not currently doctoral or research, whether they are to be encouraged, forbidden, or merely permitted to aspire to the presumed goal of many colleges, which is to become ever more oriented to the norms and configurations of the research university. Arguably, the need is for systems to resist further "research drift."

This determination (or alteration) will be made through campus and system strategic planning and the building of consensus among the key parties, including the campus heads, faculty bodies, individual governing board members, the governor and key legislative leaders, and other state leaders. Such planning and priority determination must consider the relative strengths of the individual campuses along with the overall coverage, within the system and the state as a whole (including the private sector and other public systems), of such critical public needs as access, basic and applied research, high quality affordable undergraduate education, and training in the advanced professions.

One of the great new challenges of systems as the millennium approaches is to devise ways of maintaining some beneficial order in the face of distance learning and other new instructional technologies that do not respect, or even recognize, regional, state, or national boundaries. Courses and even whole degrees are increasingly available electronically, through public, private, and proprietary deliverers, quite beyond the reach of state educational regulatory agencies. These courses can be received by student consumers who have no time for, and little interest in, such traditional academic amenities as campuses, classrooms, libraries, laboratories, or student life itself. Gordon Davies, former head of the Virginia coordinating board, wrote of the imminent end of "systems as cartels . . . dividing a state into regions and assigning each member institution a piece of the action" (A68). Future systems, if they are to be useful, will have to learn how to build alliances with other systems and with competing electronic providers.

2. *To appoint, nurture, evaluate, and if necessary remove the chief executive officer (chancellor or president) of the system and of the constituent campuses or institutions.*

This is the most important single function of any governing board of just about any organization or entity. At the same time, it requires of the system board a special sensitivity to the nature of academic governance and the absolute need for effective academic leadership to carry, at the system level, the support of the campus heads, and at the campus level the support of the faculty.

This role is most perplexing and oftentimes frustrating to the governing board members of large systems in which the system board, simply by the very large number of campus presidential appointments, must delegate the exceedingly time-consuming task of the frequent campus head searches to some combination of local faculty and lay persons, guided and certified as to the quality and integrity of the process by the system head and his/her officers. The purpose of the actual appointment being reserved to the system governing board, which will presumably act only on recommendation of the system head, is to allow the system head, in case of a bad or corrupted campus search, to abort the process and start the search anew.

3. *To advocate to the legislature, governor, and other key opinion leaders and patrons the needs of the system.*

The advocacy by the system head, system lobbyist, or even governing board chair cannot replace the advocacy of the separate campus presidents, faculty leaders, and local lay persons; after all, most politics is still local. However, it is critical for all advocates to sing from the same page. Ideally, this should be for a system budget that is realistic, given state resources and competing needs, yet is still "aspirational" and a "reach" for the governor and legislature. If the campuses are allowed to advocate individually for only their own budgets, the function of the system to allocate state tax dollars fairly and appropriately among the respective campuses will be lost; and campuses forced to engage a zero sum battle in which the campuses with the most legislative clout—perhaps the ones in the home districts of the most influential legislators—are bound to win. At the same time, to give the campuses something more concrete for which to advocate, and the individual legislators something to bring home to their constituents, it is appropriate for local campuses to advocate for special campus-specific appropriations, such as capital projects or board-approved single campus programs.

4. *To advocate to the constituent campuses the needs of the state.*

At the same time that the system advocates on behalf of the institutions to the governor and legislature, the system must advocate to the institutions on behalf of certain state needs and perspectives that may not otherwise hold high priority with faculty and campus presidents. These may be needs such as accessibility, or racial and gender diversity, to which some faculty may give lip service but believe to be mainly the responsibility of some other campus. Or, the state need may be less politically controversial, but merely a burden or distraction—like public service—that the faculty (usually correctly) perceive will take them away from the teaching and scholarship for which they were hired and will be rewarded. In such a case, the governing board must insist (one must hope in full knowledge of the opportunity costs involved) that resources be allocated, and faculty efforts be rewarded, in such a way as to make, say, contributions to state economic development or public health needs the object of real faculty time and attention.

The more difficult role for both the board and the head of the multicampus system is to convey the values and priorities of the government (and the larger public that the government supposedly represents) when these values are not compatible with, nor welcomed within, the prevailing values of the academy. This is where the role of the governing board and head of a public multicampus system diverges most from the role of a governing board of a single private institution. The latter kind of board can insist on measures of accountability and long-run fiscal prudence that may seem less than fully sympathetic to the faculty—but these postures are still imposed with only the long-run interests of that college or university in mind. On the other hand, the governing board of a public multicampus system and its appointed system head also need to defend the campus from the short-term, sometimes thoughtless and shortsighted political noise that may emanate from the legislature—and even at times from the governor who appointed the board. But they cannot ignore the genuine, thoughtful expression of a particular ideology or set of priorities clearly sought by an appointing governor and/or an approving legislature, even when these are different, or less generous to the established academy than those that may have operated in the past.

In this regard, probably the most difficult "state need" to convey to campuses is the need for greater efficiency. The natural trajectory of colleges and universities is to spend all that is available, and to believe not only that it was spent well, but that even more could have been spent, with even greater (although largely immeasurable) benefits. At the same time, public higher education is particularly vulnerable to budget cutting for three reasons: (1) the other possible sources of revenue, such as tuition and private giving, that are not available to other competing state agencies; (2) the relative political ease of imposing a single very large cut on the public multicampus system, allowing the governing board and system head to take most of the heat for where the actual damage may fall; and (3) the difficulty of demonstrating conclusively (at least to the satisfaction of the governor and legislature) the real damage done by budget cuts that may leave the university weakened but still able to teach the same number of students. Consequently, the system head and governing board must be prepared to advocate strongly for the resource needs of the system, even while working to facilitate efficiencies and difficult reallocations throughout the system.

It falls to the system head to broker and translate these sometimes differing perceptions and values between the governing board and its political base, and the campuses, further splintered by differences among campus heads, the faculty, and the students, and sometimes even further by different campus sectors. While the system head clearly serves the governing board, he or she must also be able to educate the board in the traditions of the academy, the purposes of public higher education, and the functions served by governing procedures that are almost bound to seem dysfunctional to most lay persons. The public multicampus university system concept is at its best when this natural tension between the traditions and priorities of the academy and those of government are in a constructive balance, with the governing board, and especially the system head, tipping in the direction to best serve the very long range public interest.

5. *To allocate operating and capital resources and missions to the respective constituent institutions and missions.*

Some system or formula, or at least set of principles, must be employed to allocate the state's tax resources among the constituent institutions and missions. The formula may be simple and largely incremental (that is, beginning from the previous year and only examining or justifying the additions). It may be based only on simple measures of workload—i.e. students and/or course credits taught. Or it may be based on some measures of performance or outcomes. The system may give a lot, or very little, room for gubernatorial or legislative manipulation. But some authority is going to allocate at least the state tax dollars, and the less involved the system governing board and head, the more

involved must be either the governor or the legislature. One of the principal
rationales for a system is that governing boards and academic system heads are
probably better entrusted with this critical function than are state budget officers and legislative committee staffs.

A critical system function that is inextricably tied to the allocation of state tax
dollars is the establishment of a tuition policy and/or the actual tuition rates for the
constituent campuses. These may seem to be quite different policy decisions, and
indeed they may be in the very short run. However, the establishment of tuition
is so politically volatile—both to the students and their parents and to the governor and the legislature—that any delegation of this authority to chancellors or
presidents will ultimately come back to the governing board.

Furthermore, any policy to differentiate tuition among the different institutions or sectors of a system will affect—or be affected by—the underlying allocation of tax resources among these institutions or sectors. This is because the
capacity of a public institution to raise tuition is highly dependent upon the socioeconomic makeup and the related academic selectivity of the student body.
Campuses or institutions that attract a traditional-age, academically able, high
socioeconomic status applicant pool can charge much higher tuition than institutions with nontraditional students or students from lower socioeconomic status
families. Thus, a decision to allocate equivalent tax revenues to two campuses differing substantially in their ability to raise tuition revenue, and then to charge, or
to allow to be charged, higher tuition in the campus that has the higher socioeconomic applicant pool, is to make a policy decision that a public institution can
spend more if it attracts a more upscale student body. This is a contestable, but by
no means an indefensible, policy. Among other points in favor of market-sensi-
tive tuition for public colleges is that it may encourage them to become more
attractive generally, for example by offering better teaching and better programs.
But it is a policy that only a governing board or state government itself can make.
And the tuition policy—for example, whether or not to charge differential tuition,
and if so on what basis—must be made in cognizance of the reasons for allocating base state tax funds differentially among the system's constituent institutions.

6. *To provide liaison between the executive and legislative offices of state government and the member campuses.*

This function is in part a service to government, both to the legislature and
to the many state agencies and offices that may have questions for the several
campuses of a system. It is also a service to the campuses, which can be shield-
ed from the almost insatiable demands of executive and legislative staff for
answers and information. With the system office playing a coordinating role,
the governor and the legislature are more likely to get information drawn con-

sistently, measuring the same thing. The campuses are saved not only some time, but also the awkwardness and occasional embarrassment of providing information to the same inquiry with different interpretations and sometimes very different levels of thoroughness and candor.

7. *To mediate disputes over programs and missions among constituent institutions.* There are three common inter-campus disputes. The first involves new program proposals that duplicate existing programs at another campus. The proposing campus is likely to say that its program is actually different, or that it serves a distinctly local need unmet by the other campus, or simply that the demand is considerable and that it ought to be allowed to compete. The campus perceiving its academic territory encroached upon is likely to claim not only damage to its program, but also a waste of taxpayer dollars.

A second common dispute is over the acceptance of students by a campus that hitherto would not have accepted them. Moving down the "academic food chain" is usually precipitated by declining applications or acceptances at the "offending" campus, which then maintains its enrollments (and presumably its state resources) by lowering its traditional standards and accepting students that it would not hitherto have admitted. The aggrieved campus is the one normally less selective in its admissions standards; it will typically claim that the lowered standards are not only unfair, but inappropriate: that the student attracted to the hitherto more selective campus will be served less well. Frequently, the encroachment happens between sectors, as when a research university begins accepting students that traditionally would have enrolled at a comprehensive college, or a comprehensive college accepts students that traditionally were acceptable only to the community college.

A third dispute may involve the encroachment of a traditional comprehensive college or university on the turf of the research university. The natural drift in American colleges and universities is in the direction of the research university. This direction includes a greater orientation to research and graduate instruction, a more traditionally prepared (and predominantly upper middle class) student body, and greater expectations for scholarship and grant production from the faculty. While the system can usually limit encroachment into the doctoral or other advanced professional programs, and can deny the richer funding that generally accompanies a doctoral mission, it is nearly impossible—and would probably be undesirable anyway—to discourage the faculty of a comprehensive institution from competing for research grants and the peer recognition that comes from quality scholarship. And an aggressive comprehensive institution with some ambitious and talented faculty, sharing the same metropolitan region with a research university, can also seem to be encroaching into academic and service realms that the research university may think more properly belong to it.

8. *To foster cooperation among campuses, which can both cut costs and enlarge options for students.*

Examples of such ventures include:

a) provision of campus legal services, information systems, financial assistance and loan servicing, purchasing agreements, statewide recruitment, and overseas programs;

b) articulation agreements and joint admission programs between two- and four-year campuses that guarantee admission to the senior institution after satisfactory performance at the two-year college;

c) systemwide general education requirements that facilitate transfer with minimal credit loss;

d) collaborative multicampus proposals in response to major research and training requests for proposals (RFPs);

e) joint purchasing, where a large order can leverage lower unit prices, or where the costs of expensive and specialized infrastructure, such as satellites, transponders, or fiber connectivity can be spread over many campuses.

It is not necessary for all of the constituent campuses to be part of every cooperative activity or consolidation of functions. Some might be large enough to obtain most possible economies of scale on their own. Others may have needs that are too specialized. Still others might have alternative partners: for example, within a region, even in combination with colleges or universities outside of the system. Nor is it necessary for consolidated services to be centralized; frequently, member campuses can serve as the lead campus, or service provider, for different systemwide operations. In fact, a rule of thumb proposed by Terrence MacTaggert, who has headed both the Minnesota and Maine systems, is that "[t]he presumption should always be in favor of decentralization to the individual campuses or units" (215). But a system board and a central system administration should serve as the goad, facilitator, and broker to provide campuses with the greater efficiency and enriched opportunities that can come from the greater critical mass of system activity.

9. *To audit and otherwise assess the stewardship of resources, including the assessment of academic programs.*

This is a period of intense interest in performance assessment, originating partly in a search for programs and activities to cut or downsize, exacerbated by a general public perception that most colleges and universities are profligate, and further encouraged by the defensive resistance of so many faculty to the call for evidence of outcomes. But this is a perfect role for the multicampus system, bridging, as it does (or should): (a) the demands of parents and students for indicia of quality; (b) the legitimate need of the public for an accounting of how their taxes are being spent; (c) the frequently exaggerated, but strongly felt and not-to-be-ignored, feelings of governors and legislators that the academy is full of waste; (d) the fact that the outputs of colleges and universities are multiple and hard to measure, at the very least; and (e) the feelings of faculty and presidents that the academy is misunderstood and an easy target for political demagogy.

This bridging is not an easy task. The general public—or at least parents whose children are potential students at public multicampus systems—want affordability and quality. "Affordability" means tuition that is manageable—that will force neither a significant reduction in current family consumption nor excessive student indebtedness. "Quality" often means prestige, which in turn is reflected by the selectivity or academic preparedness of the entering students. Quality in this sense is most easily assessed by the kinds of measures used by the popular magazines in their rankings of "top colleges." These are dominated by average entering SAT scores, high school rank in class, and average time-to-degree—all correlating overwhelmingly with socioeconomic class and the academic preparedness of the entering freshmen class and having little to do with the college's or university's contribution to student learning. In the meantime, state governments are looking for measures of efficiency and productivity and finding their indicators in time-to-degree, student-faculty ratios, teaching loads, and the generation of other-than-tax revenues.

Presidents and faculty are sensitive about the misuse of simplistic performance measures by students, journalists, and politicians alike. But they often have little to offer as alternative indicators, other than protestations about the difficulty of measuring what they do—protestations, however valid, that often sound limp, self-serving, and even arrogant. So it may be up to the system head to resist the heavy-handed, sometimes misleading and even invalid measures of quality and output, while at the same time urging upon faculty and campus leaders both the validity and the inevitability of some kinds of performance measures.

Management and Leadership Challenges for Multicampus Systems

The above description of the functions of multicampus systems presumes some continuity in the basic patterns of governance, finance, and curriculum that have guided public higher education—indeed, all of higher education—in the last half of the twentieth century. Such patterns include, for example, the delivery of most undergraduate instruction didactically, by lecture and professor-led discussion, in units known as "courses" of a given duration, usually extending 14 or 15 weeks. Degrees are granted after an accumulation of courses, allowing easy "stop outs" and the frequent prolonging of the time to degree, as well as permitting easy transfer between institutions. Legal authority for all decisions in both the public and the private sectors is held by an outside governing board, patterned after the traditions of lay governance borrowed from Scottish, Dutch, and Irish sources by the early American Colonial colleges. However, traditions of academic governance place de facto responsibility for curriculum, instructional methodology, and key decisions on appointments and promotions in the hands of the faculty.

Many influential leaders—politicians, business and civic leaders, and many within the academy, including both faculty and administrators—believe that these patterns must be fundamentally changed. Universities and colleges (especially public ones), according to this view, must radically restructure. Tenure must go, at least in all but a few of the most scholarly institutions. Most noninstructional services, according to this view, should be out-sourced or otherwise privatized. Faculty at all institutions must teach much more and much better— a fundamental change in professional workstyle—and spend less time trying to gain disciplinary recognition and playing at academic governance (that is, getting in the way of good, decisive management). Institutions should teach what is demanded by students and employers, not what the faculty is comfortable teaching. If students (or whoever is paying the bills) are more satisfied with what can be downloaded from Internet deliverers in self-paced instructional modules, then this is the direction that public higher education must go in—or lose out to institutions, public or private, that will. Most importantly, according to this view, higher education systems and their leadership will have to either facilitate this radical change or stand in the way of progress and become part of the problem, to be radically altered or done away with.

However, if the current and familiar patterns of higher education are to continue into the foreseeable future, as this author ("Patterns of Finance") believes they will, then systems as described in this chapter will survive, even though the political road may be rough. System boards and system heads will take much of the blame from those who are deeply unhappy about the course of American higher education and presume it to be profligate, insufficiently oriented to the undergraduate or to teaching, insufficiently rigorous in standards of both entry and exit, and slow to adapt to new needs and new technologies.

But these charges, while containing important elements of truth, are both overstated and tired. Some of the unhappiness comes from ignorance or misunderstanding: a failure to appreciate how dramatically so many institutions have changed over the last decade, or how overwhelmingly oriented most (not all) faculty at most (not all) institutions are to teaching rather than to research. Much of the unhappiness also stems from the dilemma of fundamental yet conflicting social and political expectations placed upon public higher education: access and opportunity, yet with high standards; great teaching and a student orientation, yet a recognition that many parents and students, just like many faculty, are looking mainly for scholarly prestige; a reverence for the liberal arts and learning for its own sake, yet an acknowledgment that most of the public is seeking practical and vocational ends from their higher educational studies.

In this more conservative view, the objectives of public higher education, for all the criticism, and for whatever restructuring will take place over time, will continue to be both multiple and exceedingly hard to measure. Universities will continue to be both repositories of culture and tradition as well as servants of change and bearers of social and political criticism. The most productive faculty will continue to be so because they operate in a context of freedom and professional autonomy: the very context that inevitably allows a few to be obstinately unproductive.

In this context—a vision of the future not fundamentally different from the present, and quite contrary to those who see, and may even wish for, the end of the university as we have known it—the challenge to system leadership is to defend the fundamentals of the academy while continuing to press for the incremental changes that will make a difference over time. But there is no single right vision, any more than there is a single reform agenda. Leadership needs to take the system where it will not necessarily go on its natural trajectory. For some institutions within some systems, this need may be to raise the standard of scholarship, to award tenure more parsimoniously, and to encourage a more aggressive faculty entrepreneurship. For other institutions and other systems, the need may be to provide a counterpressure against these very propensities: to turn faculty away from a preoccupation with research and a search for scholarly prestige, and more toward students and one's own institution.

Leadership needs to counter the inherent tendencies toward administrative aggrandizement. Leadership needs to attend to those faculty, however few, who give the professorate a bad name and jeopardize both faculty governance and the principle of academic freedom. But in this admittedly conservative view, the greatest single challenge to the leadership of public higher education may be to counter the view that all public colleges and universities need dramatic, truly fundamental, change, without becoming captive to the status quo or losing credibility with governors, legislators, and governing board members. This is a role best played in the future, as in the recent past, by multicampus systems, properly led.

2

MANY VOICES, ONE CHOIR

Managing External Affairs

Kevin J. Boatright

Multicampus systems continue to be useful for communication and a greater sense of balance between public higher education and government. The relationship between the system and its campuses is changing, however, from that of ventiloquist to that of high-value service provider.

The "Constant Conversation"

When he wasn't talking about baseball, or Renaissance literature, or his beloved Yale, the late Bart Giamatti was a philosopher of higher education. In this "free and ordered space," which is how he described the academy, there is a "constant conversation" going on. It occurs, he wrote, "between young and old, between students, among faculty; between faculty and students; a conversation between past and present, a conversation the culture has with itself, on behalf of the country" (24). This helps explain why American colleges and universities are what they are: awe-inspiring temples to the search for truth, set amidst roaring, unruly marketplaces of haggling, blather, and surmise. The conversation Giamatti described is how we settle the differences, how we come to distinguish sense from nonsense, and how we conduct the business of teaching and learning.

Encouraging, managing, and (sometimes) refereeing that conversation is at the heart of the multicampus system external affairs mission. In this respect, little has changed since the publication of Lee and Bowen's landmark study, *The Multicampus University*, in 1971. Whether such a mission is still viable today is a question that remains in search of an answer.

PARK BENCH DEBATES

A Giamatti-style conversation is going on right now in every state. It involves a professor and a politician, each squirming uneasily on a bench that overlooks the quadrangle. As they talk about the college and what it means to each of them, a heated argument ensues.

In its search for truth and quality, says the professor, the college ought to be free to add every imaginable academic program. Never mind that another state college, 50 miles away, wants to do the same thing. The state should simply pay for this growth, and be grateful for the privilege, argues the professor. At the same time, he says, the state could further ensure quality, and the search for truth, by permitting higher admissions standards and providing regular faculty sabbaticals in exotic locales. Smaller classes and substantial annual pay increases for the staff would also be a refreshing change, and would be consistent with the college's selfless, relentless urge to rise a notch in the annual national magazine ratings.

The politician listens patiently to the professor, all the while calculating in his head the cost to taxpayers of the professor's generous pension plan. As they sit together on the bench, watching the sunlight shimmer on the dappled ivy, the politician responds that the state can't afford and doesn't need the very same programs at every campus. Economic conditions make big pay increases unthinkable, and politically untenable. Further, higher standards and smaller classes would upset constituents. They pay their taxes and they expect their children to get a degree, maybe even an education. So forget about sabbaticals spent anywhere but in a dimly lit study carrel, because professors don't teach enough as it is. Also, any degree program that isn't redeemable for a job the day after graduation should be reevaluated, perhaps by a special joint committee of the legislature. And constituents aren't too keen about the class being offered in "Trans-Gender Social and Political Perspectives on Post-Capitalist Amerika." The loonies who insist on teaching that stuff are going to regret it come budget time. Yessiree Bob.

Giamatti said the conversation was constant. He didn't say it would always be dignified, or logical, or even civil.

PARTNER, BROKER, AND BUFFER

As this argument swirls back and forth on the bench, with rising irritation and loathing on both sides, an anonymous-looking figure in a modest gray suit comes strolling by. After listening to the bickering for a moment, and after an exchange of pleasantries, the figure sits down and settles into the no-man's-land between the professor and the politician. Neither has invited her to sit down, but neither asks her to leave. Their argument resumes, volleying back and forth between the poles of unlimited growth ("the search for truth") and unlimited restraint ("we won't pay for it").

The anonymous figure listens a minute longer, clears her throat, and then begins to talk. Turning to the politician, for example, she suggests that academic freedom is a very good thing. Squelching it would also surely strangle an economic golden goose, and we wouldn't want that. To the professor, she suggests that academic planning and the pooling of resources with those of other colleges makes good sense. The alternative is for all of the colleges to add new, marginal programs that none of them can truly afford to sustain, and we wouldn't want that.

To the politician, she says "here's what the professor needs from you in order to succeed." To the professor, she says "here's what the state really needs from you, and can afford to provide." Frankly, neither the politician nor the professor much cares for the anonymous-looking figure in the modest gray suit. She is, after all, not quite a politician but not quite a professor. Gradually, however, she becomes useful to both of them. After a decade or two, both come to agree that having her sit between them on the bench has the effect of lowering their blood pressure (as well as the decibel level). The uninvited guest is certainly an advocate for the needs of the college. At the same time, she is also an advocate for the needs of the state. Her role between the two has evolved into that of interpreter, partner, broker, and buffer, so that their "constant conversation" can continue without either the professor or the politician resorting to violence. And, no small feat, all have agreed to at least stay seated together on the bench, even when the three-way conversation grows heated, or frigid, or eerily silent.

Maintaining the Balance

It is possible to describe the multicampus system external affairs in quite complex ways, such as with affinity charts, fishbone diagrams, and extended narratives. It may help, however, to think of the external affairs function of a system as it's described in this allegory: as the anonymous figure imposed precariously in the often-hostile space between the campus and the government. The system is thus positioned both to facilitate the conversation and to moderate the worst excesses of each participant.

Imagine there are as many benches as there are state colleges, each of them containing the inflammatory potential for unlimited expansion and unlimited constraint. In the arena of external affairs, the goal of the multicampus system is to coordinate these many conversations as an honest, if often unloved, mediator. With the system in the middle, recognizing and communicating what both parties need in order to function, the result can be the access and efficiency that the state demands and the freedom and resources that the university requires. When neither party gets everything, and both parties get something, the ultimate beneficiaries are usually the students, the taxpayers, and the state.

It is the state's bench, after all, but it's not worth much without a professor willing to sit at the opposite end. Balance is everything, and the system helps maintain that balance. This, at least, is one historic rationale for the multicampus system: it gives politicians one ear in which to scream when public priorities are not being well served. And it gives public universities one relatively united voice with which to badger politicians concerning budgets, regulations, academic freedom, and a host of other issues.

Created during an era of vast and costly expansion, systems provided a politically useful way to manage that expansion while ensuring a mutually acceptable balance of access and quality. Indeed, "The ability of a group of campuses to communicate with the governor and the legislature through a single spokesman" was early on described as being "close to the core of any working definition of a multicampus university" (Lee and Bowen, *Multicampus University* 341). That definition retains its validity today.

SYSTEMS AS POLITICAL CREATIONS

Far from having simply stumbled upon a park bench conversation, systems came into being as convenient structures for heading off wasteful political warfare on behalf of competing campuses. Systems have political, rather than educational, roots, and their continued existence is a political balancing act. Indeed, it has been argued that "multicampus systems were often constructed purposely to create coalitions among regions in order to compete in the state political process," and that "states will continue to turn to systems as means to manage regional economic and political imbalance and to sustain political coalitions" (McGuinness, "Model" 208).

Wisconsin provides an example of this. The 1971 merger that created the present University of Wisconsin System combined a group of four largely urban campuses in the populous east with a group of nine rural/small-city campuses in the less populous west and north. In Wisconsin, as elsewhere, the resulting "geographical diversity [was] an obvious political benefit" (Lee and Bowen, *Multicampus University* 341), in that all factions in the state acquired a vested interest in the one system's welfare.

As a result, politicians are less able than they might otherwise have been to hold individual campuses hostage for unrelated political gain. It also ensures that university-related economic and educational benefits are distributed statewide. Having statewide, rather than regional, scope for advocacy purposes also works to the advantage of the system. A flagship campus may have alumni in every community in the state, but that is less valuable politically than the presence of system campuses in all quarters of the same state, busily functioning year-round as centers of economic development, cultural events, athletic prowess, and education. It may also double the number of alumni who have a stake in some part of "their" system, though it has been noted, accurately, that "Alumni loyalties run to ivy-covered halls, not to the system administration building" (Lee and Bowen, *Multicampus University* 345).

In politics, then, a multicampus system functions within the American tradition of checks and balances. In addition to continuing (and containing) the conversation between freedom and restraint, a system spreads the academic benefits of access statewide while giving the state a tangible presence in places that might otherwise feel neglected.

SYSTEMS AS SERVICE PROVIDERS

Increasingly, then, the simple notion of strategically situated systems providing "one ear and one voice" is an inadequate metaphor for what takes place when the politician and the professor sit down together on that bench. Systems are not disinterested parties, after all, nor are they passive two-way conduits of information. They assess and articulate the needs of the state, in part to establish an agenda for lobbying state government. In external affairs, the system is always an advocate for, and eager to both protect and build, public higher education.

In an era of slow growth, however, with states showing greater reluctance to support public colleges, a further imbalance has developed. The state may feel that the "ear" isn't listening, and isn't accountable enough. The college may feel that the "voice" isn't speaking forcefully enough, or isn't saying the right things. Both may begin to believe that merely keeping their conversation going does not, by itself, add enough value to justify the existence of an extra layer of bureaucracy. Evidence of this can be found in states' recent enthusiasm for quantifiable accountability indicators, cost-shifting from appropriations to tuition, and the gnawing feeling on campuses that states are abandoning them to a semi-public fate.

One result of this imbalance has been a changing role in external affairs for multicampus systems. With experience gained over the past 40 years, the mission of a system administration is gradually changing. In an environment that favors decentralization and deregulation, systems have begun to view themselves less as buffers, less as campus police officers (wielding a nightstick to forestall mission creep), and more as an efficient provider of selected, high value services.

It's an entrepreneurial vision, superimposed uneasily on organizations that still retain a traditionally bureaucratic and political outlook.

Legal counsel is one example of this. It makes little sense to have an attorney trained in the intricacies of higher education law on staff at every public campus in the state. Creating a central staff to provide advice and counsel systemwide saves money, ensures adequate representation, and protects the state's interests. Rather than acting solely as a reactive mouthpiece when problems arise, however, a central system's legal counsel today is just as likely to spend part of its time holding workshops on campus in an attempt to help prevent legal problems from occurring. That's a slowly emerging service orientation that adds value to the system as a whole.

The same is true with external affairs staff. In a multicampus system, few individual institutions can afford (or need) to staff a full-time government relations function, which involves a regular presence in the state capital, frequent excursions to Washington, D.C., the capacity to analyze bills and draft testimony, and fully developed advocacy plans. It makes more sense to focus this activity in the central system office, where a small group of specialists can do all of the above on behalf of all institutions, all of the time, with a fair degree of objectivity.

SYSTEMS AS CONDUCTORS

Service implies negotiation, however, not the imposition of a single, monotone voice on campuses that often vary widely in their histories, resources, needs, strengths, weaknesses, and missions. Far from functioning as ventriloquist for these campuses, forcing them all to speak with one voice whether they wish to or not, a more apt description would be to think of the system administration as the conductor of a choir.

For a choral concert, the conductor chooses the music to be sung and decides how it will be interpreted. The tempo, the volume, the breathing, and the points of emphasis are not questions for the choir to vote on, ultimately, though a good conductor will take into account the range and vocal abilities of the singers at every stage in the rehearsal and performance.

So it is with multicampus system external affairs. The institutions take their cue from the conductor, but only they can do the actual singing. Only they have the four things most worth singing about: *students* in academic *programs* who are transformed by *faculty* into outstanding *alumni*. When they are in fine voice, and are all reading off the same page of music, the effect can be glorious. If any of them sing off-key, or at the wrong time, or forget to make their entrance, the effect on the group's performance can be calamitous.

The music is the external affairs message, carefully composed of themes, motifs, choruses, and arias. There may even be a few very Wagnerian cymbal crashes and drum rolls to enliven the recital. The audience is the public, composed of politicians, alumni, students, their families, taxpayers, and every imaginable stakeholder.

Some are critics, some are fans. Some will cheer like proud parents, regardless of what's sung or how well it's performed. Others will make catcalls, utter rude remarks during shaky, high-pitched solos, or walk out of the hall in a huff. On truly memorable occasions, the audience may be moved to sing along, and will head for home humming the tune. At all times, however, the public is a difficult house to read, reach, or satisfy for long.

At the center of this tension, and these distractions, the conductor is once more the anonymous figure in the modest gray suit, waving arms, imploring the singers, and adapting to the audience reaction in mid-concert. She chose the music, and she settled on its interpretation with the audience, acoustics, and available singers in mind. She did this not as a tyrant, but as a colleague; as someone motivated by service rather than control; as someone who can provide for the system what no single campus would ever be permitted to provide: a sense of balance among competing colleges.

The reviews are written in the form of appropriations, statutory language, enrollment figures, levels of charitable giving, and executive career paths. The reviews influence the next concert, which begins before all the reviews are actually in. As a result, the conductor will still be scanning the critique of last night's concert while she tries to lead the choir in tonight's performance. The same will be true tomorrow, *ad infinitum*.

CONDUCTING THE CHOIR

All politics is vocal. Politicians respond more readily to local campus messages and messengers than they do to systemwide exhortations. On any given day at the statehouse, the system staff may be more visible but the campus could be more influential. For elected officials, success at the polls is largely a product of how well they are regarded by local voters. As the choir performs, the politician is listening for and responding to the local campus voice, as well as to the overall combination of sections and parts. So is every other politician in the audience. The multicampus system does well to encourage strong local (and vocal) connections with politicians, while retaining its necessary role as conductor. The result is that campuses have their distinctive voice, while the system as a whole enjoys a more harmonious sound. Usually.

Lee and Bowen had it right when they observed that "campus executives are in a particularly difficult position: if they actively court legislators and other political figures, they are viewed with suspicion by the system executive and ... staff. If their activity does not rise to the level of meriting such suspicion, however, they are accused of failing to pull their weight along with their colleagues" (Lee and Bowen, *Multicampus University* 339).

In other words, more balance is needed. While the system may free campus executives to concentrate on their campus, those executives still cannot entirely forget about the legislature. And a sure path to an early exit is for a campus executive to ignore system (and board) positions and priorities in pursuit of his or her own. In most systems, such "end runs" usually lead to the edge of a cliff.

How do systems function as conductors in this environment? Typically, in systems as large as Wisconsin's or as small as Nebraska's, each campus identifies someone on the staff to function as the legislative point person. His or her (frequently part-time) duty is to represent the campus viewpoint in strategy sessions with system staff, and to then articulate both the system strategy and the campus viewpoint to selected legislators. The campus staff reports to the campus chancellor/president, but also relates to the system staff by reporting back the results of legislative contacts. In this division of labor, both the system head and the campus executive maintain a role that neither should surrender and which neither can entirely delegate.

There is some tension to this relationship, however, precisely because it is of the "dotted line" variety. Like trapeze artists, the campus executives, system president, and board must function in the area of external affairs without having to guess at the whereabouts of their allies. And there's also no net between floor and ceiling.

Yet, whereas "the governing board is, essentially, the only constituency a system president has," it has been noted that "campus chancellors are assessed by their constituencies on their success in obtaining resources in a competitive environment. Being considered a good team player by the system administration may win you high marks with the president and board, but on your campus, you may appear to be weak and a poor advocate" (Kauffman, 129).

For the campus executive, having your own voice in the choir is important, for both internal and external political reasons. It is to the advantage of the system conductor to recognize this and to be generous, when applause comes, in letting the campus singers collect the bouquets. The system must be equally generous, when brickbats come, in catching or deflecting as many as it can.

Systems as Stabilizing Factors

In external affairs, systems maintain balance in other ways as well. As Aims McGuinness has noted, "Systems may help meet the need for stability, continuity, and long-term perspective in an increasingly turbulent political environment" ("Model" 212). Statutory term limits, statewide initiatives, and self-imposed early retirement means it is the university, increasingly, that is better positioned to take the long view in policy matters. It is the university, and not the legislature, that may have the stronger sense of history and the clearer premonition, based on past experience, of the future results of present trends.

"In these circumstances," writes McGuinness, "multicampus systems may be a critical means to provide for long-term, consistent attention to a public agenda that connects higher education to states' major social and economic challenges, and they may be the only means to develop and implement long-term policies that will stimulate and support institutional responses to these public concerns" ("Model" 213).

This is another reason why, for multicampus systems, the job of external affairs keeps on growing. There are several other reasons that deserve mention:

1. At the state level, public universities have had to compete with a host of other demands on the public purse. Most notably, Medicaid, prisons, and K–12 school aids now draw funds that, in earlier times, might have been used to support higher education. The competition for funding has increased in response to public fears about crime, property taxes, and failing schools. Public higher education should be flattered: taxpayers are relatively confident of the quality and value of these institutions.

2. The perception also exists that 1) state universities have deep pockets and can readily absorb budget setbacks, while 2) college graduates are (or will soon be) wealthy enough by virtue of their degree that no increase in tuition will deter them from paying a bigger bill.

3. An increasing challenge for system external affairs staff is to demonstrate the often subtle impact of budget decisions made by unwary legislators over a span of years. In this effort, the campus liaisons provide the necessary examples and can best describe the resulting pain.

4. The system must also remind the state of its historic partnership role, and of the positive effect on the whole of society (not just graduates) when the state invests in its universities. This latter argument is harder to make with legislators whose constituents, increasingly, are concerned only with the present benefits of present actions. The result in all these cases is a tougher assignment for the external affairs staff.

Seeking a Federal Mission

The much-discussed "reinvention of government" in recent years has not yet meant there's less of it. In many cases, the work load has simply shifted to other levels.

One example is the State Program Review Entity (SPRE), a program authorized by Congress in 1992 but never funded. If SPREs had come into existence, the function of policing high student-loan default rates at postsecondary institutions would have passed, in part, from the federal to the state government. While this might have reduced the size of the federal bureaucracy slightly, 50 new state agencies would have been created. The external affairs staffs of multicampus systems (as well as some campus staffs) would have had yet another agency to monitor and relate to.

The whole federal relations arena is also something new, and extra, for higher education. Smaller state-supported institutions and comprehensive systems once relied on the national higher education associations or other consortial arrangements to help represent their relatively modest interests in Washington. Larger, research-intensive campuses (both public and private) tended to manage their own federal affairs, which consisted largely of advocacy on behalf of science and medical research funding. Multicampus systems might lend support to the flagship campus research agenda, and they certainly took note of the expansion of federal student aid programs as they evolved over the years. But the need, or the opportunity, for a *system* approach to federal relations was not obvious until recent years.

The 1992 reauthorization of the federal Higher Education Act (containing the SPRE program), followed by the assault on federal student aid programs that took place during the 104th Congress, caused some systems to reconsider (and increase) their profile in Washington. Whereas the National Institutes of Health appropriation might directly affect only the flagship campus, the Pell Grant and Stafford Loan programs affect the entire system. The need for systems to advocate on the federal level became a higher priority. The question was how?

If systems conduct choirs of campuses on state-level issues, the national higher education associations (e.g., ACE, AAU, AASCU, NAICU, NASULGC) perform a similar role at the federal level. During the 1990s, they began to encourage campus presidents to become more vocal with members of Congress, a role for which many smaller campus presidents were unprepared and unstaffed. As a result, many public institutions turned to their system administration for assistance and advice. The result was a new and larger external affairs job for the system, usually managed through the reassignment of existing staff.

Some systems, notably the University of Colorado, the University of Maryland, the University of Illinois, the University of California and California State University, have had a strong federal agenda for some time. For others, federal relations remains largely a matter of monitoring issues and responding with calls, letters, and other contacts in concert with the higher education associations.

Whereas systems are well-positioned for state-level government relations, it remains true at the federal level that "with limited exceptions, the multicampus university [does] not have any special role in the national Capital. . . . Broader policy issues at the federal level are on a scale that does not bring the multicampus structure as such into focus. . . . System staff in Washington may assist in mobilizing support for an 'institutional' position, but their activity in this regard does not differ from that of representatives from individual campuses or associations" (Lee and Bowen, *Multicampus University* 344-45). More than 25 years later, systems are still searching for ways to have as much impact at the federal level as they do at the state level, and in ways that reflect their particular mission as systems.

STABILITY IN THE POLITICAL AGENDA

Higher than normal turnover of elected officials has meant that the external affairs staff of the multicampus system are often dealing with relative neophytes. Legislators elected on anti-government platforms may possess little knowledge of intricate higher education issues. Initially, the needs of the university tend to carry little political weight with them or their constituents.

High turnover, after a period of higher than normal stability, and dramatic shifts in the control of Congress and statehouses, means getting to know a constant influx of new officials and their fresh-faced aides. It means attempting to educate them (through campus visits, informal meetings with campus and system leadership, one-page briefing papers) in the fleeting moments between floor sessions, hearings, elections, and vacations. This is especially perilous when, for example, the chair of the education-related committee is only in her second or third term, has promised to retire after four terms, and owes her election to a splinter group that opposes the university's use of laboratory animals for research purposes.

The need to spend a lot of one-on-one time with newcomers, few of whom regard the university as much more than an economic boon for their district and a never-ending source of constituent complaints (admissions policies, party noise, parking problems, the distribution of football tickets, etc.), is relentless. And it can be frustrating when the members you've invested effort in, and who've begun to emerge as the system's legislative champions, are rewarded by term limits, electoral defeat, or an ulcer-induced early retirement.

For all of these reasons, the task of system external affairs has grown. The shift toward "service provider" and "conductor" may unconsciously reflect the fact that the resources available to do this expanding job have remained largely static. Public concern about the cost of higher education results in a demand for flat organizational charts and leaner administrations. The public is especially skeptical about using tax dollars to pay for "lobbying." This is especially true when the full-time professional at the system office and the one-eighth-time campus liaison are both identified as "lobbyists" in local news media accounts of "political wallowing at the public trough."

Necessary Leadership Qualities

The job of advocacy on behalf of higher education has become a high burn-out occupation, comparable to fund-raising. If you, or your institution, come to be too closely identified with one side of the aisle or the other, prospects are good that a change of party control may result in a change of careers.

In addition, the spiritual rewards of system-level external affairs are not bountiful. As the "anonymous, gray" advocate at the capitol, spending time far from the campuses and students for whom you labor (locked in rapt conversation with a page while waiting to see a 22-year-old aide to a 25-year-old freshman legislator), it's easy to imagine another line of work. This is especially true when you realize that the other person in the waiting room, a high-powered lobbyist for the Forces of Darkness Association, makes enough money to be able to afford to send his children to a school that charges twice the tuition yours does.

This raises a question about the most appropriate staffing for external affairs at the multicampus system level. Because you're competing for attention and funding in a much more sophisticated environment now than was the case when the system was created, it's tempting to think you need as your lobbyist the same person who would happily work for the Forces of Darkness Association. That's probably a temptation it is wise to resist.

Former legislators and staff aides are often hired for this purpose. Their knowledge of the legislative process, their capacity to sit for days at a time, and their acquaintance with legislative members all prove useful, assuming there is a more than superficial devotion to the university's mission.

It used to be that lobbyists were often recycled deans and professors, whose intimate knowledge of academe balanced out their initial political naiveté. That is less often the case today. Advocacy has become a profession, at the system level and at the larger campuses. While that is a positive move overall, one result may be a loss of passion for the institution and a loss of the gentility that sometimes compensated for a lower level of political savvy. Another consequence is that higher education can now be viewed by politicians as a special interest, rather than especially interesting by virtue of its place in society.

Whoever fills the system external affairs positions, what does matter most is devotion to the mission of public higher education. It is sometimes easier to "teach politics" to a university person than it is to "teach the university" and its mission to someone who is first and foremost a politician.

If the politician is also an alumnus or, even better, a former member of an education committee, the need to teach the university may not exist. Disaster portends when the external affairs staff regards the university as just a client. The relationship has to be more intense than that or the marriage is likely to be a short and rocky one.

SYSTEM LEADERSHIP

Perhaps more important than the staffing of external affairs is the leadership of the system as a whole, since the system chief is always the principal external affairs person as well. When systems first came into being, the top position was often viewed as a logical step up for the president of the flagship campus. This was probably true at the time, even though it inevitably reduced the presidents of the other campuses to a state of vassalage, with an attending loss of internal balance. It wasn't until the 1970s that one system (Wisconsin) appointed as its president someone who had been a system president elsewhere (Missouri).

Today, such a move is not uncommon (Charles Reed from the State University System of Florida to the California State University System in 1997), nor is it impossible for the head of a nonflagship system campus to be appointed to the top spot (Richard Atkinson from the University of California-San Diego to the University of California System in 1996).

In most cases, system leadership still demands some level of academic credentials and experience. This is true even though it is well understood by governing boards and campus executives that the position is more akin to the administration of a state agency than it is to stewardship of a teaching and learning community. In appointing the state senate president, William Bulger, to its system presidency in 1996, Massachusetts was recognizing the fact that system presidents spend more time in the capitol and the board room than they do in the classroom.

Joseph Kauffman has described the system presidency as "the least stable of higher education presidencies and often the least satisfying chief executive position." They are "caught between the often ambiguous expectations of system boards and the tendency of the respective campuses to blame all ills on the system's administration." For their trouble, "system heads are often disparaged as politicians rather than respected as educators" (128). Nonetheless, system presidents are rewarded and regarded more highly for the budgets they get passed than for the scholarly articles they publish.

In their pioneering study, Lee and Bowen found that "System executives felt [the] lack of a 'constituency' of students, faculty, or alumni." They wrote:

> This lack was most evident and troublesome to those who, having only recently relinquished their direct campus responsibilities, found that their new position carried little of the traditional and symbolic author-ity they enjoyed as a campus executive. At the same time, there was no corresponding decrease in external responsibilities to the governing board or state government to offset their loss of support "in the power struggle." Compared with his single-campus counterpart, the system executive finds himself faced with an increasingly complex external environment but with a decreasing ability to mobilize his internal resources. (*Multicampus University* 386–87)

More recently, Gordon Davies has written about these being "tumul-tuous times for the executive officers of state systems of higher education, more than a fifth of whom are being or have been replaced within the past two academic years." He added that this turnover "rarely elicits much regret, given the inevitable tension between these officers and the administrators of individual institutions." He interpreted the large number of changes as an indication "that state systems as we have known them are in trouble. I think they are also obsolescent" (*Higher Education* A68). In other words, the exter-nal affairs role of the system president remains a challenge for anyone who takes it on.

OTHER CHARACTERISTICS

It is also essential that the system president recognize that external affairs cannot really be delegated. He or she is always responsible for government relations and it's always one of the highest priorities. This is true even though there's a vice president and staff ostensibly assigned for this purpose. At a campus, especially a smaller state college, the executive also bears some responsibility, but can often put it on the back burner. The system president doesn't have that luxury.

It may also help if the system president and external affairs staff are peo-ple who are comfortable sitting on that bench between the politician and the professor. Those whose personality adds fuel to fires, or whose ego demands constant maintenance, may not enjoy the roles of mediator, conductor, and service provider. It is possible to be very successful as both a celebrity and a system executive (Barry Munitz, formerly with the California State University System, is one example), but it's no coincidence that system presidents are often little known figures, even in their own state.

It's a position that usually places a premium on diplomacy, balance, patience, and the ability to hold (or bite) one's tongue when necessary. The system president and external affairs staff must also be able to personify and stand up for the whole system. They must be prepared to extol the simple virtues of the smallest campus, as well as the economic dynamism of the flagship research university. Even wearing the "wrong" school color may offend those who read such things as though they were tea leaves. Is the campus out of favor with the system? Is the flagship getting too much (or too little) of the attention it rightfully deserves?

The system president speaks both to that large, internal audience of faculty, staff, students, and friends and to that larger, external audience of officials, trustees, employers, foundations, parents, and the news media. The president must speak in both directions, and explain each to the other. In this regard, Donald Langenberg of the University of Maryland System has compared central administrations to Janus, the twin-faced Roman god of gates and doorways ("Why?" 9).

Structures that Work

Rudyard Kipling once wrote that "There are nine and sixty ways of constructing tribal lays, and every single one of them is right" (Rudyard Kipling, "In the Neolithic Age," Stanza 5) Much the same can be said of system external affairs organizational structures. All of them are "right," within the context of a particular system's mission, staffing, history, and institutional relationships.

Some system structures include alumni relations. Others include development. Still others encompass oversight and events related to the system president's residence. In general, however, the system external affairs function is largely limited to two main areas: government relations and public information.

In a typical structure, a vice president for university relations reports directly to the system president. In turn, a public affairs unit that is responsible for system-level news releases, media relations, publications and design, and web-site management reports to him. Also reporting to the vice president is a government relations unit that includes separate state and federal relations staff.

The public affairs unit has an advocacy function in addition to an information function. In the University of Wisconsin System, this unit produces an annual admissions viewbook that is used statewide. It also publishes a system "fact book" and administrative directory, and a news and features tabloid that is distributed during the academic year to all faculty and staff in the system. The latter often serves an internal advocacy role, explaining major issues to persons who are directly affected by them.

The public affairs unit supports, but inevitably plays a secondary role to, the government relations unit at the system level. Lee and Bowen spoke of universities having "such a multiplicity of goals that their interpretation is very difficult," with "little agreement on the priorities of the diverse goals and activity" (*Multicampus University* 331). This tendency is magnified at the system level, with the result that "public relations officers are at the outpost line when inevitable disputes arise. They are asked to clarify the intangible, and with a straight face." Their conclusion was that "public relations is not a major achievement of the multicampus university *as a system*" (Lee and Bowen, *Multicampus University* 330, 337). One reason for this, they suggested, is the paucity of staff and budget allocated for the purpose. While public affairs staffs at the campus level have ballooned in size in recent years, the level of resources devoted to this task at the system level remains modest.

The state relations side of external affairs typically includes someone who is recognized (from past experience) as a Democrat and someone who is recognized as a Republican. This enables the unit to maintain trust and communications with both parties, regardless of which one is in power. Most systems cannot afford to have more than one federal relations person on staff, and it is often a part-time assignment, so being viewed as nonpartisan is an advantage.

The 16-campus University of North Carolina recently adopted a new structure for its system-level external affairs function. In many respects, it is typical of the ways in which most systems have chosen to organize this function. Called the Division for Public Affairs and University Advancement, the structure encompasses state and federal government relations, communications and media relations, and related advancement functions. The vice president reports to the system president and oversees associate vice presidents for state governmental affairs, federal relations, and communications. In addition, the vice president "provides support to the constituent campuses and other components of the University in the further development of their fund-raising and other advancement programs, and provides leadership to the University in building coalitions with business, educational, civic and governmental agencies" (position description).

SEEKING ALTERNATIVE ADVOCATES

In some systems, fund-raising and alumni relations are jealously guarded campus prerogatives. In others, coordination of major development works takes place at the system level. Elsewhere, as in North Carolina and Wisconsin, the system's support of fund-raising is yet another service function—a form of objective, in-house consulting with campuses (where the real fund-raising actually takes place) that encourages capacity building.

While few systems attempt to orchestrate alumni relations from a central office, most do attempt to identify and mobilize alumni and other friends as statewide networks of political advocates. Indiana University and the University of California System are among those that have made significant investments in such networks.

Systems can be effective in mobilizing other "alternative advocates," as Gordon Davies described them. In his own state, the ad hoc Virginia Business–Higher Education Council successfully lobbied the legislature for increased funding at the behest of the state's college and university presidents, "who perceived that the system's coordinating council had surrendered its informal authority and its effectiveness as an advocate for higher education in Virginia" (*Twenty Years* 27). While the Council was effective, and welcome, Davies regards the emergence of such alternative advocates as "a sign that the official higher education structure is not working satisfactorily." Such groups "try to establish communication with elected public officials and others by circumventing bureaucratic processes that would inhibit it" (*Twenty Years* 26–27). Nonetheless, he argues that these new relationships are important and should be encouraged. Can system external affairs offices "conduct" these alternative advocates as well as they do their own campuses? Probably not, but it's a risk worth taking.

Conclusions

In asking the question, "What must a system do to encourage a university to greatness?" Frank Newman responded with two achievements that specifically involve external affairs. "The system must buffer the campuses from inappropriate intrusion and not create more of its own," he wrote, and "where necessary, the system must campaign to eliminate unnecessary bureaucracy from the state or from itself" (Newman, 98–99). There is a sense in Newman's remarks of systems being a "mixed blessing" for higher education.

Clark Kerr said as much in his foreword to Lee and Bowen's 1971 book, *The Multicampus University*. He wrote that "the American multicampus system . . .

has some great advantages," one of which is that "it concentrates certain external relations, particularly with state and federal authorities, in a single office where they can usually be better performed" (xiii). Just as quickly, he added that "the central question about any multicampus system is whether it improves results . . . [including] the successful representation to external authorities—more than it impedes the processes of governance. Is the value worth the cost?" (xv).

Patrick Callan, writing in 1994, asked provocatively "are the systems, as is sometimes asserted, buffers against . . . intrusion. Or do they simply function as convenient levers for state budget cutters and legislative micro managers providing 'one number to call' for the implementation of budget cuts and the imposition of control. If one of the principal functions of systems is to simplify the lives of state officials, is this a luxury that can be afforded at a time of reduced services to students?" ("Questions" 5–6).

Lee and Bowen themselves observed that "common membership in a university system . . . does not necessarily create a more favorable and effective relationship with state government than would otherwise be the case" (*Multicampus University* 417). Further, "the multicampus system is not always an effective buffer against undue political pressures from state government. On the contrary, by its very size and importance, it often attracts political attention, at times interference, which might be less likely were each campus a separate entity" (*Multicampus University* 419).

Anyone who has worked for a multicampus system in external affairs will admit to having entertained similar doubts from time to time. The criticism reflects, I think, the fact that neither the politician nor the professor is entirely reconciled to having the anonymous-looking figure in a modest gray suit as a party to the constant conversation. Nor is either quite satisfied by the notion of a system functioning as the conductor of a choir of campuses in the area of external affairs. Both might like to dispense with the intermediary so that they can speak frankly and directly with each other.

Too much "frankness," and too much "directness," are why systems and their external affairs staffs came into being, however. On the whole, systems (and system boards) may not always be the cheerleaders that campuses would like them to be. Neither are they always the watchdogs that government would like them to be. In fulfilling their Janus-like role, sometimes they are most useful when they prevent the worst excesses of freedom and restraint from playing out, to the ultimate detriment of students.

I've suggested, in the form of two analogies, ways in which multicampus system external affairs can be viewed less as members of the Politburo and

more as providers of high-value service. I have been influenced in this by
Donald Langenberg's 1994 article, "Why a System?", in which he outlined five
functions that systems are uniquely positioned to perform: Synergy, Strategy,
Efficiency, Accountability, and Integrity (8–9).

To these, in 1996, Katharine Lyall of the University of Wisconsin System
added two more: Advocacy, "for the value of sustaining educational opportunity and affordable access if we are to be optimistic about the collective future of our
society," and State Government Reform, because "public universities can change
only as much as the governments of which they are a part will permit" (45).

Jim Mingle has added a further observation, which fits well my assertion that maintaining balance in external affairs is justification enough for
the existence of multicampus systems. In response to a stinging critique
(James Fisher's 1995 article, "The Failure of Statewide Coordination"),
Mingle wrote:

> The dilemma for systems is this: the more rules created, the lower the trust
> in the system. But without the rules, free riders cannot be controlled. The
> answer for systems is to create a new modus operandi within a system frame-
> work. In a recent seminar for the president and chancellor of the University
> of Wisconsin System, I asked the campus chancellors to list the "value
> added" by the system president. "Civility," they responded. What they were
> saying is that the system creates, in the words of [Francis] Fukuyama, "social
> solidarity" against a hostile environment. ("The Case" 9)

Of all the reasons cited for continuing to focus external affairs at the system
level, I think Langenberg offers the most telling. "The system structure," he
wrote, "creates an important and rarely appreciated line of defense against
efforts that might compromise institutional integrity—whether from a legislature intent on dictating curricula, an executive branch seeking to influence
appointments, a corporation trying to circumvent procurement processes, or
irate citizens demanding curbs on academic freedom. Shielding the institutions from such assaults so they can flourish may be a system head's most
important task; it is certainly the most thankless" ("Why?" 9).

In the process, it must be noted, those same institutions are held more fully
accountable, and the legitimate interests of society are better served. This happens, I would suggest, only because the "constant conversation" has a chance
to continue, and the choir of voices has a chance to be heard, with help from
multicampus systems that provide high-value services to the public, the institutions, and the students for whom they work.

3

MULTICAMPUS SYSTEMS

The Challenge of the Nineties

Joseph J. Burke

*Systems generally decentralized their
responsibilities and learned to live with less in the
nineties; the expected widespread system-led
reforms did not emanate from budget cuts, and
campus leaders demonstrated more creativity,
innovation, and reform than did system officials.
Sweeping synergistic changes did not occur, but
several lessons were learned for future reference.*

Public higher education, once untouchable, seemed an easy target for budget cutters and external critics in the first half of the 1990s. Commentators predicted that
the cuts and criticisms could produce dramatic changes on campuses. "The 1990s
promise to be a time of wrenching transition for American colleges and universities," said the *Christian Science Monitor* in 1992. "With budgets declining and criticism rising, many universities . . . find they may have to make sweeping changes
to stay in business" (Boot). In 1993, Edward Hines, editor of *State Higher Education
Appropriations*, saw bleak budgets leading to "the beginning of a fundamental
reshaping of higher education"(Jaschik, 21). Elaine El-Khawas in *Campus Trends
1994* claimed that "reorganization and redirection may be the defining themes of
the 1990s for American higher education" (1). Clark Kerr, architect of the California
Master Plan that fixed the goals of access and quality for all of public higher education, echoed this theme in 1993. " I believe that these few years of the middle
'90s will be a defining moment in the history of higher education." He spoke of
California but could have been talking about the country. Kerr believed this defining moment required "someone or some group in higher education . . . to step forward and take the responsibility and the burdens of leadership."

Leaders of multicampus systems seemed the obvious candidates to step up to
Kerr's challenge. Though differing widely in size, organization, and authority, sys-

tems seemed tailor-made for the task. They could provide collective responses from constituent campuses in place of random reactions from individual institutions. System boards could make comprehensive policies and plans that accommodated budget cuts in ways that protected access and quality and produced efficiency and effectiveness. Systems set the missions, allocated the resources, and approved the programs of their campuses. They possessed the information on personnel, programs, and productivity that could inform coordinated responses to the calls for reduced costs and improved performance. If higher education had an organization that could meet Kerr's challenge, university systems seemed the clear choice.

The classic case for multicampus systems came in 1994 from Donald Langenberg, Chancellor of the University of Maryland System. "It is important, particularly in this era of financial constraints," said Langenberg of university systems, "that we exploit their strengths to help achieve the best results possible with the resources available" ("Why?" 8–9). Synergy, strategy, efficiency, accountability, and integrity constituted for Langenberg the essential objectives of university systems. "These are the areas in which the system model can 'add value' to the educational enterprise." Synergy stood for their "enormous potential for enhancing, even transforming, the performance of individual institutions through coordinated effort." Strategy, by setting "common goals" and "complementary roles," ensured that constituent institutions could fulfill their individual missions while making unique contributions to common purposes. Strategy also allowed systems to reduce redundant academic programs and reallocate resources to priority areas in ways that could never happen with independent institutions. Langenberg insisted that systems had a greater potential for efficiency than autonomous colleges and universities acting on their own interests. "For . . . public higher education in particular 'accountability' is the watchword for the '90s," declared Langenberg. Systems could assure accountability for meeting the needs of the states and not just the desires of clients of individual institutions. Integrity represented the capacity to resist the "undue and inappropriate" intrusions of outside groups, including government officials, into educational affairs. Langenberg had no doubt that the collective weight of multicampus systems could resist such pressures better than single colleges or universities (8–9).

The Maryland Chancellor conceded the difficulty of reaching these objectives. "Realizing a system's potential . . . requires creative design and decisive leadership capable of overcoming the strong centrifugal forces that characterize most systems." Despite these problems, Langenberg insisted that systems had the potential and represented the best hope for achieving his objectives. "Synergy, strategy, efficiency, accountability and integrity," he declared, " are the objectives to which systems should be dedicated and against which they should be judged" ("Why?" 8–9).

It is hard to image five objectives more suited to success in a period of declining budgets and rising criticism for public higher education. It also seems reasonable to judge the value of systems by assessing how they responded to the challenges facing state colleges and universities in the first half of the 1990s.

Both system champions and critics appeared to agree with this judgment. Bruce Johnstone, former Chancellor of the State University of New York and an advocate of university systems, thought the true test was how they dealt with budget cuts. "The . . . raison d'être of a multicampus system is that the system board and its central administration . . . is better able to make the critical and difficult resource allocation decisions . . . than are . . . strictly political or regulatory offices" ("Central" 11). Patrick Callan, then Executive Director of the California Higher Education Policy Center, did write an article questioning the usefulness of multicampus systems. On the other hand, his Center constantly criticized the leaders of the University of California and California State University for failing to protect access in the face of large budget cuts and soaring enrollment demands ("Gauntlet" 16-19). Callan charged that their lay boards and central offices "have neither taken nor stimulated major initiatives to set program priorities, to eliminate duplication, to streamline campus missions, or to encourage cooperation among campuses" ("Introduction"). In practice, he seemed to quarrel not with Langenberg's objectives but with the will of system leaders to pursue them.

How did university systems respond to the budget problems of the first half of the 1990s? How well did they translate the ideals of synergy, strategy, efficiency, accountability, and integrity into the real world of policymaking, planning, programming, and budgeting? Did they redirect priorities to meet the changing needs of their students and their states? Did systems develop plans for cutting costs and bureaucracies and improving productivity and performance? Did they redesign campus missions, restructure central administrations, and reduce redundant programs? Did they develop long-term strategies that encouraged the cooperation, efficiency, and productivity of their campuses? How well did systems protect the hallmarks of public higher education, quality and access? Of course, system leaders were not the only actors in the arena of higher education. Success also depended upon the actions and attitudes of state and campus policymakers as well as system trustees and officers. The fairest test is not whether systems succeeded, which they could not do alone, but the extent to which they sought Langenberg's objectives.

The Study States

To seek answers to these questions, this study examined system actions from 1990 through 1997 in California, Florida, Massachusetts, New York, Texas, and Wisconsin. Although system actions in just six states cannot stand for system performance in all the states, these six states included the largest systems in the nation and represented the full range of system types and numbers of constituent campuses. They covered the major regions of the country and exhibited divergent attitudes toward public higher education and different patterns of state funding. Massachusetts and New York had strong private sectors, while public institutions dominated in Florida and Texas. Some of the states had segmental systems with campuses of similar missions, such as the University of California and California State University. Others had comprehensive systems with the full range of campus types, such as the City and State Universities of New York. Still others mixed institutional types. The Universities of Massachusetts and Wisconsin included research universities along with comprehensive institutions, while Texas offered an array of institutional clusters. Some of the twelve systems studied had a history of centralized decision making, while several seemed collections of fairly autonomous institutions. State funding during the period ranged from drastic reductions in California, Massachusetts, and New York to budget constraints in Florida, Texas, and Wisconsin. California, Florida, and Texas anticipated soaring enrollments, while Massachusetts, New York, and Wisconsin expected modest growth.

Budget cuts for higher education hit hardest in California, Massachusetts, and New York. From 1990 through 1997, state appropriations in current dollars to higher education fell 11.9 percent in New York and rose only 3.5 percent in Massachusetts and 6 percent in California. Subtracting inflation shows their real plight. In constant dollars, appropriations plunged 30.5 percent in New York, 18.3 percent in Massachusetts, and 16.3 percent in California. Florida, Texas, and Wisconsin appeared to have much less of a problem. Appropriations in current dollars climbed 29.5 percent in Florida, 21 percent in Texas, and 21.6 percent in Wisconsin. Funding in constant dollars presents a different picture. Appropriations grew during the period only 4.4 percent in Florida. They actually fell by 4.5 percent in Texas and 4.1 in Wisconsin (Hines). These figures included appropriations for private as well as public institutions. An increased share of diminished funding went to student aid to cover at least part of the big tuition increases in many of the six states. All of the states experienced anti-tax sentiment, which often produced tax cuts and constitutional limitations on spending. Competition with mandated services such as corrections, public schools, health care, and welfare meant diminished increases or deeper cuts in one of the largest discretionary items in state budgets, higher education. Appropriation as a percent of tax revenue fell in these six states by a minimum of 13 to a high of 36 percent.

The Surveys

To discover the reactions of university systems in these six states to the problems of the period, separate surveys were sent to the finance officers of state coordinating or planning agencies, university systems, and comprehensive campuses and research universities. The surveys were administered in October 1997, and the replies returned in November and December. Though the surveys were sent to finance officers to ensure a single, knowledgeable contact, the answers from systems and institutions required input from officers in academic affairs and institutional research. Discussion with a number of the respondents confirmed that their replies represented collective responses, composed with input from several offices. The surveys sent to the three groups of respondents differed depending on their organization, but all included questions about system strategies and actions for dealing with budget problems from 1990 through 1997.

The questions for system officers sought to determine the extent to which their organizations, in practice, pursued the objectives prescribed by Langenberg. Did their systems prepare comprehensive plans for dealing with the diminished shares of state support, issue guidelines to shape institutional plans, or allow full discretion to campuses for preparing their own plans? Did system boards or officials reserve the right to approve campus plans? Were the required institutional plans short- or long-term, or a combination of these approaches? Did systems allocate funding cuts to campuses primarily across-the-board or selectively? Did the relative importance of funding factors, such as base budgets, student enrollments, and salary and inflationary increases, shift during the period, and if so, in what ways? Did system governance change; and if it did, in what directions—toward more centralization or decentralization?

The survey also asked whether systems used their authority over campus missions and programs during the period. Did campus missions change; and did systems initiate those changes? Did system officials propose or suggest campus closures and program eliminations? If so, how many were achieved, and if not, what was the reason for the lack of success? Did systems alter their enrollment strategies during the period to raise or reduce their student numbers? Did they restructure their administrative organization and operations? Finally, what type of actions best characterized system and campus responses during the period, from raising revenues and reducing expenditures to restructuring operations and refocusing missions?

Questions for state higher education and institutional finance officers asked their appraisal of the system's role in shaping campus responses to the budget stringency of the 1990s. The first question requested both groups to evaluate the importance of the system's role; the second sought from campus officers an assessment of its positive or negative impact. The surveys requested all three groups of respondents to evaluate the impact of the period on undergraduate access and the quality of undergraduate and graduate programs and research and public service activities. They also queried all three groups on funding levels and tuition revenues. To what extent did state funding in the period create a problem, and to what degree did tuition and fee increases fill the gap between the needs of public colleges and universities and the levels of state funding?

All five State Higher Education Finance Officers responded. (Wisconsin has no statewide coordinating or planning body.) All of the finance officers of the 12 systems surveyed also replied. The institutional response rate reached 65 percent, running from a high of 90 percent in Florida to a low of 54 percent in Massachusetts and Wisconsin. The returns included a representative sample of research universities and comprehensive campuses, as well as a good mix of institutional types and a reasonable number of units in each of the 12 systems.

The Collective Response

Respondents for all of the University Systems, except those from Texas, considered the budget problem large or very large. Even the Florida System, whose state funding for the period more than covered inflation, called the problem large. The Universities of California and Massachusetts described the budget problem as very large. Institutions tended to see the problem as somewhat more serious than their systems. Of the twelve systems surveyed, eight felt that tuition and fees significantly filled the gap between their state funding and their financial needs. Despite large fee increases, both of the California Systems thought student charges made only a moderate contribution. The Florida State System said tuition helped only slightly; and the Texas State System described it as no help. In both of these states, legislatures limited tuition increases. The campus responses claimed that tuition and fees made less of a contribution. A third described the assistance as significant, 32 percent as moderate, and 28 percent as slight. The State Higher Education Officers tended to rate the funding problem as slightly less serious and the contribution of tuition as more significant than did system or campus officers.

Contrary to expectations, given their assessment of the budget problem, only four of the twelve systems developed systemwide plans for dealing with the funding cuts or constraints. One system with a plan commented that it allowed full discretion to the campuses. Three additional systems developed guidelines, but one of these also cited full discretion to campuses. Apparently, a majority of the systems left the budget problem largely to their colleges and universities. Even a majority of the systems in California, Massachusetts, and

New York, which had the worst budget problems, adopted this approach. Seven of the systems did not retain the right of approval of campus plans. For those systems that did prepare plans or guidelines, the planning groups included a range of participants, but system officers clearly dominated the process.

Of the nine systems responding to the question, seven said they allocated funding reductions to campuses primarily across-the-board. Only one distributed them selectively throughout the period and a second for most of it. The campuses took a different approach. Over half of the institutions made their internal allocations selectively. The relative importance of funding factors for allocations from systems to campuses shifted only slightly during the period. Base budgets remained first, enrollment rose from third to second place, while salary and inflationary increases fell from second to third. Institutional missions became less important, and performance slightly more important. The severity of the budget problems in the states seems to have had little effect on these rankings. State funding factors for public higher education follow a similar pattern. Some states, according to their higher education officers, showed more interest in performance funding based on institutional results, but it ranked in the top three factors only in Florida, which had a legislated program.

Only one of the systems proposed and closed or consolidated a campus, though several comments suggest that more might have recommended closures, if they perceived such actions politically possible. The one consolidation amounted only to a minor administrative merger. Five of the twelve systems did propose program eliminations and achieved a considerable number of program closures, although not as many as initially identified. Respondents most often cited resistance from campus presidents and local communities as reasons for the failure to win approval for all their proposals. The replies from institutions indicated that 38 percent of the campuses surveyed eliminated academic programs. The closures did come mostly in the states with the worst budget problems. In spite of the fiscal constraints of the period, only a third of the systems indicated a change of campus missions, and these came primarily from institutional initiatives.

Seven of the systems had governance changes, with five moving toward more decentralization. Three of the five systems that did not alter their governance were already fairly decentralized. Only the City University of New York and the University of Massachusetts became more centralized. Seven of the 12 systems restructured their central administrations; six closed or consolidated offices and functions; five devolved functions and services to campuses; four reduced senior officers; and two contracted out services. Apparently, restructuring and downsizing central administrations represented one of the few steps systems could take that would win approval on campuses and in state capitols.

Half of the systems surveyed altered their enrollment strategies during the period, with half increasing and half decreasing their student numbers.

According to the system respondents, raising revenues (75%) and restructuring organization and operations (50%) best characterized the system responses to the budget problems. They cited restricting expenditures (75%) and raising revenues (67%) as best representing the campus responses. The replies from the institutions confirm this assessment. They suggest that the top three actions taken by institutions were restricting expenditures, restructuring their organization and operation, and raising revenues. Revising campus mission and restructuring teaching and learning were not the actions of choice of the campuses in any of the systems and states. Only 16 percent of the institutions said they changed missions and just seven percent altered their teaching and learning processes.

Most of the system respondents claimed that quality and access in undergraduate education was maintained, but a third conceded that access decreased and 17 percent that quality diminished. Of the five state finance officers, two (California and Massachusetts) saw a loss of undergraduate access, one an increase (Texas), and the other two cited maintenance. Two (Massachusetts and New York) perceived a drop in quality of undergraduate education, while the others thought it was maintained. The campuses provided a harsher assessment. Forty-one percent admitted a fall of undergraduate access and 30 percent a drop in the quality of undergraduate education. Most of the replies from systems, campuses, and higher education officers indicated maintenance of quality in graduate education and research and service activities.

Although the systems as a group adopted a rather passive approach to the budget problems, most of the replies from coordinating or planning agencies and the institutions considered the systems important in shaping the response to the budget problem. Four of the five State Higher Education Finance Officers rated the role of system boards and administrations as important or very important. Only one considered them of slight importance. Although two of these officers considered their importance equal to campus officers and one above, two ranked them below campus officials. Fifty-nine percent of the institutional replies rated their system's role as important or very important. As expected, graduate and research institutions considered the system role as somewhat less important than comprehensive institutions did. Although institutions saw the system role as important, 43 percent viewed its actions as negative and only 36 percent as positive.

The responses from their own finance officers suggested that most systems did not use their authority over planning, policy-making, and budgeting to forge collective responses to the budget problems of the period. On the other hand, the state and campus officers rated the role of systems as more important than the replies from system officers would suggest. Perhaps the latter were loath to admit making centralized decisions at a time when decentralization appeared in vogue. Or, perhaps, system officers influenced campus actions in informal ways rather than through official decisions. Systems did restructure their organizations and operations, which probably encouraged the considerable administrative restructuring that occurred on their campuses. They also moved to eliminate duplicative programs. On the other hand, the funding factors in budget allocations to campuses showed only slight shifts during the period. Most systems relied on tuition increases as a major strategy and some reduced enrollments, which many systems, and most campuses and state finance officers, conceded caused a decline in undergraduate access.

The survey responses do not confirm the predictions of the first half of the '90s as a "defining moment" that could reshape public higher education. Most systems seemed to treat the problems of the period as temporary difficulties rather than long-term challenges. Apparently, they decided to cope rather than change. Raising revenues appeared the preferred reaction from systems. Few systems cited refocusing missions or reallocating resources. Systems did take more aggressive actions to restructure their central administrations and to eliminate duplicative programs. They also changed enrollment strategies, with half reducing student numbers. Most system leaders concluded that the fall in state support called for a choice between access and quality, and nearly all chose the latter.

Most of the systems in this study failed some of Langenberg's tests. Most fell far short of synergy, for few tried to enhance or transform "the performance of individual institutions through coordinated effort." Few seemed to set the "common goals" or "complementary roles" required for strategy, although most moved to reduce program duplication ("Why?" 8–9). Systems did achieve the objective of efficiency by cutting the costs and the bureaucracy of their central administrations. Accountability suffered from the *laissez faire* approach of leaving the budget problems to campuses, which encouraged institutional interests over collective needs. On the objective of integrity, the appointive power of governors over trustees in at least one state revealed that systems could become conduits for political intrusion as well as buffers against political influence. Perhaps the cuts were so sudden and sharp in some states that coping was the best they could do, and were not so severe or serious in others to justify radical actions.

The States

A collective analysis of system responses allows some insights, but overall averages obscure individual differences. Only a state by state and system by system assessment can reveal the significant variations among these six states and twelve systems. The states and their systems are considered in two groups, based on the extent of their budget problems. The first group of states includes California, Massachusetts, and New York, which had deep budget cuts during the period. The second presents Wisconsin, Texas, and Florida, which experienced budget constraints.

CALIFORNIA

The worst recession since the great depression hit California in 1990, sharply cutting state revenues and creating huge deficits. With revenues falling and costs rising for mandated programs in health care, welfare, corrections, and public schools, California, along with most states, made disproportionate cuts in the discretionary area of higher education. From FY 1991–92 through 1993–94, annual cuts slashed state funding for the University of California (UC) nearly 17 percent and for California State University (CSU) 13 percent. The public systems responded with huge hikes in student charges. Fees for resident undergraduates more than doubled at UC and CSU from 1990–91 to 1994–95 (Washington State Coordinating Board). Beginning in 1994–95, state funding started a slow climb toward previous levels of state support, which was not reached until 1996–97. Along with funding cuts, California colleges and universities faced a tidal wave of nearly half a million more students than in the previous decade. This combination of budget cuts, tuition increases, and enrollment demands threatened to swamp that State's fabled master plan, which promised both access and quality in higher education. Unfortunately, the promise demanded generous state support and low student fees, both of which disappeared during the first half of the 1990s (Gold 104–40; Martinez and Nodine 81–106).

During his first few years as Governor, Republican Pete Wilson showed little interest in higher education, aside from proposing deep budget cuts and encouraging huge fee increases. The legislature, especially its Democrat members, tried, with limited success, to soften the cuts proposed by the governor. The governor and legislature mandated cuts but left the systems and campuses to determine how to accommodate them. As the recession receded and resistance to fee increases rose, Governor Wilson negotiated a compact with the public systems that increased funding, raised enrollments, and—at legislative insistence—froze tuition.

The California model for public higher education combined equality with elitism. Equality dictated low tuition, which was called fees, although it supported instructional as well as student services. Elitism shaped the structure of public higher education. California chose to ensure quality and access through a hierarchical system that divided public higher education by institutional type and admission standards. The UC system, with nine doctoral, research universities admitted high school graduates in the top 12.5 percent of their class. The 22 campuses of California State University (CSU) offered comprehensive programs through the master's degree, stressed teaching, and accepted undergraduates from the top third of their high school class. Over one hundred community colleges fulfilled the promise of access through open admissions. California lacked the statewide coordinating agency found in most states. The California Postsecondary Education Commission (CPEC) provided only planning and advice for the legislature. The UC system had constitutional autonomy and left most budget and program decisions to its universities. CSU had a tradition of more centralized control of its campuses by its central administration.

Three actions undermined the credibility of UC leadership during the first half of the 1990s. First, the public learned of the huge retirement package given in 1992 to retiring President David Gardner. Then his successor, Jack Peltason, lost influence with the publication of a transcript of a teleconference where he criticized prominent legislators. Finally, the third president during the period, Richard Atkinson, became embroiled in the Regent's controversial decision to end affirmative action. Barry Munitz, the chancellor of the CSU system for the entire period, had the reputation of providing stronger leadership for that more centralized system.

The budget cuts in California seemed to call for a choice between quality and access, and UC and CSU and their campuses clearly chose to protect quality by sacrificing access. Both systems responded to the budget crisis by raising fees and by using short-term measures such as salary and vacancy freezes and early retirement programs. The USC System also reduced enrollments, as did several of the UC campuses. The actions of both systems appeared to be based on the belief that the past levels of state support would come back and that the fiscal crisis called for temporary coping, not fundamental change.

CALIFORNIA STATE UNIVERSITY SYSTEM

From 1990–91 through 1996–97, state general appropriations for CSU rose 4.3 percent in current dollars but fell over 13.4 percent in constant dollars. The survey response from the CSU System labeled the budget problem as large and claimed that fee increases only moderately filled the gap. Eighty percent of the institutional responses called the problem very large and twenty percent called it large. The CSU institutions held divided opinions on the contribution of student fees. Thirty-six percent checked moderate, the same percent marked slight, and twenty-seven percent labeled it significant. Despite the decline in funding and its reputation for centralization, CSU prepared neither a systemwide plan nor guidelines to shape campus responses to the budget crisis. Instead, it allowed campuses full discretion to develop their own plans and did not retain the right to approve them. CSU also allocated the cuts to its campuses primarily across-the-board.

Although it is understandable, given projected enrollments, that the system would propose opening a new campus at Fort Ord rather than closing existing ones, it is surprising that CSU did not recommend program eliminations. The response from CSU finance officers suggested that campuses closed programs on their own but not as a consequence of budget cuts. Forty-five percent of the responses from CSU institutions said they closed programs. The system also did not initiate mission changes, but 18 percent of the institutions surveyed noted such a change, with an increased emphasis on undergraduate education. The CSU official noted that system governance shifted during the period in the direction of more decentralization. This response certainly countered the traditional image of CSU as a centralized system closely controlled by the chancellor and senior staff.

CSU altered its enrollment strategy during the period by cutting admissions and shifting more students to community colleges. (The latter part of this strategy failed, since the community colleges, due to their own fee increases, lost students.) The system administration restructured its organization and operations by closing or consolidating offices and functions, contracting out services, and devolving activities to campuses, but it did not reduce senior staff. The finance officer of CSU stated that restructuring administrations, changing enrollment strategy, and raising revenues best characterized both system and campus actions during the period. The campus responses said restricting expenditures, reducing enrollments, and raising revenues best described their actions. Despite CSU's *laissez faire* approach to the budget crisis, three-quarters of its campus correspondents called the system role very important or important. On the other hand, fifty-five percent of those institutional replies saw the system actions as negative.

The response from the CSU System claimed that the quality of undergraduate and graduate education and of research and service activities was maintained, but conceded that undergraduate access declined. Nearly three quarters of the institutional responses reported that undergraduate access declined, while nearly half indicated that the quality of undergraduate education also fell. The decline in access is understandable, since 73 percent of the campuses decreased enrollments. The budget factors in system allocations to campuses before 1990 and after 1996 showed significant shifts. Base budgets rose from fourth to first, enrollments slipped from first to second, and salary increases and inflation fell from second to fourth. Special projects and programs remained third.

UNIVERSITY OF CALIFORNIA SYSTEM

From 1990–91 through 1996–97, state general appropriations to UC fell 4.4 percent in current and 20.6 percent in constant dollars. The response from the UC System characterized the problem created by funding cuts as very large and claimed that fee increases significantly filled the gap, covering about a quarter of the loss in state support. The description of the problem as "very large" compared with CSU's characterization of "large" conflicts with the common claim that outside income made UC less dependent on state revenues. Half of the campus responses also described the budget problem as very large and another third as large. The campus replies divided on the question of the contribution of tuition, with 36.4 percent calling it slight, 36.4 moderate, and only 27.3 significant.

The UC response stated that the central administration did not allow full discretion to the campuses to prepare their own plan, but prepared a systemwide plan and "some" guidelines for dealing with the diminished level of state support. However, the written comment suggested full discretion to the campuses. "Budget cuts of $433 million were distributed to the campuses. Campuses were given discretion as how to take the cuts." The UC System did not reserve the right to approve campus reduction plans. Though University Regents, system officials, campus officers, and faculty and students are listed as participating in preparing the system plan and guidelines, system officials from the President's Office played the lead role. UC required a combination of short- and long-term plans from the campuses, but distributed the cuts primarily across-the-board to its universities. The response stated that the system distributed the reductions: 50 percent budget cuts, 25 percent salary freeze, and 25 percent fee increases. No changes occurred in the relative importance of the factors used in budget allocations to campuses during the period. Base budgets remained first; salary and inflationary increases, second; and enrollments, third. The UC respondent indicated that no governance changes occurred during the period, although campuses did receive more flexibility in budget matters.

Despite responding that the system did not restructure its organization and operations, the reply noted a reduction of senior officers and a delegation of some functions and services to campuses. The President's Office of UC did not propose campus closures, but it recommended elimination of academic programs and closed "several" of those suggested. The reply cited opposition from legislators, regents, campus chancellors, faculty, and local communities as stopping some of the proposed eliminations. The only option not checked was the governor. Only 17 percent of the UC campuses said they closed programs, little more than a third of the percentage reporting closures in CSU.

Campus missions did not change nor did the system's enrollment strategy, although several of its universities reduced student numbers. The system cut the state subsidy for its five teaching hospitals, and UC San Francisco and Stanford merged their teaching hospitals. UC's finance officer thought that raising revenues best described the response of the system during the period, and restricting expenditures that of its universities. Restricting expenditures, changing enrollment strategy, and raising revenues constituted the most common responses from the campuses. The system reply asserted that undergraduate access and the quality of undergraduate and graduate education was maintained, but admitted that the quality of research activities and public service declined. Half of the replies from institutions reported that both access and quality declined in undergraduate education during the period. A third also thought the quality of graduate education and research declined and two-thirds believed the quality of public service fell. The UC campuses rated the importance of their system considerably lower than the institutions in CSU. Half of the UC universities considered their system important or very important and half moderately important. The replies from UC units also rated their reactions to system actions as more negative than the CSU campuses, with 60 percent unfavorable and only 20 percent favorable.

The finance officer of the California Planning Commission considered the role of System Boards and Administrations during the period as important, but below campus officers, which he rated very important. California represented one of the two instances where the reply from the coordinating or planning agency considered campus officers as more important than system officials. The planning officer called the budget problem large and considered tuition as significantly filling the loss in state funding. He saw no change in the budget factors used by the state in allocating resources to the University Systems. They ranked base budgets, enrollments, salary increases and inflation, and institutional missions both before and after the period. The Commission official believed that the systems stressed changing enrollment strategy, raising revenues, and restricting expenditures, while their campuses emphasized restructuring of organization and operations, changing enrollment strategy, and raising revenues.

MASSACHUSETTS

The recession hit earlier and harder in Massachusetts than in other states. The free fall in the state economy led to huge cuts for higher education. From FY

1989 through FY 1992, state appropriations plunged nearly 40 percent. Each of these years brought deep annual cuts, followed by mid-year recessions. Once again, higher education was one of the biggest losers among state services. The Systems of Higher Education responded with huge hikes in student charges. Between 1987–88 and 1993–94, tuition jumped 48 percent at public colleges and universities and fees soared 240 percent (Gold 270).

Massive deficits after the collapse of the "Massachusetts Miracle" meant that Governor Michael Dukakis could only raise taxes and slash spending before leaving office in January 1991. His successor, the Republican William Weld, a social moderate but fiscal conservative, won election on a platform promising both spending and tax cuts. In his first term, Weld pushed for spending reductions, tuition increases, and restructuring public higher education, including closing some state colleges. Although the legislature blocked some of the restructuring and all of the closings, it approved huge budget cuts and tuition increases. In 1994, a Task Force mandated by the legislature reviewed the large funding cuts and tuition increases and proposed a five-year plan for a fairer sharing of the funding of higher education between the state and students (Massachusetts Task Force). In his second term, Governor Weld accepted this advice and reversed course by pushing higher education's contribution to economic development and by stemming falling enrollments through increased funding and reduced tuition. Weld's initial attitude toward public higher education was hardly surprising. Private colleges and universities always dominated in Massachusetts, the only state with more students enrolled in the private than in the public sector (Gold 252–95; *Almanacs*).

Massachusetts divided its public colleges and universities into two systems. The University of Massachusetts System (UMASS) had five campuses (two of which joined the system during the period). The state coordinating board also acted as the governing body for the nine state colleges and fifteen community colleges. It underwent a series of reorganizations and title changes during the period: from the Board of Regents of Higher Education, to the Higher Education Coordinating Council, to the Massachusetts Board of Higher Education. The budget crisis ravaged the leadership of both the UMASS System and the Board of Higher Education. The former had six presidents from 1989 through 1995 and the latter, five chancellors. The Almanac of the Chronicle of Higher Education in 1995 declared: "A 'jump ship' mentality has existed for some time in public higher education in Massachusetts" (62). At times it seemed there might be no ship to jump from, since proposals circulated to abolish both boards and their central administrations. Toward the end of the period, politics produced strong leaders for the UMASS System and the Board of

Higher Education. The UMASS Board of Regents appointed as its President William Bulger, the long-time leader of the State Senate; and Governor Weld named a close associate, James Carlin, as Chair of the Board of Higher Education. Both leaders raised state funding, cut student tuition, and pressed for improved efficiency and performance *(Almanac,* 1996, 65).

UNIVERSITY OF MASSACHUSETTS

The system finance officer reported that state general appropriations for the UMASS System from 1990–91 through 1996–97 rose 19 percent in current dollars but only 1.7 percent in constant dollars. In spite of the improvement in the later years of the period, this officer considered state funding a large problem, while conceding that tuition and fees significantly filled the gap. Two-thirds of the UMASS institutions responding to the survey also called the problem large, but a third cited it as very large. Two-thirds of the campuses felt tuition contributed only moderately and a third only slightly to relieving the budget problem. The system prepared guidelines rather than a plan. Although system and campus officials participated in preparing the guidelines, the former took the lead. The system also retained the right to approve the required one-, two-, and three-year plans from its five universities and allocated reductions to these campuses primarily on a selective basis. Beginning in August of 1989, UMASS System implemented a three-year retrenchment plan that cut spending and enrollment by 10 to 15 percent. This initiative represented merely the first of a series of retrenchment and revenue plans. Given this activist approach to planning and budgeting, it is not surprising that UMASS was one of the two systems in this study that moved toward more centralization during the period. Perhaps increased centralization explains why this system was also one of the few that did not restructure and downsize the organization and operations of its central administration, despite complaints about its size and cost.

The UMASS System proposed no campus consolidations or closures, although its Boston campus closed—with much controversy—its downtown center. The system proposed 150 programs for elimination, but closed only 25. The respondent did not answer the question of why so many of these proposals failed. According to the system official, campuses themselves initiated and eliminated three undergraduate, four master's, and two doctoral programs. Two-thirds of the campus replies to the survey reported closing programs. The system office skipped the question of what actions best characterized the system's response to the budget problems of the period, but stated that raising revenues and restricting expenditures best described the institutional responses. The campus returns accepted this assessment but added restructuring their organization and operations. The system adopted the strategy of decreasing enrollments and approving huge tuition increases. The campuses, which controlled fees, raised them to levels higher than tuition. No campus mission changes occurred during the period. Though its Worcester campus had a teaching hospital, UMASS neither cut its state subsidy nor changed its state status. The system made major changes in the funding factors that determined budget allocations to campuses. It abandoned base budgets as a determinant and added enrollments, although salary increases and inflation remained the number one factor. This abandonment of base budgets was unique among the systems, for almost all of them kept it as the top consideration in allocations to campuses.

The UMASS finance officer admitted that access decreased during the period but gave no assessment on what happened to the quality of undergraduate education. The response asserted that the quality of research increased, while the quality of graduate education and public service was maintained. Two-thirds of the campus replies saw a decline in undergraduate access and a third cited a drop in the quality of undergraduate and graduate education. On the other hand, two-thirds of the respondents felt the quality of graduate education, research, and service actually increased. Two-thirds of the UMASS universities rated their system as very important in fashioning the response to the budget crisis. Despite its activist approach, two-thirds of the respondents also reacted positively to the system actions.

STATE COLLEGE SYSTEM

The finance officer of the State College System reported that state funding from 1990–91 through 1996–97 increased 18.5 percent in current dollars and 1.2 percent in constant dollars. He described the budget problem as very large from 1990 through 1992 and as moderate for the rest of the period and admitted that tuition and fees significantly filled the gap. Although the campus responses agreed with this analysis of tuition's contribution, two-thirds called the budget problem very large.

The State College System took a much more decentralized approach to planning and budgeting than UMASS, in part because each of the colleges had its own governing board. It developed no systemwide plan and gave the colleges full discretion in preparing their own strategies. The system also failed to retain the power of approving campus plans and allocated budget cuts primarily across-the-board. Governance moved toward more decentralization according to the survey response. The appointment of a new activist Chair of the Massachusetts Board of Higher Education came at the end of the period. The Board did implement a major restructuring of its executive offices, probably in response to criticism of its large administrative payroll. It cut senior officers, closed and consolidated offices and functions, contracted out services, and devolved functions and services to campuses. The system did not recommend campus closures, despite the early proposals from the Weld Administration to close several of its colleges. It did propose eliminating 39 programs and closed 23 of them. Campus appeals explain the difference, according to the respondent. A quarter of the campuses responding to the survey eliminated programs.

The period produced no campus mission changes. The system did change enrollment strategies by reducing admissions at its baccalaureate campuses and shifting more students to its community colleges. The Board of Higher Education also approved huge hikes in tuition. The system finance officer saw some shift in the relative importance of funding factors for allocations to campuses between 1990 and 1996. Performance rose in importance from sixth to fourth and institutional missions fell from fifth to seventh, but base budgets, enrollments, and salary increases and inflation remained the top three components. The officer of the State College System felt undergraduate access declined but the quality of academic programs, research, and service was maintained. The replies from campuses supported most of this assessment, although only 28.5 percent felt that access declined. Half of the college replies rated the system's role during the period as slight, but the other half considered it either important or very important. Half of the campuses marked "none" as their reaction to the system actions during the period. The other half split evenly between a positive and a negative reaction.

A finance officer of the Board of Higher Education responded on its behalf as the coordinating agency in Massachusetts. This response labeled the budget problem for public higher education as very large, with tuition significantly filling the gap. This officer thought the coordinating agency, systems boards and administrations, and the governor and legislature had only slight influence in shaping the response of public higher education in the state. This reply rated campus officers as very important and institutional boards of trustees and faculty as important. It depicted decentralization as the governance change during the period. This officer may have been thinking primarily of the State College System, for the strong role in planning, budgeting, and eliminating programs by the UMASS System suggests that it surely had more than slight importance. The citing of institutional boards, which the state colleges had but the universities did not, confirms that conclusion. Although the two system responses claimed that no campus mission changes occurred, the reply from the coordinating board lists such changes as the action that best characterized the system's response to budget problems. The finance officer of the coordinating board believed that both access and quality in undergraduate education decreased. This response also said quality declined in public service but was maintained in graduate education and research activities.

NEW YORK

The recession also arrived earlier and lasted longer in New York than in most of the states, bringing massive deficits in its wake. Once again, the soaring costs of health care, welfare, and corrections demanded state funds that once had gone to higher education. Big cuts in appropriations for higher education came in the beginning, moderated in the middle as the recession receded, and then returned at the end of the period. From 1990–91 through 1996–97, state funding for City and State Universities of New York fell by 21 percent in current, and 34 percent in constant dollars. Their tuition, which once had fallen below the national average, moved toward the high rates of the Northeastern states.

New York had a balance of private and public higher education. Private colleges and universities enrolled forty percent of the students, yet the State and the City Universities (SUNY and CUNY) constituted the first and third largest public systems in the country. Proponents of public higher education claimed that no New York governor since Nelson Rockefeller had supported that sector. Presidents of independent institutions believed their sector fared no better in the first half of the 1990s. Both sectors complained about cuts in their state funding from the Democratic Governor, Mario Cuomo, and his Republican successor, George Pataki (Bracco and Sanchez-Penley, 198–228).

SUNY and CUNY, with different constituencies and clienteles, had to confront contrasting complaints. Critics claimed that CUNY's ten senior and six community colleges and a four-year technical institution admitted too many unprepared students, spent too much on remediation, and graduated too few of those it enrolled. They yearned for a return of a bygone era when its senior colleges educated the poorest but the brightest students and produced renowned scholars and corporate leaders. Though many SUNY campuses had built a reputation for quality in undergraduate education, critics charged that the system was too big, dispersed, and diverse for effective and efficient management. Its 64 campuses, which spread throughout the state and stretched from two-year colleges to doctoral centers, lent credence to this charge. So many units, often located in rural areas, meant that many SUNY campuses had lower enrollments and higher costs than had national peers of the same institutional types.

CITY UNIVERSITY OF NEW YORK

CUNY's Chancellor, Ann Reynolds, responded aggressively to the complaints and the cuts. While vigorously defending CUNY's mission of serving the city's underprivileged and its tradition of low tuition and ready access, she launched plans and programs to raise admission standards and institutional perfor- mance. Her initiatives expanded college preparatory courses in high schools, limited remedial programs, increased admission standards at the senior col- leges, and developed a planning process to close weak and duplicative pro- grams. She dealt with the budget crisis through two declarations of fiscal exigency, which allowed faculty and staff layoffs (City University of New York, 1995). Though Chancellor Reynolds eventually prevailed in the courts on the legality of these declarations, they insured the opposition of the powerful faculty union, the Professional Staff Congress. The union accused the chancellor of acting repeatedly without faculty consultation and of centralizing authority at the expense of campus autonomy.

The CUNY Board of Trustees steadfastly supported her aggressive actions against the complaints of the faculty union and of some campus presidents. That support vanished in 1997 when Governor Pataki and Mayor Rudolph Giuliani packed the Board with new appointees. The new majority, and especially its new Chair Anne Paolucci, was anything but silent about its conservative political and educational goals and its opposition to Chancellor Reynolds. Ironically, the new chair publicly and repeatedly attacked the chancellor with the same agenda that Reynolds had championed—higher standards, less remediation, and improved performance. These criticisms echoed the complaints of the mayor and governor. In September 1997, Chancellor Reynolds left to become the President of the University of Alabama at Birmingham (Mathews, 1, 15–16).

CUNY's chief financial officer depicted the budget problem as large, but admitted that tuition significantly filled the gap. Forty-three percent of the responding campuses considered the problem very large and the same percent called it large. Forty-three percent also thought tuition and fees helped only mod- erately in offsetting state cuts, as opposed to 29 percent who felt they made a sig- nificant contribution. CUNY prepared systemwide plans for dealing with the diminished level of state support and issued guidelines for the campus plans. Although campus officers participated with the system trustees and officers in developing the systemwide plans, the latter clearly dominated. The system required two-year plans from campuses and reserved the right to approve them. Given its centralized budgeting and planning, it is surprising that the CUNY sys- tem distributed the funding cuts to its colleges primarily across-the-board. System governance definitely concentrated authority in its Central Administration.

With this emphasis on centralized direction, it is not surprising that CUNY only consolidated some offices in its Central Administration and did not reduce its senior officers or its functions and services. The system finance officer felt that restructuring organizations and operations, revising degree requirements, and raising revenues best characterized system actions during the period, while the first two along with restricting expenditures best described the institutional response. The campus replies endorsed this characterization.

The CUNY System moved aggressively to eliminate duplicative academic programs. Its planning process mandated regular reviews, with the goals of closing programs with low enrollment and questionable quality. CUNY officials claimed that this process led to the suspension, consolidation, or closing of 128 programs and the strengthening of 91. Eighty-six percent of the campuses responding to the survey said they eliminated programs, by far the highest percent of any system. Fifty percent also redesigned their undergraduate curriculum. The survey replies from both the system and the institutions indicated that campus missions did not change during the period, although the chancellor pushed the Senior Colleges to concentrate on their high-demand, high-quality programs.

Whereas some systems cut enrollment in response to budget cuts, CUNY increased its student numbers to accommodate a growing student demand, especially of new immigrants in New York City. The CUNY finance officer claimed that access was maintained, but conceded that the quality of both undergraduate and graduate education declined. He believed the quality of research and public service remained stable. CUNY was the only system in the study that seemed to choose access over quality. However, 43 percent of the campus responses said both access and quality in undergraduate education declined. The same percent cited a decline in graduate education.

The CUNY System also altered its approach to campus allocations more than most systems. Although base budgets continued as the top factor, salary increases and inflation and institutional missions fell in importance. Enrollments increased from third to second and performance rose sharply from seventh to fourth. Special projects, which the Central Administration generally developed, moved from fifth to third.

A survey high of 72 percent of the CUNY campuses rated the system's role as very high. An additional 14 percent called its role important. As might be expected with an aggressive Central Administration, the institutional assessment of system actions was much more divided. Campus reactions split 57 percent negative and 43 percent positive.

STATE UNIVERSITY OF NEW YORK

SUNY's Chancellor, Bruce Johnstone, led his system in the opposite direction from his CUNY counterpart. His canon was decentralization. Traditionally, SUNY had been run by its Central Administration as a single university with constituent campuses. Johnstone declared: "SUNY is not a university in the sense of a single institution, but a university system—of substantially autonomous campuses" (Johnstone, "Budget" 9). Senior officers even tried to change the title of the organization from Central Administration to System Administration, with mixed success in practice, especially in campus parlance. As so often happens with moves toward decentralization, SUNY presidents, especially from its University Centers, called for more autonomy, including determining their own tuition, enrollment levels, and academic programs (Greiner). Center presidents complained that the Central Administration still controlled tuition revenues and budget allocations to protect small rural colleges with falling enrollments. They also charged that the Central Administration remained too big, too costly, and too bureaucratic.

Johnstone also devoted his chancellorship to disproving the recurring charge that SUNY was overbuilt, unplanned, and inefficient. He wrote a series of system monographs to prove his point. His administration also answered these criticisms with a white paper called *SUNY 2000* ("Chancellor's Letter"), five-year reviews of campus missions, and a Performance Report that detailed system results on efficiency and productivity indicators (Burke, "Preserving"). An expert on higher education funding, Johnstone also reversed a SUNY tradition of supporting low tuition by urging that students pay a larger, but specified, share of educational costs. Though Governor Cuomo had initial doubts, both he and his successor Pataki—responding to revenue fluctuations rather than rational arguments—adopted huge hikes in tuition, often followed by tuition freezes when student protests produced legislative resistance (Bracco and Sanchez-Penley).

When Johnstone resigned because of illness in 1994, the SUNY Board appointed Thomas Bartlett, former Chancellor of the Oregon System, who had presided over a reorganization and downsizing in response to state budget cuts. The Pataki Administration treated Bartlett as a Cuomo appointee, because the SUNY Board announced his appointment before the gubernatorial election in 1994, which many observers thought Cuomo would win. Pataki swiftly selected new Trustees to fill vacant or expired positions and soon gained a conservative majority on the SUNY Board. When the new majority rejected Bartlett's recommendations for senior system posts, he resigned in June 1996. The Board finally persuaded John Ryan, former president of Indiana University, to become interim chancellor and later made that appointment permanent when a national search failed to attract acceptable candidates.

The new Board majority endorsed Pataki's first budget proposal in 1995, which mandated huge budget cuts and tuition increases. The next year, it rejected a budget request recommended by system officers that followed guidelines from the governor's own Budget Division, because it proposed a slight increase rather than a budget cut. The Pataki Trustees issued their own planning paper, *Rethinking SUNY,* late in 1995 (State University of New York). It criticized SUNY as too centralized and the System Administration as too big and bureaucratic and proposed devolving to campuses most decisions on budgets, tuition, enrollments, and programs. On the other hand, Board members seemed set on determining admission standards, curriculum requirements, and presidential appointments—matters that had long been left largely to the campuses (Mathews, 1, 15–16). The Board's attitude toward the System Administration seemed to shift over time. Instead of downsizing as it favored in *Rethinking SUNY,* it filled vacant positions and created new senior positions after most of the top officers left in 1995 and 1996.

The SUNY finance officer described the financial problem of the period as large, with tuition significantly filling the gap. However, forty-three percent of the campus replies called the budget problem very large. Twenty-three percent said tuition contributed only slightly to ease the problem, and forty-three percent only moderately. The system prepared a series of annual plans for dealing with the decline in state support, but left campuses with full discretion to decide their own reductions. It did not require system approval of campus reduction plans. Though campus officers participated in preparing the system plans, the real direction came from board members and system officers. The system allocated reductions to campuses selectively from 1990 through 1994 and across-the-board for the remaining three years. System governance clearly changed toward more decentralization. Although senior officers prepared several plans for downsizing the system administration during the period, the Board did not approve them. The total staff declined mostly through attrition by eliminating vacant positions.

The reply to the survey states that the System Administration did not propose formally or suggest informally campus consolidations or closures. Privately, senior staff developed several scenarios for consolidations and closures, which responded to recurring complaints about too many campuses with low enrollment. Prior to the Pataki appointments, the SUNY Board threatened to close unspecified units if the legislature approved the cuts proposed in the governor's first budget. Although the budget passed largely intact, fear of legislative opposition and community resistance led the Board to avoid closures. The system administration did not propose program eliminations, but it did periodically identify programs of wide availability, high costs, and low enrollments and asked campuses to justify their continuance. This review process contributed to campus decisions to close 35 undergraduate, 14 master's, and 3 doctoral programs. Survey replies from SUNY colleges and universities said 53 percent of them eliminated programs. The system finance officer stated that a "program driven master plan" changed campus missions during the period, but institutional replies reported that only 16 percent of the campuses altered their missions. Although the system did not change enrollment strategies during the period, enrollments fell overall, allegedly because of large tuition increases. A number of campuses tried to increase enrollments, especially of transfer students, but with mixed success. The system slashed the state subsidy to its three teaching hospitals. This action constituted a major source of budget savings during the period. SUNY also tried unsuccessfully—because of legislative opposition—to convert its teaching hospitals into public benefit, or private, corporations.

The finance officer thought that raising revenues and restricting expenditures best characterized the system and campus responses to the budget problems. The campus replies added restructuring their administrations to raising revenues and restricting expenditures. The factors for budget allocations to campuses remained the same throughout the period: base budgets, salary and inflation increases, enrollments, and institutional missions. The SUNY finance officer perceived that undergraduate access declined, while the quality of undergraduate and graduate education, research activities, and public service was maintained. Half of the campus replies saw a decline in undergraduate access and 37 percent a drop in the quality of undergraduate education. Although the System Administration decentralized during the period, half of the campus returns to the survey called its role important or very important, yet almost two-thirds gave a negative or highly negative reaction to system actions. Surprisingly, the comprehensive colleges were slightly more negative than the University Centers.

The finance officer from the coordinating agency, the State Education Department, also described the budget problem as large and agreed that tuition significantly filled the gap. This officer rated the importance of various groups in shaping the response of public higher education to the budget cuts as follows: governors, legislators, and their staffs are cited as very important; and system boards and administrators as important. The influence of coordinating staff and campus officers is seen as slight. If the systems maintained base budgets as the top factor in their allocations to campuses, this reply noted considerable changes in the factors influencing state allocations. The importance of base budgets, salary increases and inflation, and institutional missions declined, while performance and productivity showed sizeable increases. The officer from the coordinating agency believed that the governance of higher education in New York State moved toward more decentralization. This belief probably stemmed from a decline in the influence of the higher education division of the State Education Department. This division suffered repeated cuts in budgets and personnel during the 1990s, and the exercise of its authority of program approval provoked considerable opposition from both the public and the private sectors of higher education. Changing enrollment strategies, raising revenues, and restricting expenditures, according to the State Education Department response, best characterized the responses of both the systems and institutions to the budget problems. This officer claimed that undergraduate access was maintained at the expense of a decline in the quality of undergraduate and graduate programs, research activities, and public service.

WISCONSIN

Wisconsin's cut in funding for public higher education came at the end rather than the beginning of the period. Funding suffered more from small increases than large cuts. Unlike other states, diminished funding did not stem from an economic recession, for Wisconsin remained fairly prosperous. Passage of a property tax proposition, similar to those in other states, did restrict state spending. In addition, the University of Wisconsin had lost some support in the legislature. Although most lawmakers graduated from a university campus, some felt that the system had abandoned its progressive tradition of service to the state, while others viewed its Madison campus as a hotbed of liberalism. The UW system also alienated some legislators with its policy of reducing enrollment to raise its funding per student to the national average. Lawmakers felt this policy, combined with tuition increases, diminished student access. Suspicion of the system grew when a report from its audit committee in 1991 charged that UW had misled the legislature about the number of course sections created by several hundred new faculty positions funded by the state. Relations worsened when the System President Kenneth Shaw fought with state lawmakers over the report. After Shaw resigned in late 1991 to become the head of Syracuse University, his successor, Katharine Lyall, improved legislative relations. Although the popular Republican Governor, Tommy Thompson, seemed more supportive of the university, the Board of Regents angered him in 1995 by increasing the salaries of top system and campus administrators against his advice. The governor proposed freezing salaries of UW administrators and cutting the budget for the university system in the 1995–97 biennium. The legislature rejected the salary freeze but approved the budget cuts for the university. Despite the complaints about the university, even the cuts in the 1995–97 biennium appeared less than those allocated to state agencies (*Almanacs*).

Wisconsin had no statewide coordinating or planning agency, but the legislature retained tight control over the university's budgeting and personnel practices. The Board of Regents governed the UW System of 13 four-year universities, 13 freshmen-sophomore centers, and a university extension. The Regents and the System President provided strong direction by stressing statewide priorities, controlling program duplication, and reducing campus competition. UW's strategic plan for 1985–95, *Planning the Future*, emphasized centralized direction to assure accountability to the state. Pressed by both the governor and the legislature, in December 1993 the system issued the first of its accountability reports of performance results (Sanders, Layzell, Boatright). In 1994, the system reversed its policy of reducing enrollment and pledged to admit 4,000 additional students and to fund them from its own resources. In return, the UW System sought in 1995, with the support of Governor Thompson, to loosen legislative control of the university budgets and personnel. The legislature rejected this request for lump sum budgeting and the request for an end to position control. It also mandated a large cut for the System and campus administrations in the 1995–97 budget and protected academic units critical to undergraduate access.

Clearly, centralization dominated policymaking through the first half of the 1990s in UW. Not surprisingly, central direction generated campus opposition, especially from the flagship campus at Madison. Two planning documents adopted in the summer of 1996 showed a dramatic shift in the direction of governance. As the legislature mandated, the Regents downsized the System Administration by 20 percent of its staff, including cuts in senior and mid-level positions. A *Restructuring Report* and a new strategic planning document, *A Study of the UW System in the 21st Century*, announced a change in emphasis from centralization to decentralization and from state accountability toward campus autonomy (Board of Regents). *The Restructuring Report* stated that System Administration should "rebalance its activities more toward assisting UW institutions in achieving their primary mission of teaching, research, and public service, with somewhat less time and emphasis devoted to monitoring control and compliance activities" (Sanders, 3). It spoke of the need to persuade state officials and the public that more autonomy with incentives could do more than centralized controls to cut costs and expand services to students and the state. The System Administration pledged to develop policies that assisted campuses in pursuing their own missions and to create "managed competition among institutions to focus resources on performance." The Report claimed that "Don Langenberg, President of the University of Maryland System, has identified the functions that systems are uniquely positioned to perform" and endorsed synergy, strategy, efficiency, accountability, and integrity as the UW System objectives (Sanders, 3).

Although state general appropriations between 1990–91 and 1996–97 grew by 13 percent in current dollars, it fell by 6 percent in constant dollars. UW's financial officer characterized the budget problem as large. "While we did not have to resort to fiscal emergency, in 95–97, we had an absolute base cut even after new compensation, for an ongoing cut of $33 million." The respondent conceded that tuition and fees helped significantly in filling the shortfall in state funding. Tuition for resident students grew by 30 percent from 1992–93 through 1996–97. These increases produced in Wisconsin, as in other states, a concern in the legislature about loss of undergraduate access. The finance officer responded to this complaint with the comment that tuition in UW remained lower than peer institutions in the surrounding states. Although most of the campuses also answered that the fall in funding created a large or very large problem, 43 percent described it as moderate. Fifty-seven percent thought tuition and fees provided only moderate help in meeting their financial needs.

The UW System prepared guidelines for campus plans and reserved the right of approval. Although campus officers participated in preparing the guidelines, the real direction came from the Regents and system officials. UW required two-year plans from campuses to fit biennial budgeting, but allocated funds to campuses primarily across-the-board. Formal governance stayed the same statutorily, but the Board delegated more flexibility to institutions and sought additional flexibility from the state. The System Administration restructured itself by reducing senior officers, closing or consolidating offices and functions, and devolving functions and services to campuses.

The Wisconsin system did not propose campus closures. The respondent claimed that the political controversy created by the past closing of a two-year college caused everyone to avoid this option. Though the system did not propose program closings, campuses on their own initiative eliminated 40 undergraduate and 14 master's programs. The system officer stated that this result came not from budget cuts but from a system policy that required campuses to fund new programs through internal reallocation. Over 70 percent of the campuses replying to the survey said they closed programs. UW set a strategy of cutting enrollment during most of the period and then reversed this approach at the end. It reduced enrollment by over 12,000 FTE from 1987 through 1995 to bring funding per student to the national average. The plan for 1995 to 2001 called for an increase of 4,000 students, supported entirely by reallocated resources. The system reduced the state subsidy and converted its teaching hospital into a public benefit corporation, with more flexibility to respond to a managed-care market.

The system officer indicated that restructuring administrations, raising revenues, and restricting expenditures best characterized UW's response to budget stringency. Campus replies said changing enrollment strategy, restructuring administrations, and restricting expenditures best described their actions. Mission changes initiated by the campuses, not the system, increased emphasis on undergraduate education at two UW institutions. The funding components used by the system for campus allocations remained unchanged: base budgets, enrollments, salary increases, and institutional missions. Rather than answering the specific question concerning access and quality, the system reply indicated that in the early 1990s the system increased support per student, due first to enrollment reductions and second to modest state funding increases. Tighter budgets in recent years slowed this trend. The two research universities, Madison and Milwaukee, did not respond to the question on access and quality. Only 20 percent of the comprehensive colleges believed that the quality of undergraduate education declined but 40 percent felt that access diminished.

All of the comprehensive institutions, as opposed to 40 percent of the graduate and research centers, rated the UW System as important. The two graduate and research universities at Madison and Milwaukee assessed the system impact as negative, while only 20 percent of comprehensive campuses gave negative ratings. Neither of the research universities reported a mission change, but 40 percent of the comprehensive colleges altered their mission, the highest by far in the survey. Eighty percent of the comprehensive institutions and even 50 percent of the research universities eliminated degree programs and redesigned their undergraduate curriculum.

TEXAS

Texas also suffered from the national recession of the early 1990s, but appropriations for higher education appeared better than in any of the study states, save Florida. This appearance proved somewhat deceiving, for the rising costs of new programs in South Texas and of remedial education absorbed much of these apparent increases. Faculty salaries and per student funding, especially in the graduate and research universities, fell considerably below national peers. Despite small declines in enrollment during the first half of the 1990s, public colleges and universities in Texas faced the prospects of educating nearly all of the projected increase of 150,000 additional students by 2005.

Both Governor Ann Richards and her successor, George Bush, generally supported public colleges and universities. More importantly, in this weak governor state, the legislature in the first half of the period provided what it considered reasonable funding given the state of the economy (*Almanacs*). The usual squabbles arose over the division of state appropriations between the flag-

ship universities and the regional campuses. Robert Berdahl left the presidency of the University of Texas at Austin for the chancellorship of UC Berkeley
after four years of frustration with the Texas legislature (Shevory). He complained that lawmakers denied the special funding, tuition levels, and admission standards required for a premier research university. At the same time,
the presidents of regional colleges and universities complained that UT's Austin
and A&M's College Station got the lion's share of state funding. Though tuition
increased sharply during the period, the Texas legislature resisted the larger
increases proposed by many systems and campus leaders.

Surveys went to four systems with several campuses: The University of
Texas, Texas A&M, University of Houston, and Texas State University. The UT
System governed seven universities, two upper-level institutions, and several
health science centers and branches. A&M contained seven universities and a
health science center. The University of Houston included two universities and
two upper-level institutions. Texas State had four universities and one upper-
level center. Governance in Texas was more decentralized than in most states,
in part because the legislature allocated appropriations directly to the colleges
and universities rather than through the coordinating agency or university systems. The Texas Higher Education Coordinating Board (THECB) and its staff
enjoyed a good reputation in the capitol and on campuses. It had rather extensive statutory authority, except for budget allocations, but exercised its powers
collaboratively under the long and capable leadership of its Commissioner,
Kenneth Ashworth. Government leaders believed the decentralization of governance and the number of systems raised costs and diminished effectiveness.
They called for expanding the coordinating authority of the THECB and for
reducing the number of university systems.

Although all of the University Systems in Texas had decentralized governance, the University of Texas, under Chancellor William Cunningham, provided more central direction than the heads of the other three systems, which
did not sit well with UT Austin. Leadership in the Texas A&M System suffered
from a financial scandal and a succession of three chancellors during the period,
and Houston experienced turnovers of system chancellors and senior staff and
campus presidents. Texas State University had only a small system office and
delegated most responsibilities to its four universities. See Tables 3.1A and 3.1B.

The finance officer of the THECB depicted the budget problem as small
and suggested that tuition and fees moderately made up for limited state funding. The UT, A&M, and Houston finance officers characterized the fiscal problem as moderate, while the Texas State official considered it no problem.
System respondents from UT, A&M, and TSU thought tuition and fees signif-

Table 3.1 A *State Higher Education Appropriations for Texas Higher Education Systems: Percent Change Compared to the Previous Year and 7-Year Percent Change Based on Current Dollars*

	1991–92	1992–93	1993–94	1994–95	1995–96	1996–97	7-year change
University of Texas	4.4	0.9	14.9	-1.9	3.0	0.6	23.0
Texas A&M University	6.8	1.3	12.0	-1.5	6.5	0.2	27.4
University of Houston	6.3	1.3	5.9	-1.9	3.1	-0.2	15.1
Texas State University	6.1	1.6	8.7	-2.6	11.8	3.8	32.3

Source: Based on Hines data.

Table 3.1 B *State Higher Education Appropriations for Texas Higher Education Systems: Percent Change Compared to the Previous Year and 7-Year Percent Change Based on Constant Dollars*

	1991–92	1992–93	1993–94	1994–95	1995–96	1996–97	7-year change
University of Texas	0.7	-1.9	11.1	-4.8	0.0	-2.3	2.1
Texas A&M University	3.1	-1.5	8.2	-4.5	3.4	-2.6	5.7
University of Houston	2.6	-1.5	2.4	-4.8	0.1	-3.0	-4.5
Texas State University	2.3	-1.3	5.1	-5.5	8.6	0.8	9.8

Source: Based on Hines data adjusted for inflation according to the Higher Education Price Index.

icantly filled the shortfall between state funding and system requirements, while the reply from the Houston System marked "slightly." The campus replies tended to support their system assessments on the size of the problem, aside from Texas State, where two-thirds of the institutions called state funding a large problem. The same held generally true for tuition, except for UT, where 57 percent of the campuses, including two research universities, claimed tuition contributed only slightly to easing the budget problem. Despite these responses, none of the four systems felt the need to develop systemwide plans, though Texas A&M did prepare guidelines. UT, A&M, and TSU did reserve the right to approve campus plans. All four systems required a combination of short- and long-term plans from their campuses. Only the University of Houston had a governance change, and it moved toward more decentralization.

UT and TSU did not restructure their system organization and operation. Texas A&M and Houston did close or consolidate some offices. The Houston system also reduced its senior officers and devolved functions and services to campuses. A&M, alone among all the systems surveyed in the six study states, proposed and achieved a campus closure or consolidation. Actually, it merely consolidated a small College of Marine Science at Galveston with the administration of its College Station campus. None of the four Texas systems recommended program eliminations; and the campus responses also list no such closures. However, the finance officer of the THECB said they cooperated in closing about 200 doctoral programs with few or no enrollments, as part of a doctoral review mandated by the legislature. UT indicated mission changes that increased emphases on graduate education and research; and Houston reported increasing slightly the stress on graduate education at one of its campuses. Both respondents stated that the campuses, not the systems, initiated these changes. Neither A&M nor TSU noted changes in mission. Only A&M altered its enrollment strategies. It increased enrollments, especially of in-state students and two-year college transfers.

The four systems gave similar answers to the question of what actions best characterized the system and institutional responses to the budget stringency of the 1990s. UT reported raising revenues for the system and restricting expenditures for its institutions. A&M said restructuring, changing enrollment strategies, and raising revenues for itself and changing enrollment strategy and raising revenues for its campuses. Houston responded restructuring and raising revenues for the system, and the same for its institutions. Texas State replied raising revenues for the system and changing enrollment strategy and restricting expenditures for its campuses.

As might be expected, the campus responses to the importance and value of their systems during the period were mixed. For A&M, 45 percent of the institutions called the system important or very important, with fairly even respons- es from research and comprehensive universities. Half of the research uni- versities give the system a positive rating, but the comprehensives split their reactions, one-third positive and one-third negative. All of the comprehensive campuses but only 25 percent of the research universities rated the role of the UT system as important. Forty-four percent of the former and 38 percent of the latter viewed system actions as positive. Its one research university called the role of the UH system moderately important, while all of the comprehen- sive campuses that responded considered its role very important. The latter also gave the system a positive rating, while the research university checked "none" in response to the question of its reaction to system actions. Two-thirds of the TSU institutions called the system role slight, but two-thirds also had a positive reaction.

UT conceded that the quality of undergraduate and graduate education decreased during the period, while claiming that access to undergraduate education and the quality of research activities and public service was main- tained. Its campuses thought that the quality of undergraduate education was maintained and 43 percent responded that the quality of graduate edu- cation increased. A&M gave a more optimistic answer. It reported an increase in both access and quality for undergraduate education and in the quality of graduate, research, and service activities. Although slightly less optimistic, its institutions agreed with most of this assessment. UH sug- gested an increase in the quality of research and maintenance of the quality of the other missions and undergraduate access. Half of the campus replies perceived a decline in quality and access in undergraduate education. TSU claimed undergraduate access increased and the quality of undergraduate and graduate education and research activities was maintained, while the quality of public service improved. The institutional responses claimed main- tenance rather than improvement in undergraduate access.

The finance officer from the coordinating agency listed the role of the fol- lowing as very important: system administrators and boards, campus offi- cers, the governor's office, and the legislature and their staff. He cited the Texas Higher Education Commission as only moderately important. The reply from the THECB noted no change in the main factors for state alloca- tions to campuses, with institutional missions first, enrollments second, base budgets third, and salary increases and inflation fourth. It also indicat- ed no change in governance during the 1990s. This response claimed that raising revenues and restricting expenditures best characterized the responses of both the systems and their campuses to state funding during the period. The finance officer of the Commission felt that access increased and the quality of undergraduate and graduate programs remained stable.

FLORIDA

The recession struck Florida in 1990. State revenues through 1992 fell far below projections, while the cost of health care, social services, public schools, and especially corrections rose sharply. To avoid tax increases, the legislature cut state spending. The economy began a slow recovery in 1993, and revenues increased gradually. After cuts in FY 1991 and 1992 and flat funding in 1993, the annual budgets for public colleges and universities brought sizeable increases. From 1990–91 through 1996–97, state funding for the university system rose by 31.4 percent in current dollars and 9 percent in constant dollars. Access constituted the big problem, for higher education in Florida had to cope with a projected surge of students second only to California. From 1990 through 1996, enrollments at public institutions grew by 7.5 percent, and higher education had to prepare for a projected 28 percent increase in high school graduates over the next decade. Rapid enrollment growth during the 1980s and early 1990s had reduced significantly the State University System's funding per student (Sanchez-Penley; Martinez and Nodine).

Florida's 28 public two-year colleges provided easy access to vocational training and lower-division education. Access to the nine universities in its State University System (SUS) became a pressing problem because of rising student demand. This led to the opening in 1997 of a tenth campus in South Florida. System and campus leaders proposed to relieve or reduce their budget problems with large tuition increases, but the Florida legislature rejected this solution, which so many other states accepted. The lawmakers restrained tuition increases to preserve student access. Resident tuition at the universities rose by only 10 percent from 1992 to 1996–97. Ever ready to legislate on policy for higher education, Florida lawmakers tried to reduce the space problem by limiting the number of credit hours of graduates and the remediation of underprepared students. They also adopted performance-based budgeting to increase graduation rates. The Master Plan of SUS for 1993–98 made improving access and quality in undergraduate education the overarching goals of the State University System.

The university system had a tradition of centralized leadership, especially under the direction of its politically astute Chancellor Charles Reed. He maintained good relations with Governor Lawton Chiles and—more important in this weak governor state—close contacts with legislative leaders. As often happens with strong system heads and centralized direction, pressure for more campus autonomy grew during the period. John Lombardi, President of the University of Florida, pressed for more institutional autonomy and won support for his views among influential legislators. The absence of a coordinating agency in Florida enhanced the authority of the system and its chancellor over planning, policymaking, and academic programming. The Postsecondary Planning Commission prepared excellent policy and planning documents, but possessed only advisory, rather than coordinating, powers.

Despite comparatively good budgets, the finance officer from the SUS claimed that state funding created a large problem, since "in terms of real (adjusted for inflation) funding per FTE student, we are still $1,300 below the 1989–90 level." Fifty-six percent of the campuses also called state funding a large problem, and a third called it a moderate problem. The system response claimed that tuition and fees filled none of the gap between funding and needs. Three-fourths of the responding institutions marked "slightly" or "none." This answer on tuition possibly stemmed from disappointment over the legislature's rejection of the larger increases proposed by the university system and advocated by its campus presidents. Though the finance officer from the Planning Commission agreed on the size of the budget problem, he judged that tuition and fee increases moderately filled the shortfall between system needs and state funding.

Contrary to its reputation for central direction, SUS prepared neither a systemwide plan nor guidelines for dealing with constrained funding. It allowed campuses full discretion to prepare their own plans and did not reserve the right to approve the required two-year plans. The ranking of budget factors in system allocations to its universities remained the same during the period: base budgets, student enrollments, and salary increases and inflation. The respondent for SUS stated that no change occurred in system governance during the period; the reply from the finance officer of the Planning Commission confirmed this conclusion.

This system constituted one of the few in this study that did not restructure its central administration, although its campuses downsized their administrations. Campus missions did change during the period by increasing the emphasis on undergraduate education and by reducing the stress on research and public services. The reply credited legislators and System Regents and officers with initiating these mission changes, which represented a unique response from the systems in this study. The Florida University System did not propose campus closures, since all of its units had rising demand, and it planned to open a new campus. The system also proposed no elimination of degree programs, probably for the same reason. Though the research universities did not eliminate academic programs, responses from 17 percent of comprehensive institutions say they closed programs. Two-thirds of both types of campuses reported redesigning the curriculum, which probably resulted from a state mandate ending state funding for excessive credit hours earned by graduates. Given the growing student demand, SUS continued its strategy of increasing enrollments. As often occurred in Florida, the legislature mandated this strategy. Its proviso language in budget bills often stipulated that funding increases carried the expectations of additional enrollments in the university system. SUS reduced the state subsidy of its teaching hospitals, but did not attempt to change their state status.

The system respondent did not indicate the steps that best characterized the system response to budget stringency during the period. Those checked for the campuses constituted revising campus missions and restricting expenditures. The respondent from the Planning Commission thought that raising revenues and restricting expenditures best described the responses of both the system and its universities to fiscal constraint. Florida was one of the two systems surveyed that claimed the quality of undergraduate education increased during the period. Its response also indicated that access to undergraduate education was maintained along with the quality of graduate education, research activities, and public service. Its universities offered a more pessimistic assessment. A third said both quality and access in undergraduate education declined. The same percentage reported a decline in graduate education and research. The officer from the Postsecondary Commission believed that the quality of undergraduate education was only maintained.

This officer also offered a different perspective on the funding problem, which he admitted was large:

> The General Revenue numbers do not tell the whole story. While General Revenue declined significantly in 1991–92, the sectors benefited from increases in Lottery dollars as well as tuition and fees. . . . These reductions were addressed by travel restrictions, unfilled positions being frozen, no raises, elimination of summer course offerings.

Contrary to the system response on allocations to campuses, the Commission officer saw a definite shift in the funding factors for state appropriations to public higher education. In 1990, base budgets, student enrollments, and salary increases and inflation ranked first, second, and third. After 1996, the first two factors kept their position, but performance replaced salary increases and inflation in the third position. Despite SUS's *laissez faire* approach to planning and budgeting, this official rated the SUS Board and System officers as important, along with the governor, legislature and campus leaders. Forty-four percent of the SUS's universities that responded considered the system's role very important, and 33.3 percent called it important. Graduate and research institutions rated the system as somewhat less important than the comprehensive campuses. Half of SUS's campuses had a negative and half a positive reaction to the system actions during the period.

Conclusion

As is often the case, changes during the period appeared far less dramatic than some commentators had predicted. The first half of the 1990s constituted considerably less than a "defining moment" for public higher education. The surveys support the conclusion of *The Chronicle of Higher Education* in 1994 (Lively, 17). It claimed that, despite cuts in the usual levels of funding and calls for radical reforms, "observers see only isolated examples of fundamental change." "There has been a good bit of hunkering down as opposed to radical restructuring," said Mark Musick, President of the Southern Regional Education Board. Though he speculated that "radical changes happen only during free falls," the survey responses indicated that even free falls in funding failed to produce radical reforms in California or Massachusetts.

The period also represented something less than the finest hour for university systems. Most systems did not seek to shape collective responses to the budget problems of the period. Most rarely used their powers over planning and budgeting to produce changes in system priorities or campus directions. Most systems did not prepare budget plans or guidelines, retain the right to approve campus plans, or allocate scarce resources selectively to their institutions. The reactions of most systems was characterized by raising revenues and restricting expenses rather than refocusing missions and redirecting priorities. Systems and campuses usually relied on tuition increases and short-term savings, such as vacancy and salary freezes and early retirements, to weather the storm in the hope it would blow over. Many systems did restructure and downsize their administrations and reduced duplicative programs. Only Texas A&M, which received comparatively good budgets, consolidated a campus; this administrative merger hardly constituted a real restructuring.

The survey responses suggested that university systems compiled at best a mixed record on Langenberg objectives. They fell far short of achieving, or even seeking, synergy, for few tried to enhance, much less transform, performance of their campuses through coordinated effort. Few systems followed the strategy of setting "common goals" and "complementary roles," which would ensure that constituent institutions fulfilled their diverse missions while making unique contributions to common purposes. Systems did push to reduce redundant academic programs, but most refrained from reallocating resources selectively to priority areas. They did achieve efficiency through downsizing and restructuring their own administrations and encouraging campuses to follow this lead. Systems hardly met the test of accountability, for nearly all sacrificed access for quality by raising tuition and fees as their primary reaction to budget stringency. Several added enrollment reductions to their strategy. Raising tuition and reducing enrollments is a reaction that champions would expect systems to resist rather than recommend. At least two systems failed the integrity test of resisting political intrusions. The experience of CUNY and SUNY showed that systems, through gubernatorial appointment of trustees, could become a conduit for, rather than a buffer against, political intrusion.

System leaders could and did argue that coping to survive represented the best of the bad options available during the period. They claimed better budgets would and did return to public higher education in most states. Radical actions do divert attention from the educational mission of higher education, disrupt the fragile consensus of the academic community, and endanger the external support of political leaders. Governors and legislators resist responsibility for controversial actions and reject pleas for increased funding from groups beset by internal battles. By coping rather than changing, system leaders could say they got through a difficult period without wrenching reforms and some would say without permanent damage. Chancellor Johnstone made such a case in a detailed defense of why he rejected radical restructuring as a response to SUNY's budget cuts (*SUNY 2000*).

Other system heads thought the times demanded radical reforms. Michael Hooker, the President of the UMASS System, saw the situation of public higher education in the first half of the 1990s as strikingly similar to that of healthcare. Both suffered from declining federal and state support, soaring costs, increasing competition from nontraditional providers, and declining public confidence.

> We cannot continue simply to "muddle through," engage in "wishful thinking," or assume a bigger state appropriation is a "divine right." . . . We live in an era of fundamental social and economic re-structuring in which all institutions must change in order to survive and compete. (Hooker, "Letter").

Shortly after presenting this tough appraisal, Hooker resigned his system post to become chancellor of University of North Carolina at Chapel Hill.

Both approaches sought to safeguard public higher education. Advocates of restraint and reform differed not on their assessment of current problems but on the future prospects of public higher education. The pressure for making drastic—possibly destructive or constructive—decisions can make either fools or cowards of system leaders, depending on future consequences.

The merits of these two approaches do depend on the future prospects of public higher education. The system tactics of the first half the 1990s may have left public higher education more vulnerable to future falls or stalls in state funding. Reliance on tuition and fee increases raised their levels to heights that not only endangered access but also diminished the potential for softening future funding shortfalls. The recent moves to freeze or cut tuition in California and Massachusetts support this conclusion. Moreover, short-term measures, such as vacancy and salary freezes and early retirement programs, aside from being temporary and indiscriminate devices, have been depleted as sources of future spending reductions. Their value diminishes with the frequency of their use. With these options increasingly unavailable, unattractive, or unproductive, radical restructuring may become the only alternative in the next decline in state funding. Though such a forecast may seem sensible, it sounds suspiciously similar to the predictions made during the first half of the 1990s. Given collegial governance in higher education and the political opposition to controversial measures, system leaders may well continue to consider radical restructuring in the same context as nuclear weapons—useful for making threats, but too devastating to use.

A multicampus system is always a house divided by the perpetual pull between state demands and campus desires. States demand systemic economies, reforms, and responsiveness. Campuses desire advocacy, funding, and freedom. University systems, without student, alumni, or community backing, lack a political constituency. Their clout comes from campus leaders, who quickly withdraw their support when systems push a collective, rather than a campus, agenda. Governors and some legislative leaders advocate strong leadership but abandon system heads when they lose the support of campus leaders. They call for radical reforms, but only on the impossible conditions that they happen quietly and swiftly with little or no campus and community opposition.

Though most of the systems did not advocate radical reforms, they did alter their governance. Decentralization became the preferred direction in a period when the states' share of the cost of public higher education declined. Several systems groped toward a new paradigm that tried to link state accountability with campus autonomy through the market forces of campus competition and consumer choice. Activist trustees with business backgrounds, rather than system professionals with academic credentials, led this movement. The new paradigm combined business practices and political conservatism. Business brought the concepts of administrative downsizing, decentralized decisions, and competitive markets. Conservatism contributed distaste for centralized authority, collective planning, and external mandates. The new approach favored delegating authority to campuses over budgets, enrollments, and tuition; downsizing the power and size of system administrations; and leaving accountability to the market discipline of consumer choices. In many ways this new decentralization reflects the conservative consensus that has captured Washington and most state capitols. Mickey Edwards, a former Republican Congressman, defined this core consensus as "limited government, low taxes, minimal regulation, a focus on the individual rather than on the collective, reliance on the market, opposition to centralized planning" (5).

Champions contend that this approach encourages campus entrepreneurship and responsiveness to changing student, state, and societal needs, which are indeed cruxes of accountability. UW, CUNY, and SUNY are proposing using a portion of state funding for financial incentives to improve, or reward, client-centered performance and productivity. The UW *Restructuring Report* suggests that campus autonomy and managed competition should replace system direction as the means of achieving Langenberg's objectives. Critics see this strategy as privatizing public higher education by viewing it as primarily a private good for graduates rather than a public good for states. They view it as a Darwinian model of campuses struggling with each other for survival. Such an approach, they say, can never satisfy statewide needs in a higher education market where the decisions of both providers and consumers are based mostly on campus reputations rather than customer services.

Although many systems adopted such a decentralized strategy, several seek to combine it with a new centralization over traditional campus issues. Some board members in SUNY, CUNY, and UW, while defending decentralizing decisions on budgets, tuition, enrollments, and programs, also advocate more system mandates on admission standards, course requirements, and campus behavior. They desire to decide issues that have long been left to institutions and their faculties. This apparent contradiction also reflects the thinking of neo-conservatives. Mickey Edwards notes that some conservative intellectuals deplore centralized power over most matters involving individuals and institutions but favor fully using government authority to enforce "proper standards" and behavior in communities and society. It is too soon to tell whether this new centralizing urge will become an integral element in the new paradigm for systems or merely an aberration.

The decentralized approach to system governance may represent the most lasting legacy of the first half of the 1990s. It holds the hope of forging a better balance between autonomy and accountability by freeing campuses to respond creatively to the changing needs of students, states, and society. It also carries the threat of tying public higher education to the momentary desires of the market rather than the long-term needs of states and society. Somehow systems and the states they serve must find a way to improve their responsiveness to changing needs while continuing their commitment to enduring, and at times unpopular, values. Market forces can achieve the first goal, but the second demands considerations beyond consumer choices. Systems should change with the times, but it is difficult to imagine a time when campuses will coordinate their activities for common goods beyond their institutional interests. As Langenberg said: "It is about as likely that a group of autonomous institutions will spontaneously take concerted action as it is that a pile of lumber will spontaneously form a house" ("Why?" 8–9). Market forces can make campuses more responsive to the needs of their own clientele, but states will want systems to help meet the collective needs of their citizens. The finding that systems did not achieve these goals during the first half of the 1990s is an argument for improving the systems, not abandoning them.

In 1994, while serving as SUNY's Interim Chancellor, I wrote that "a public university system should do for all its campuses only those functions that no single campus could do, should do, or would do" (Burke, "Unity"). Systems should do less and campuses more than they once did, but multicampus systems remain essential to the survival of public higher education. Despite recent efforts to erase or blur the distinction, there is a fundamental difference between public and private higher education. Public, as opposed to private, higher education must deliver to the general public that funds them more than a collection of the random results of campus and client choices. Systems offer the best hope for providing this essential coordination with an understanding of campus concerns and without neglecting statewide considerations.

PART TWO

MANAGING TODAY'S SYSTEM

When resources are plentiful most enterprises, including multicampus systems, can flourish and avert crisis, and the need for developing exemplary planning, budgeting, and productivity systems is not so pressing. Unfortunately, as Burke, Layzell, and Caruthers point out in this volume, the decade of the nineties has not been one of higher education's finest hours in terms of resources received. This is largely because other social objectives such as prison construction, health care, and the reform of K–12 education are competing successfully for public dollars that have traditionally subsidized public institutions. This fact has forced higher education systems to respond with greater imagination in their planning and budgeting techniques to avoid further eroding program quality, increasing tuition, and limiting the number of available enrollment places in the public system.

Thus, today's university systems are being confronted with a series of new management dilemmas. On the one hand they are affected by growing enrollments, by taxpayer criticisms about value received for resources provided, and by competition from new costly campus electronic technologies. On the other hand they are being asked to accommodate more nontraditional, lower-income, ill-prepared, and historically bypassed students—yet also to cut costs, maintain quality academic programs, and enhance new nonfunded missions such as community service.

Greater attention to planning, budgeting, and productivity techniques serve as one means to meet these new challenges. Unfortunately, very little of the literature on these topics focuses on multicampus systems, despite their dominance of higher education. In this section, three chapters offer an up-to-date and comprehensive survey and an exploratory view of planning and budgeting activities in the knowledge age. Within this assemblage of topics, a chapter on system instructional productivity points out that multicampus systems of all types do provide large amounts of instruction, despite strident public allegations about an intransigent, poor learning atmosphere dominated by research and uncaring faculty.

4

HIGHER EDUCATION SYSTEMS AND STRATEGIC PLANNING

Joseph J. Szutz

Some of the challenges being faced by university systems are being addressed through strategic planning; different systems use different approaches to shape their future but most have elements and themes in common, and all are pragmatic in nature.

According to Clark Kerr, president emeritus of the University of California, "the freestanding campus with its own board, its one and only president, its identifiable alumni, its faculty and student body, all in a single location with no coordinating council above it, is now the exception whereas in 1945 it was the rule" (*Transformation* 257). In the Association of Governing Boards special 1993 report, *Four Multicampus Systems: Some Policies and Practices that Work*, Marian L. Gade says: "More than one-half of all college and university students are enrolled on campuses within systems" (ix), and, "Nearly three-fourths of the students now enrolled in public colleges and universities attend schools that are part of a multicampus system" (1). There is no dispute that the predominant model of public higher education governance in America today is the system.

However, there are divided opinions about the future of the higher education system: Will systems become even more prevalent as we enter the next century, or will they become obsolete in the face of rapid and dramatic change in the nature, technology, and delivery of higher education? Either of those potential futures will present challenges that will require college and university systems—and higher education in general—to proceed deliberately and with the utmost consideration of all possibilities. It is the premise of this chapter that strategic planning is the most effective mechanism with which higher education systems can cope with challenges and opportunities alike.

Proceeding from that premise, this chapter will examine the basic nature of college and university systems and some of the primary challenges they face. It also will discuss strategic planning as a mechanism for addressing such challenges and shaping the course of higher education. The discussion will include observations about strategic planning as it is practiced in a number of state university systems and about its potential to deal with what promises to be a challenging future for higher education and the higher education system.

University Systems

A college/university system is in many respects more a concept than a tangible reality. It is a whole that consists of many largely independent parts, and much of what comprises it is borrowed from the separate entities of which it is composed.

Although higher education is about teaching and learning (faculty and students), scholarship and research (faculty and students), and service (faculty and agency personnel, such as extension), only the individual entities of which the system is comprised possess the human and physical resources from which those activities emanate. The technicality that each member institution's faculty and students are part of the parent "system," notwithstanding, neither diplomas nor football cheers nor alumni take their primary identity from the parent system. Students proudly proclaim their enrollment at the institution/campus they attend, and are often entirely unmindful of the role—or even the existence—of the system to which it belongs.

There are two basic varieties of college and university systems: the multicampus institution and the multi-institution system. Lee and Bowen define the multicampus university as the "coexistence of geographically distinct communities" (Lee and Bowen, *Multicampus University* 2), a capsule definition that applies equally to both kinds of systems. Multicampus systems commonly consist of separate campuses all of whose names begin with that of a parent college or university, followed by "at" and the name of a geographic location, e.g., University of California at Santa Barbara, Florida Community College at Jacksonville, University of North Carolina at Greensboro. While ostensibly branches of a single institution, the campuses that comprise such a system are, for the most part, separate and unique institutions, each with its own inventory of academic programs, special strengths and limitations, problems and challenges, and most importantly, faculty and student body.

The primary thing such institutions have in common is the first part of their names, their primary source of funding, and a single source of overall policy leadership. In the case of funding, the larger, more diversified research campuses may actually obtain a large proportion of their funding from grants, contracts, alumni support, and other private giving that the diversity and prestige of their faculties and programs can attract, and which their smaller, more modestly endowed sister institutions cannot.

The multi-institution system consists of several separate institutions—not campuses of a single university—all of which are governed by a single board of regents, trustees, governors, etc. All that was said above about branch campus systems also applies to separate institution systems. Both types have one governing board, one system chief executive officer reporting to the board, separate branch/institution chief executive officers (CEOs) reporting to the system executive, the same primary source of funds, and overall policy leadership. As with the branch campus system, the separate institutions of the multi-institution system have their own faculties, programs, strengths, and weaknesses. Although there certainly are variations on these two models, e.g., "systems" of freestanding institutions under strong coordinating boards, the great majority of systems fall into one category or the other.

If, as maintained earlier, college and university systems are more conceptual than concrete, then why are colleges and universities organized into systems, and what purpose do they serve? With respectful sympathy to the random college or university president who is stumped by that very question, there is an answer, and it lies in the two common denominators mentioned above: funding and overall policy.

The institutions belonging to higher education systems, whether public or private, university or community college, are funded from a single primary source. This discussion will be framed in terms of public systems, with apologies for variations that may exist in the private sector. For the public system, the primary source of funds is the government. State systems go to the legislature to obtain funding; community college systems may obtain funding from both state and municipal governments, while some have their own taxing authority.

WHAT SYSTEMS BRING TO THE TABLE

The process of obtaining fiscal support in sufficient quantity to fund ongoing operations as well as change and improvement is a complex and interesting topic. The aspect of that process that is germane to this discussion is the advantage of the system over the individual institution approach. The system approach to budget making might be compared to the *modus operandi* of the large political lobby in relation to the legislative and executive branches of the federal government. Another apt metaphor might be our national motto: "one from many."

Conversely, numerous public institutions lobbying the same state legislature for funding brings to mind the phrase: "divide and conquer." With the latter approach, the flagship and a few other "top rung" institutions in size and/or range of programs will commonly feast more heartily at the public table than their less influential or prestigious fellows. While it may be true that the presence of a system will not completely eliminate variations—even inequities—in budget allocations among institutions, the unified appeal to the legislature will, in most cases, be more effective than the cumulative results of individual institutions competing with and often undercutting one another. If the system approach produces a larger pie for all the institutions, then each institution's share of that pie is likely to be larger as well.

The budgetary role of the system is linked in almost *quid pro quo* fashion to its other fundamental purpose, the setting of overall policy for its institutions. The role of formulating, implementing, and managing statewide (or private systemwide, or city/countywide for a community college system) higher education policy creates the leverage the system brings to the budget appropriation process. Conversely, effectiveness of the system administration in producing healthy budgets enables not only the effective operation of its institutions, but is also the major factor in achieving and sustaining both internal and external "buy-in" to the system's budgetary and policymaking agenda. Such buy-in is the adhesive holding the multiple, independent, and often disparate institutions together in a united front.

In that ongoing dynamic, the system must continue to be effective in "implementing and managing" systemwide policy to remain effective in the budget-making arena. Whatever the broader public agenda, the system must constantly reassure the appropriate external constituencies of its fiduciary responsibility, regard for and demonstration of educational quality, correct choice of priorities, and the overall performance of the higher education sector. The system can maintain the optimum external perception of its performance in all of these regards only through the collective efforts and consistent (and one might even say, persistent) buy-in of its institutions.

Studies of the higher education system, such as D. Bruce Johnstone's "Central Administration of Public Multicampus College and University Systems," offer long lists of the core functions of higher education systems, but budgeting and overall policy-making constitute the essential umbrella under which the rest fall. Aims McGuinness adds the following prescription for how the system should function in behalf of its constituent institutions: "The system should have explicit objectives that relate to both external state and societal priorities and internal system priorities ... [and it] ... should maintain a distinct balance between its role in representing the public interest to the academy and its role in presenting the academy to the public" ("Model" 215).

These views of the higher education system's primary roles serve as the backdrop against which to examine the critical and related function of strategic planning. Having provided a working definition of the system, it is important next to consider the challenges it faces in the broader higher education and societal context. It is these challenges with which the strategic planning process is designed to cope.

CHALLENGES AND OPPORTUNITIES

Some major higher education figures hold conflicting views about the future of the system as the dominant organizational model in higher education. A brief overview of such opinions will serve well to delineate the planning challenges the system will face. Writing over a decade ago, Lee and Bowen suggested that although "multicampus systems . . . continue to be the fastest growing pattern of university organization in the United States . . . both the multiversity and the multicampus system are under severe challenge" (*Multicampus University* 1). In his op-ed piece, "Higher Education Systems as Cartels: The End is Near," Gordon K. Davies takes that notion to the next level, asserting that state systems "are obsolescent" (*Chronicle* 3 Oct. 1997). According to Davies:

> Almost all state-university systems are subject to increased political interference these days. Even the ones that traditionally have received ample funds from their state governments are losing ground to other state spending priorities such as prisons, health care, and schools. And broad access to higher education — the central reason that state university systems were created — is being called into question. On top of this, higher education is becoming a retail industry, in which new providers of electronic instruction are beginning to offer their services anywhere at any time.
>
> As a result of all these changes, the era of the "system as cartel" has ended, even if the strongest state systems in the nation do not yet recognize their own vulnerability. Systems will no longer be able to control what education is offered, where, and for whom. (Davies A68)

To put Davies' argument in a nut shell: "state systems . . . can no longer try to function as cartels . . . [because] technology respects none of the protective devices—such as regional service areas—that have been used by higher-education systems" (A68).

In contrast to Davies' dire prognostications, Aims C. McGuinness, Jr., thinks that "systems are likely to be more, rather than less, a feature of

American higher education a decade from now" (*Restructuring* 204). As evidence for that conclusion, he suggests that there are "four essentially negative reasons why systems will be exceptionally difficult to eliminate and, in fact, may be even more in demand in the next decade":

1. States will continue to turn to systems as means to manage regional economic and political imbalance and to sustain political coalitions.

2. Legal issues, pressure for "shared governance" at the system level, and collective bargaining will make disaggregation of systems exceptionally difficult.

3. Worldwide pressures are accelerating to merge nonuniversity sectors with university sectors.

4. In difficult economic times, political leaders can be expected to resort (or revert) to traditional alternatives aimed at increasing expenditure controls, eliminating duplication, and centralizing in an effort to achieve economies of scale. (212)

It is not the purpose of this chapter to make the case for either viewpoint, but rather to explore against that backdrop the way systems address challenges to their continued success. McGuinness strikes the theme for this discussion when he says: "the relevant issue is not the abstract question of whether systems should exist but rather how systems should be designed and structured so that they stimulate, support, and sustain an outstanding, highly diverse, and responsive higher education enterprise" ("Model"). It is the premise of this chapter that strategic planning is the key to successfully achieving that highly demanding and multidimensional goal.

As this discussion proceeds, some of the threats to modern systems as well as some of the strategies alluded to above will be reflected in the strategic agendas of various state systems. But first, let us establish a working definition of strategic planning.

Strategic Planning

Peter F. Drucker says that "the mission and the plan—if that's all there is—are the good intentions. Strategies are the bulldozers. They convert what you want to do into accomplishment . . . they also tell you what you need to have by way of resources and people to get the results" (*Managing,* 59).

Strategic planning, which has its roots, as the name implies, in the military, has been in vogue in higher education, at least as the term of choice, since the early 1980s. As the favored approach to aligning current and anticipated resources with anticipated challenges and opportunities, it is the successor to "long-range planning," "five-year planning," "master planning" (a term now most often associated with facilities/infrastructure planning), and even "program planning and budgeting" (PPB), an idea whose latter day manifestation may be "performance budgeting." Some of those terms are still used interchangeably with "strategic planning" to signify planning in a longer time frame than operational planning, the annual budget cycle, etc.

The basic features of the strategic planning process are empirical analysis of the internal and external environments of the organization, the identification of a vision of the future that is congruent with those environments and the mission of the organization, the development of strategies or action plans through which to attain the major elements of that vision, and continual renewal; i.e., strategic plans "roll forward" by revising their priorities and goals in response to critical new information obtained from ongoing environmental analysis.

When features of the existing plan are no longer congruent with the facts of the environment or the vision of the most likely future for the organization or when acceptable progress is not being made in achieving existing goals, the plan is revised. Outdated or inappropriate components and goals that have been achieved are replaced by new ones that more adequately reflect the current and projected circumstances. While the mechanisms of strategic planning can be employed at the department/division level, the concept is normally associated—and the focus of this discussion is on—macro, i.e., broad organizational planning.

There are a number of ways in which the strategic planning process is conducted from organization to organization. In some institutions and systems, the process is conducted by the chief executive and his/her senior staff. In others, the process is much more bottom up, seeking broad input from faculty and staff, and sometimes from students, alumni, and members of the external community as well. In most institutions/systems the board of regents is nominally responsible for strategic planning; in many cases it is directly and actively involved in the process. Generally speaking, the higher in the organization the locus of control, the greater the *external* credibility and the internal "authority" of the process. Conversely, the broader the control and the more widely participative the process, the greater the *internal* credibility and the more enthusiastic the buy-in of the institution or the system to the purposes and goals of the process.

Strategic planning can serve the college, university, or system administration as a useful tool in several ways, from supporting management functions, to achieving high priority institutional or system goals, to responding to political pressure. Arguably, strategic planning's most fundamental utility resides in the process itself, in its focus on environmental scanning and needs analysis. The empirical foundation provided by those activities brings greater clarity to the administrative context of the institution or system with respect to both its immediate and prospective interests.

Another basic purpose of strategic planning is setting priorities for resource allocation. With more options for expenditure than resources, some structured process for making choices among worthwhile alternatives is necessary. On the operational level, of course, this is in the domain of the annual budget process. Strategic planning is the means by which the leadership creates a larger context of overall institutional or system vision, strategic priorities, and policy directions that transcend the strictly internal, practical, and often short-term considerations that characterize the annual budget cycle. In this regard, strategic planning's potential for obtaining and integrating a range of relevant viewpoints is especially valuable.

Strategic planning is also the means by which institutions and systems can formally promise certain outcomes or achievements that are in high demand by important constituencies, such as the governor, legislature, or board of regents, and then credit the system with the moral victory of timely and appropriate policy goals well in advance of their attainment. What are the political hot buttons for higher education: graduation rates, the length of time to a baccalaureate degree, the cost of a college education? Are there critics of the system's performance or boosters who are dissatisfied with its stance on growth or its posture with respect to emerging innovations?

A well-developed strategic planning process can produce an effective response. It can articulate desired future scenarios on a firm foundation of research and with a plausible expectation of realization. The well-conceived strategic plan can credit the value of accomplishment to an institution's or system's account before the accomplishment itself, thus satisfying—or at least responding to—its more vocal and influential constituencies. However, no matter how much credit might be earned by a well-conceived and politically astute strategic plan, the value of the plan ultimately is in its achievements. And a valuable strategic plan, one that is open on the desk at least as much as it sits on the shelf, is built around a plan of action that not only demonstrates the feasibility of the plan before the fact, but also proves its worth after the fact by attaining goals on schedule and as promised.

Action plans are Peter Drucker's bulldozers. They narrow the aim down to the who, when, and how questions that must be answered before the first strategic goal can be reached. They are the difference between good intentions and accomplishment.

SYSTEM VERSUS INSTITUTIONAL STRATEGIC PLANNING

For the most part, everything that has been said about strategic planning pertains equally to institutional-level and system-level planning. The critical difference is the context in which the process is conducted, and the tension between the institutional and system contexts is the dynamic variable in system versus institutional strategic planning. Because strategic planning is conducted separately at both levels, and because the planning contexts are different, system priorities will differ from institutional priorities to some degree. In a large and complex system, institutions may vary greatly in their level of agreement with system priorities. While some system priorities will be consonant with institutional priorities, others will not be, and some may even "crowd out" priorities that an institution places higher on its list.

In considering the potential conflict between system and institutional strategic priorities, it is important to remember that the system does not formulate its overarching priorities arbitrarily or in a vacuum. In most systems, strategic priorities arise through consultation with the institutional/campus chief executives, and in some the consultative process is even broader, with representative campus and systemwide committees involved in system-level planning. Of course, even in a highly democratic model, the will of the majority is always a compromise that will fail to satisfy the more (or less) ambitious aspirations of some participants.

If, for example, the highest priority of the system's primary public constituencies is undergraduate education, then instructional excellence will have a higher overt priority than academic scholarship and research. Those essential components of the higher education mission need not be abandoned or their pursuit even be significantly impaired, but neither will they be high on the list of priorities that appear in the system strategic plan or in the system budget request. A strategic emphasis on undergraduate instruction is highly suitable to the two-year and liberal arts college whose mission is strongly focused on that aspect of higher education. The research university, on the other hand, has "strengthening its research mission" at the top of its own strategic priorities and will feel frustrated, and possibly impeded, in pursuit of its plans by the system's emphasis on undergraduate instruction.

Such a conflict will, of course, be even greater if funds are allocated among institutions according to system priorities. If the system implements its strategic emphasis on undergraduate instruction by redistributing funding among the institutions accordingly, the fundamental roles and responsibilities of the system and its individual institutions are mostly at odds, and the danger of open dispute is greatest.

With the premise in mind that system strategic planning is focused on the optimal *collective* performance of its institutions, a favorable general perception of the system and higher education, and effectively addressing relevant issues to insure funding success, let's explore some current system strategic plans for insights into planning practice at the system level.

HOW SYSTEMS PLAN—STRUCTURE AND PROCESS

The strategic plans of nine major higher education systems were reviewed and analyzed: California State University, State University of New York, State University System of Florida, Texas Higher Education System, University of California, University of Maryland, University of North Carolina, University of Wisconsin, University System of Georgia. All were state university systems; both coasts and the southeast, southwest, and midwest regions of the country are represented. Three of the nine systems include two-year, junior-community colleges. Six are multicampus systems, and three are multi-institution systems. One of the nine is headed by a statewide coordinating board. Although this is a coordinating rather than a governing board, and its chief executive does not exercise line authority over the institutional presidents as in the other eight examples, it does exercise the same academic program and capital planning approval and budget review authority over the state's public two- and four-year institutions and is also responsible for statewide higher education planning. The prevailing model of strategic planning among the systems reviewed involves broad input from a variety of constituencies. While the governing board or a steering or planning and policy committee of the board (along with the system chief executive) leads the process and shapes the final recommendations to the full board, in almost all cases, formal and informal structures are used to solicit input from throughout the system and from relevant sources outside the system.

Formal structures for this purpose include committees and subcommittees of faculty, institutional officers and staff, students, alumni, and business and industry representatives. Informal approaches include soliciting input from existing groups and organizations, e.g., faculty senates, student government organizations, and systemwide councils, and holding local and regional hearings and focus groups around the state to obtain the viewpoints of key leaders and rank and file citizens alike.

The board committees established for strategic planning purposes (with the logistical support—as well as the judgment and perspective—of board staff) then sift, analyze, and organize the responses into an agenda of strategic priorities. Other common features of the process include a focus on a system vision statement, institutional missions, structural and operational issues, and benchmarking. Benchmarking is an aspect of the empirical research base of strategic planning. It establishes comparative levels, e.g., of funding, infrastructure, and performance, to which the system will aspire in its strategic plan or against which the system will measure its baseline for planning purposes.

So, descriptions of the system strategic planning process consistently present a pattern of broad input that goes into the formation of a strategic agenda for public higher education. The more varied and broadly representative the sources of that input, the more likely it is to collectively represent the hottest issues and the prevailing political priorities of the state with respect to higher education. The University of California (UC) takes a uniquely broad, participatory approach to planning, reflective of its strongly collegial administrative style and the strength and organization of its faculty. In fact, although some might claim that UC does not have a strategic planning process, *per se*, it does have many of the same planning priorities as the other systems in this review.

The legislature is not only the primary source of system funding, but also the official source of representative public opinion on all state matters, including higher education. Therefore, independent assurance that those priorities will be incorporated into the system strategic plan is provided by the board's and central administration's role and experiences in the budget making and public/legislative affairs arenas.

SYSTEM ISSUES AND STRATEGIC PRIORITIES

Whether termed priorities, goals, planning principles, or strategic initiatives, system strategic plans contain clear priorities grouped around educational, political, operational, and social themes. The major priorities to which a system commits its energy and resources reveals much about the status and direction of higher education in that state. The collective focus of several state systems may provide insights into public higher education's view of the future as well as the "hot buttons" that currently command the attention of system planners.

The strategic plans of the state systems reviewed here share a number of strategic priorities. This is not surprising in view of the structural, operational, and mission characteristics public higher education systems have in common, and the strong congruity of American higher education from coast to coast and region to region. Popular perceptions and political trends often sweep the nation. Accrediting organizations, regional boards and commissions, and national higher education associations—not to mention the Internet—cross-pollinate the fields of higher education governance and administration with the latest ideas. In a shrinking world, one state's or region's dilemma is often the stimulus for surrounding—and even distant—states' preemptive policy initiatives. Legislatively mandated performance measures are a good example of that phenomenon.

The following eight themes or planning priorities were featured in six or more of the nine system plans reviewed:

Access	Adequate Funding
Economic Development	Efficiency/Effectiveness
Enrollment Planning	Differentiation/Diversity
Quality	Technology

In addition, collaboration among system institutions and between institutions and other government and private sector entities was explicitly included in five of the nine plans. The following priorities were each identified by at least four systems:

1. The decentralization of system management.
2. Keeping higher education affordable.
3. Public accountability.
4. Forming linkages with the K–12 and the technical and adult education sectors.

Only two priorities were shared by all nine state systems: technology (i.e., technological development) and efficiency. Technology refers primarily to the expanded use of instructional technology to increase teaching effectiveness and program quality, and of distance technology to increase statewide access to higher education services. Technology is linked to quality, efficiency/effectiveness, and access. Efficiency is traditionally defined as getting the greatest impact for the dollar, or using system resources to the greatest advantage. Efficiency is linked to technology, accountability, and inter-institutional collaboration.

The next most frequently endorsed strategic planning priority was quality. Higher education quality is a generally desirable goal, but in these statewide plans it is most frequently related to undergraduate education and seems to be an extension of the public's broader concern with the quality of K–12 education. Quality is often paired with the concept of "national standards of excellence," indicating that the parameters of educational quality are comparative and should be measured against national benchmarks. Educational quality as a planning priority relates to public accountability, efficiency/effectiveness, enrollment planning, and funding.

Access, enrollment planning, and economic development were next in frequency of adoption. Access to the state system's publicly funded educational services is fundamental to the mission of the state system. It is about putting higher education services within reach of the great majority of—if not all—state residents, and is linked with enrollment planning, technology, and institutional diversity. Enrollment planning includes strategies to recruit students, streamline the application and registration processes, facilitate the transfer of college credit, improve student retention, shorten time to degree, etc.; and is linked to access, efficiency, and funding. Economic development pertains to applying the system's knowledge, skills, and resources to the economic growth and prosperity of the state and involves such areas as applied research, technology transfer, public-private partnerships, and the educational needs of the job market. Economic development is linked with efficiency/effectiveness and adequate funding.

Institutional differentiation/diversity and obtaining adequate funding for higher education were the last two strategic planning priorities adopted by two-thirds or more of the systems reviewed. Institutional diversity refers to mission differentiation among system institutions, emphasis on unique institutional strengths and attributes, and diversity of educational opportunity for students. Institutional differentiation is closely linked to inter-institutional collaboration, as well as to quality and a more decentralized administration. Adequate funding pertains both to more imaginative and aggressive private fund raising and to more effective public funding, and is linked in a causal relationship to the whole spectrum of operational and planning activities.

Four categories of system planning themes were mentioned earlier:

Educational   Political   Operational   Social

Working definitions of these categories might be:

1. Educational: primarily based on educational principles and standards.
2. Political: arising from the concerns and demands of the representational political sector.

3. Operational: related to the operation and management of the system.

4. Social: pertaining primarily to the needs and interests of the state and its citizens.

Table 4.1   *System Planning Themes*

System Priorities	Theme Categories			
	Educational	Operational	Political	Social
Access	X		**X**	X
Adequate Funding		**X**	X	
Economic Development			**X**	X
Efficiency/Effectiveness		X	X	
Enrollment Planning	X	X		X
Differentiation/Diversity	X	X	X	
Quality	**X**		X	
Technology	X	X	**X**	

These are not exclusive categories, but offer a matrix within which to understand system strategic planning. Consider Table 4.1

Sufficient rationale could undoubtedly be found to include all eight priorities in each of the theme categories: none of the priorities and themes are completely unrelated. The priority-theme relationships shown in Table 4.1 merely indicate one point of view as to which themes provided relatively more significant influence on the adoption of each planning priority. To go further out on that limb, the primary theme behind five of the priorities is indicated by a check mark. Again, the purpose of this exercise is to organize our observations about strategic planning in state university systems. The reader is invited to reconfigure the matrix and draw his or her own conclusions.

Having hedged our speculation with those caveats, we observe that political impetus is a significant driver for seven of the eight planning priorities, and is arguably the primary impetus for three of them. Considering the public context of state higher education systems, it is difficult not to find at least a recognizable political thumbprint on virtually every system planning decision, but, for the sake of argument, enrollment planning will remain the lone holdout.

Educational and operational themes underlie five separate strategic priorities, and each category is primary to one priority. Although what is politically and educationally optimal is implicitly good for the state and its citizens, only three system priorities are felt to be significantly influenced by social motives, and social motives were not felt to be primary for any of the system priorities. For three system priorities, efficiency/effectiveness, enrollment planning, and differentiation/diversity, none of the themes was considered primary, i.e., two or more of the four causal factors seemed to work in combination to bring those priorities to the forefront of the planning process.

So, while it may not be accurate to say that state university systems operate according to predominantly political agendas, its seems clear that the political necessities of operating as an element of state government, with considerable tax dollar support, founded and dedicated to serve the needs of the state's citizens, institutions, corporations, and government, impose a distinct "political" imprint on the public higher education strategic planning process. The words of Aims McGuinness again come to mind and provide an accurate perspective on this point: "The system should have explicit objectives that relate to both external state and societal priorities and internal system priorities . . . [and it] . . . should maintain a distinct balance between its role in representing the public interest to the academy and its role in presenting the academy to the public" ("Model").

It is also revealing to group the top university system planning priorities according to their primary identification with either the present or the future. Present and future, in this regard, should be viewed as distinct, but again not mutually exclusive. Even the most futuristic planning is conducted in the present with whatever available data and information promise the most probable picture of the future. Just as importantly, there really is no way to avoid conducting planning with (despite?) the values and the mind-set of the present. At the same time, planning is, by definition, about what will (or what can, or what may) happen in the long-term future, i.e., beyond today, tomorrow, or next month. As Peter F. Drucker has said: "Long-range planning does not deal with future decisions, but with the future of present decisions" (*Management Tasks* 125).

So, while present and future intermingle in the process of planning strategy to effect change, it may add a dimension to the above categorization of planning priorities by theme to categorize them a second time by their primary orientation to either the present or the future, as follows:

Planning Priority Orientations

Present	*Future*
Efficiency	Technology
Quality	Institutional Differentiation
Access	Economic Development
Funding	Enrollment Planning

The priorities listed in the Present column are more focused on immediate needs, and those in the Future column, at least to a relatively greater extent, on future goals. Technology, the archetype of obsolescence, seems perennially somewhat ahead of our capacity to utilize it effectively and is notably about future potential. Institutional differentiation, after a few decades of follow-the-leader, is a work in progress, and economic development is still seeking its proper form as well as its full potential. Enrollment planning is a process of shaping student bodies to reflect and capitalize on emerging developments in higher education strategy, and is therefore primarily oriented to change and the future.

Conclusions

While we commonly think of planning, especially strategic planning, as a means to visualize and bring about a specific future, it seems reasonable to conclude from this review that, in the real world, strategic planning is characterized by pragmatism and the necessities of the present. The best, most exciting strategic plans do aggressively probe the future and set goals based largely on carefully calculated future needs, pressures, and opportunities. Some plans evaluate those needs and pressures primarily from the perspective of educational principles and ideals, formulating strategies that promise maximum avoidance of compromise with demands and concerns that are peripheral to the enterprise of scholarship, teaching, and public service. But, in the last analysis, college and university systems, especially publicly supported systems, prosper or languish in the very real world of politics, economics, public opinion, budget exigency, downsizing, external competition, and numerous other vicissitudes. Thus, it is not surprising that the priorities shared by the public higher education systems reviewed here are largely operational and politic in nature and relatively immediate in orientation.

As systems strive to maintain their dominant role in the face of challenges from alternative models of governance and delivery and an uncertain future for higher education itself, strategic planning will remain an important tool. As a mechanism for organizing and understanding the present and visualizing the most probable alternative futures—and devising the most effective strategies to deal with both—it will continue to play a vital role as American higher education pursues its many missions and goals.

5

SYSTEMWIDE STRATEGIC PLANNING IN THE KNOWLEDGE AGE

Donald M. Norris

The higher education industry is in the throes of a fundamental transformation. The traditional focal points of strategic planning in multicampus systems are changing as campuses adjust to confront the emerging challenges and opportunities of the Knowledge Age.

My purpose is simple: to describe how strategic planning for multicampus systems will change in the face of new opportunities and challenges in the twenty-first century. Examples of these new planning practices have already appeared and are scattered throughout this chapter. But to understand their full impact, we must look into the Knowledge Age future, and then plan from the future, backward.

Enter the Knowledge Age

Every organization in our society is undergoing profound transformation. Educational institutions and other learning enterprises are no exception. A global, knowledge-driven economy has emerged, based on information technology (IT) and telecommunications. As this "telecosm" develops further and becomes ubiquitous, it will change the way we work, learn, entertain, recreate, and develop personally. It will enable citizens across the world to "fuse" activities and live their lives in ways never before possible. My colleague Ted Malloch and I describe how we will live and learn in this new age in *Unleashing the Power of Perpetual Learning*.

We are on the threshold of a true "Knowledge Age." We can see its leading edge today, in increasingly common examples of digitization, democratization,

and deregulation, but the Knowledge Age will not reach its full potential immediately. We are in for a ten- to fifteen-year transition, or perhaps even longer.
Several characteristics of this new age are already changing our organizations
and educational practices:

1. Information and knowledge flows freely across political, geographical,
   and cultural boundaries;

2. Consumers of all kinds (including learners) are coming to expect
   greater responsiveness, timeliness, convenience, coherence, and customization in their products, services, and experiences;

3. Traditional notions of quality that focus on the inputs and quality of
   processes are changing to a focus on outcomes and competencies;

4. Existing mechanisms for accreditation and certification are being questioned and confronted with new challenges;

5. Existing distinctions between levels, types, and forms of learning are
   blurring; and

6. Virtually every industry across the globe is being realigned to the standards of performance of the emerging Knowledge Age Economy.

What are the implications of this emerging Knowledge Age for higher education? And for multicampus systems? Put simply, learning will be a substantial
growth industry in the Knowledge Age, but the learning industry of the twenty-
first century will differ dramatically from today's higher education industry.

The Emerging Learning Industry

The new learning industry is emerging from the fusion of the current education
industry with parts of the information and entertainment industry. This will
create learning and discovery experiences that are highly engaging. Distinctions
between learning products and services for different levels of learners will blur.
The learning industry of the next century will be global, pre-K through 99, and
rapidly growing. Learning initiatives will involve a far broader range of participants than today's educational activities. Figure 5.1 portrays the range of participants in twenty-first century learning solutions.

This new learning industry will involve larger-scale initiatives, which will
require greater investment, new competencies, and new forms of strategic
alliance. Most of today's colleges, universities, and multicampus systems of
institutions are accustomed to learning initiatives in which they own the whole
value chain—and where they "own" a particular geographical and/or disciplinary "franchise." It will be impossible to protect "franchises" in the Knowledge

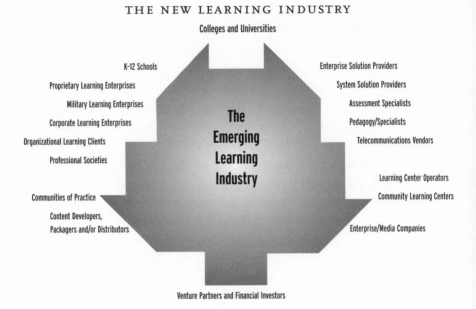

THE NEW LEARNING INDUSTRY

Figure 5.1

Age—as Gordon Davies so trenchantly illustrated in his article "Higher Education Systems as Cartels: The End is Near."

But the most important point about the emergence of the new learning industry is that the real boundary breaking practices will come from outside the higher education industry. As Gary Hamel suggests in "Killer Strategies that Make Shareholders Rich," during periods of realignment, the basic assumptions of the industry are changed and three principles hold:

1. *Analysis of existing industry conditions is not the key to success.* Where will the industry begin and end? How is it changing? These are the essential strategic questions for planners in the midst of realignment.

2. *The focus on current competitors is misplaced.* New competitors will surprise you and rewrite the rules of the industry. New perspectives and practices will be needed.

3. *It's not you against the world.* Working with strategic allies is critical to acquiring new competencies and developing fresh strategies for the future.

These principles are especially applicable to higher education today. It is no accident that the most significant new developments in today's higher education industry have emerged because the solutions suggested by educational leaders schooled in the old paradigm fell woefully short of the mark.

The Western Governors' Virtual University was launched because the governors of the western states grew weary of the inability of the leaders of public education to suggest breakthrough strategies for addressing the tidal wave of students in the western states. Other virtual initiatives such as the Michigan Virtual Auto College, the Southern Regional Virtual University, and the California Virtual University emerged because existing models were inadequate to approach the new challenges and opportunities. New approaches, new strategic alliances, and new sources of funding were needed.

The Instructional Management System (IMS) Project of the National Learning Infrastructure Initiative arose because the traditional approach to learningware development had failed to create scaleable learningware that met the gestating needs of the Knowledge Age learner. The IMS Project, launched by Educom, involves many leading universities, technology companies, the U.S. Department of Defense, and other strategic allies. New formulations are needed in the context of the new learning industry.

Planning from the Future Backward

System planners on the brink of the Knowledge Age need a new tool kit. The old tools of master planning and extrapolative strategic planning are still necessary, but not sufficient. Indeed, the old tools of demographically driven strategic planning have been decisive in clarifying the massive learning challenges and opportunities awaiting us in the twenty-first century and the accompanying inability to meet future learner needs under the existing paradigms for educational delivery and human and financial resources.

AN EXPANDED PLANNING TOOL KIT

A new generation of planning tools is described in *Revolutionary Strategy for the Knowledge Age*, by Donald Norris. These new tools will help system planners frame a variety of futures, chart migration paths toward the Knowledge Age, and build, or acquire through partnership, new families of competencies.

STRATEGIC PLANNING IS ABOUT EXTRAPOLATING FROM THE PRESENT, FORWARD

During periods of realignment, it is necessary to conceive of futures that are very different from today's experience. System planners that are steeped in

MAKING THE BLUE SKY MEET THE ROAD

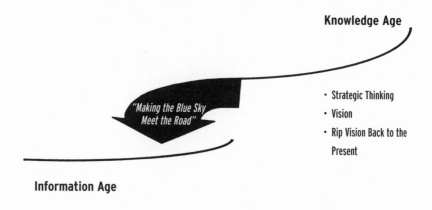

Knowledge Age

- Strategic Thinking
- Vision
- Rip Vision Back to the Present

"Making the Blue Sky Meet the Road"

Information Age

- Identify Strategies to Overcome Barriers
- Launch New Initiatives and Redirect Existing Processes
- Reallocate Resources/Identify New Resources

Figure 5.2

their experiences and traditions find it especially difficult to make the leap to genuinely different plans of operation. They literally "cannot get there from here." They are not alone; most planners in large, structured organizations find such leaps difficult.

THINKING IN THE FUTURE TENSE

At times such as these, it is necessary to "think in the future tense" and be able to envision truly different learning futures. This requires "strategic thinking," which is defined as "planning from the future, backward." System planners need to consider truly revolutionary futures and visions for how multicampus systems could respond to different learning opportunities in the Knowledge Age. The same planners that could not get there from here find that, by planning backwards, they can "get here from there."

MAKING THE BLUE SKY MEET THE ROAD

Once the future visions are formed, planners should rip those visions back to the present to identify the barriers to achieving the vision. Strategies to overcome these barriers typically require the creation of new learning initiatives or entirely new cultures, outside the boundaries of existing learning organizations. Figure 5.2 illustrates how to make the blue sky meet the road.

CHARTING ASSURED MIGRATION PATHS TO THE KNOWLEDGE AGE

System planners need a tool kit that enables them to prepare their systems for success in a variety of futures. They need to position their systems to deal with a wide diversity of learning options—traditional learning on campus, virtual variations on traditional learning, transformed learning that creates new learning experiences, and distributed learning that combines physical and virtual learning. Assured migration paths require the development of systemwide IT and learning infrastructures and the development of faculty skills to create new approaches to learning.

But the most important aspect of building migration paths is nurturing the capacity of institutions, teams, and individuals to craft "expeditionary" approaches to new learning experiences (Norris, *Revolutionary Strategy for the Knowledge* Age 15–17). An expeditionary strategy enables us to launch low-cost probes into the future and continuously improve our new learning experiences so we can position them for success.

Most of the major learning initiatives launched by multicampus systems and new multi-institution partners are decisively expeditionary in their approach. They are inventing new practices as they go. All of the major virtual university initiatives are exploring the principles of expeditionary development. The major distance learning and distributed learning projects at multicampus systems, such as the University of Wisconsin, Indiana University, and the University of California, are also expeditionary in character. See Figure 5.3

BUILDING COMPETENCIES FOR KNOWLEDGE AGE SCHOLARSHIP

Expeditionary product and service initiatives are critical to acquiring the competencies necessary for success in the Knowledge Age. These are not "core" competencies, which are those few distinctive competencies that define a particular institution and differentiate it from its competitors. Rather, these are six families of competencies that will be essential to successfully provide tomorrow's learning opportunities. They include:

1. *Leadership.* The capacity to frame new futures, envision the new learning industry, develop expeditionary strategy for Knowledge Age learning, and illuminate the shortcomings of existing systemwide approaches to planning and strategy.

2. *Information technology, telecommunications and learning infrastructure.* The competency to plan and develop robust infrastructures that support expeditionary learning initiatives. This includes skills development in the use and deployment of new tools.

CHARTING ASSURED MIGRATION PATHS

Knowledge Age

**Charting Assured
Migration Paths**

Information Age

- Develop "Expeditionary" Products and Programs
- Use New Initiatives and Redirected Processes to Build Basic Competencies for Knowledge Age
- Take Decisive, Even Revolutionary Action

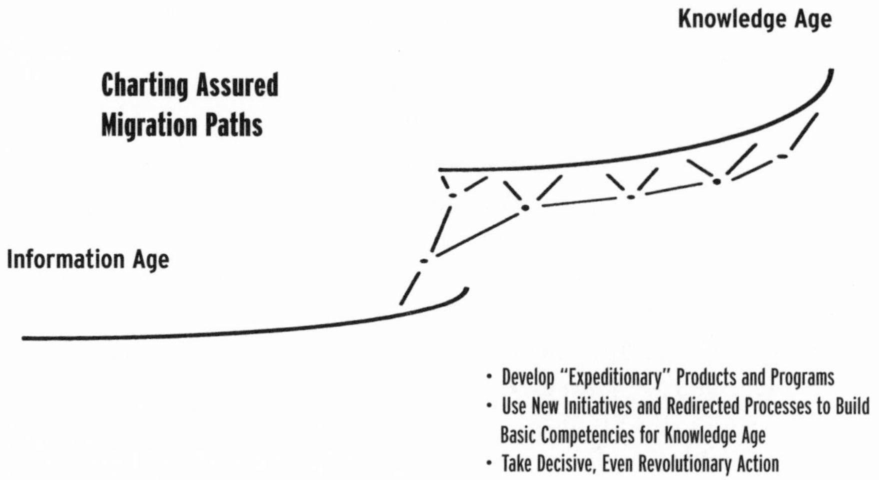

Figure 5.3

3. *Academic culture.* The capacity to create academic cultures that are responsive and timely and can roll out new academic products and services. This typically requires the establishment of new units and skunk works. It also requires expanding the reward system and providing incentives and resources for innovation.

4. *Expeditionary products, services, and learning experiences.* The ability to create a new generation of learning experiences that are distributed, interactive, and collaborative. Also the ability to deploy a trinity of expeditionary products, new financial paradigms, and supercharged strategic alliances in launching learning initiatives that are more ambitious and far-reaching.

5. *New financial paradigms.* The capacity to invest in IT and learning infrastructure and in new program/product development. Use investment partners to mitigate risk and seek broader markets. Create new sources of revenues and resource pools to support innovation.

6. *Supercharged strategic alliances.* Strategic allies bring new competencies and broaden the reach of educational institutions or systems. Relationship development and management will be essential competencies.

Part of the planning challenge facing systems of institutions is how to muster the vision, resources, and initiatives to develop these families of competencies.

Many of these initiatives will build on existing institutional strengths; others will require new approaches. Realigning and refocusing some of the basic tenets of systemwide planning are required.

Realigning the Focal Points for Effective Systemwide Planning

The principles for effective planning in multicampus systems have been clearly articulated as systems have expanded to meet growing needs over the past forty years. Farris W. Womack and Richard S. Podemski described "criteria for effective planning in multicampus systems" in the 1985 edition of *Planning for Higher Education*. As a complement to the criteria for effective planning at the individual institution, planning at the systemwide level requires the planning team to:

1. Articulate appropriate goals for a diverse, multicampus system;
2. Demonstrate relevance to society, the state, local community, and students;
3. Preserve individuality, avoid artificial conformity;
4. Create a framework for resource allocation to campuses driven by mission and need;
5. Coordinate decision-making among disparate groups; and
6. Foster cooperation among campuses.

These principles are still appropriate today, but the context has changed and the desired outcomes have shifted.

CHANGING CONTEXT AND OUTCOMES FOR SYSTEMWIDE PLANNING

In an article on the establishment of the Western Governors' University, Governor Michael Leavitt of Utah describes a conversation with President Clara Lovett of Northern Arizona University on the barriers to linking Utah's and Arizona's higher learning systems via distance education. Lovett cited four obstacles: "The first is bureaucracy; the second, tradition; third, regulation; and fourth, turf" ("Learning" 3). This list captures the essence of the challenges facing multicampus systems that can only be solved by changing the context for, and the outcomes from, systemwide planning. Planning must be a vehicle both for structuring traditional responses and for framing boundary-busting solutions.

First, systems must find ways to support nonbureaucratic, adaptive responses to new learning needs and opportunities, even if it means creating new "skunk works" for that purpose. These new enterprises can be created within existing institutions or as subsidiaries. Second, they must move beyond tradition to adopt new learning initiatives, financial paradigms, and strategic alliances. Third, regulations must be changed to deal with new learning and competency assessment modes that aren't measured on seat time and process. Fourth, issues of turf and service areas will become moot as distributed learning erodes existing boundaries. These developments will not happen overnight, but they are coming.

Focal Points for Systemwide Planning for the Knowledge Age

Systemwide planning on the threshold of the Knowledge Age is utilizing the following focal points. These will become even more important over the next decade.

FRAME NEW CHALLENGES AND OPPORTUNITIES AND CALL FOR NEW APPROACHES

Demographically focused strategic planning has proven critical in framing the need for massive investment in higher education in states experiencing hypergrowth. California, Arizona, Utah, Georgia, Florida, and Texas, as well as others, have launched new campuses and virtual/distributed learning initiatives based on strategic planning that framed future needs. Such master planning efforts have demonstrated the impossibility of meeting future needs with existing models of delivery and financing. They have stimulated genuine strategic thinking about different modes of learning interactivity in the Knowledge Age. This strategic thinking has spawned a number of significant new virtual and distributed learning initiatives such as the Western Governors' Virtual University (Johnstone and Jones, 8–11) and the California Virtual University (Vines, et al., 11–14).

These developments have not been limited to multicampus systems in states experiencing explosive demographic growth. Indiana University has developed a major initiative in distributed learning, driven not by explosive growth but by its strategic intent to enhance its competitive position. The University of Wisconsin has spawned a UW Learning Initiatives unit to leverage its distance learning assets. Major technology-supported learning initiatives have been developed in multicampus systems in New York, Minnesota, Pennsylvania, and other low-growth states. Indeed, few major multicampus systems have not developed such plans.

NEW MODELS FOR CAMPUS FACILITIES PLANS

A new breed of plans for future campuses is emerging. Not only are these new campuses rich in technology infrastructure, but their planning also has focused on distributed learning and its importance in the design of facilities. The new downtown campus of the University of Texas at San Antonio and new state university campuses in Florida and Georgia celebrate a new type of campus in metropolitan or suburban areas.

ESTABLISH STRETCH GOALS

System planning efforts have established "stretch goals," challenging their constituent institutions to increase enrollments, raise their level of diversity, enhance productivity, develop new competencies, and expand revenues from sources other than government and tuition. Multicampus systems in all parts of the country have utilized such stretch goals.

DEVELOP STRATEGY FOR INFRASTRUCTURE DEVELOPMENT AND MIGRATION PATHS

Infrastructure development has been a major focus of systemwide planning. This has included information technology and telecommunications, learning, and collaborative infrastructures. Successful infrastructure development has employed the tactic of building technological and application migration paths to the future.

Most multicampus systems have developed systemwide technology plans and strategies. The University of Texas System engaged Andersen Consulting in a major strategic planning process for all campuses and health sciences centers. This effort established systemwide goals for infrastructure development and enhancement, and it is stimulating a variety of campus-level initiatives.

The efficacy of technology strategies as a mechanism for rethinking approaches to learning has been discovered by many practitioners (Daniel, *Mega-Universities and Technology Strategies*).

FOCUS ON NEW REVENUES AND PROVIDE RESOURCES FOR NEW INITIATIVES

Multicampus system planning has always provided a basis for allocating and reallocating resources for strategic purposes. Many recent systemwide plans have included explicit goals to increase revenues from nongovernmental, nontuition sources, in both absolute and relative terms. They have also provided resource pools for distance learning and distributed learning initiatives.

Indiana University is a case in point. A blue ribbon task force on distance learning developed a vision for distributed learning that would position the eight-campus system to serve Knowledge Age learners. Working with a consulting team from Coopers & Lybrand, the task force suggested three selected areas for investment. The university has committed several million dollars to invest in these new initiatives and intends to continue this investment into the future.

SUPPORT INTERINSTITUTIONAL COLLABORATION AND NEW STRATEGIC ALLIANCES

Recent multicampus planning activities have emphasized the importance of interinstitutional cooperation, especially in new distance and distributed learning initiatives. They have also discussed the importance of strategic alliances involving not just other institutions, but technology companies, businesses, and other learning enterprises.

The new generation of virtual learning enterprises demonstrates this point. Michigan Virtual Automotive College was formed in 1996 by a collaborative effort among the University of Michigan, Michigan State University, the State of Michigan, the state's other colleges and universities, and the automotive university. It is a 501(c)(3) corporation that serves as an interface between higher education institutions, training providers, and the automotive industry.

The Western Governors' Virtual University is governed by a blue ribbon board of corporate leaders and educators. Eighteen Western states and possessions are participating. Major contractors/partners include IBM, Monitor Company, National Center for Higher Education Management Systems, Western Cooperative for Educational Telecommunications, University of New Mexico (on-line library access), Washington State University (registration and billing), and Follett Express (on-line bookstore).

SUPPORT GENUINELY NEW APPROACHES TO KNOWLEDGE AGE LEARNING

Over time, systemwide planning has built on the strengths of individual institutions. Recent planning efforts have also spawned a number of new initiatives that leverage the assets of multiple institutions and create new mechanisms for cutting through the impediments presented by bureaucratic structures and policies.

The University of Wisconsin is an internationally recognized leader in continuing education, cooperative extension, distance education, public radio and television, and other outreach activities. Even so, it has found it difficult to mobilize and leverage its considerable competencies and resources to address the needs and market opportunities in distributed learning. The "coefficient of friction" associated with attempting rapid change within existing academic cultures has been a problem, even in units such as Continuing Education which are more adaptive than most. The restrictions associated with state procurement and accountability standards have made expeditionary program development difficult.

The UW Regents recently approved the creation of UW Learning Innovations, a subsidiary unit with an attached 501(c)(3) corporation, to address this opportunity. Michael Offerman, UW-Extension's Dean of Continuing Education, will lead UWLI. It will serve as a utility enabling faculty throughout the UW System to develop, market, and distribute learning products and services worldwide through technology. Its aim is to set new standards of responsiveness, competitiveness, timeliness, and customization in the development of Knowledge Age learning materials.

Systemwide Planning Will Not Be Transformed Overnight

No educational or political leader expects multicampus systems to be transformed overnight. Indeed, one school of thought holds that the only way to transform multicampus systems is to create "skunk works" and new units that can bypass the organizational drag of state bureaucracies, policies, and structures.

The fact remains: multicampus strategic planning—especially for large, public university systems—will continue to be a powerful instrument for shaping our visions of the future and redirecting resources for investment in new learning initiatives. Such planning will continue to define the limitations of our existing tools and techniques in order to address the learning challenges and opportunities of the Knowledge Age. By expanding on the new directions in strategic thinking and strategic planning discussed in this chapter, we can advance the state of the planning art in multicampus systems.

6

BUDGET AND BUDGET-RELATED POLICY ISSUES FOR MULTICAMPUS SYSTEMS

Daniel T. Layzell

J. Kent Caruthers

The authors present analyses and examples of several important budgeting practices— examining revenues, expenditures, different initiatives, and programmatic trends—and interpret this information. They recommend applications for systems and campuses of today and the future.

Budgeting for multicampus university systems is a topic that has received little treatment in recent years. However, this is a topic of great importance given that multicampus systems are the dominant form of governance for public higher education in the United States. The purposes of this chapter are to describe budgeting practices and current budget-related issues for multicampus systems and then to introduce additional issues that are likely to increase in importance for systems in the years ahead. Topics covered in this chapter include:

1. Budgeting and budget processes;

2. Perennial budget-related issues for systems; and

3. Emerging budget-related policy issues faced by systems.

Budgeting for Public University Systems

A central function for most public university systems is the development of the systemwide budget and the articulation of related policies. In this section, we discuss the typical roles of the system board and its staff in budgeting. We also review the major sources of revenue available to public universities and the types of system oversight related to each; the mechanisms used by systems to request and distribute available funds; and policies and approaches for budget control.

BUDGET ROLES OF THE BOARD AND SYSTEM OFFICE

The role of each system board in the budget process is dictated by the laws and customs of the state in which the system is located. As such, no two systems should be expected to approach their budget responsibilities in exactly the same way. Nonetheless, a number of common features can be observed in making comparisons across numerous systems.

The two most common roles for lay boards in the budget process are to establish policy and to render official approvals of institutional proposals. In developing guidelines for use by institutions in making requests for state appropriations or preparing annual operating budgets, boards often express system priorities and policies on such matters as rates of salary increases, rates of tuition and fee increases, goals to enhance instructional equipment or eliminate deferred maintenance, etc. These budget policy agendas usually arise from strategic plans that have previously been adopted. An important role for the system budget, then, is to serve as the board's principle vehicle for policy implementation.

Virtually every board must take official action to approve both the system's requests for state appropriations and the annual operating budget of each constituent institution. The approval process mostly involves checks to ensure conformity with the board's policy guidelines, as described above, as well as with various directives from the governor and legislature. While the final approvals may appear as "rubber stamping" to the outside observer, the board's influence is more directly (and appropriately) felt in the earlier development of policy guidelines.

A major difference in budget responsibilities across the systems concerns whether the legislative appropriations bill identifies specific amounts for each institution or grants a lump sum to operate the overall system. When the appropriation comes as a lump sum, an additional role of the board is to determine an allocation of the system budget among constituent units. Concerns for equity, adequacy, and stability guide the board in carrying out its responsibilities.

MAJOR REVENUE SOURCES

Public universities receive operating funds from a variety of sources for a variety of purposes. In some cases, use of certain revenues is intended for a specific purpose (i.e., restricted funds) while in other cases the institutional management and its board have much more discretion over how to best use the funds to achieve established goals and objectives (i.e., unrestricted funds).

As seen in Figure 6.1A, the state appropriation is the largest single source of revenue for the typical public institution of higher education. Nonetheless, state funds account for only 40 percent of total revenues. The relative importance of state funds in supporting public higher education has diminished greatly over the past several years, dropping from 50 percent of all revenues in 1980 to just 40 percent in 1995 (see Figure 6.1B).

Other major revenue sources (i.e., those that account for more than 10 percent each) are in descending order of share: tuition and fees; federal grants, contracts, and appropriations; and auxiliary enterprises. The nature of system-level involvement in budgetary oversight varies significantly by revenue source.

1. *Treatment of State Appropriations.* By far, system offices are more concerned with the management and use of state appropriations than with any other revenue source. In fact, most campus personnel would describe the primary budget-related role of the system office as assisting in securing the state appropriation.

The state appropriation is also the focus of most legislative interest in university system budgets. Special provisions included by the legislature in the state appropriations act may dictate salary increase expectations, tuition increase limits, quotas for the enrollment of out-of-state students, and the extent of budget flexibility. When such directives exist, the system's budget staff is frequently charged with whatever implementation and/or compliance efforts may be required.

2. *Treatment of Tuition and Fee Revenues.* The principal role for systems with respect to tuition and fees is the development and approval of a schedule of charges to be levied on the students. This role is especially evident for the general-purpose charges that are assessed to all students, including any general-purpose surcharge for out-of-state students. Many systems require that each

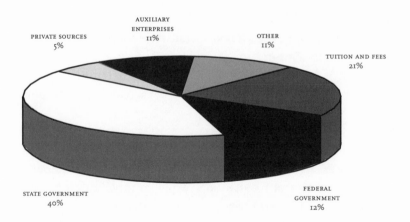

Figure 6.1A

Major Sources Of Revenue For Public Colleges And Universities: Fiscal Year 1995.

Note: Excludes hospital-related revenues.

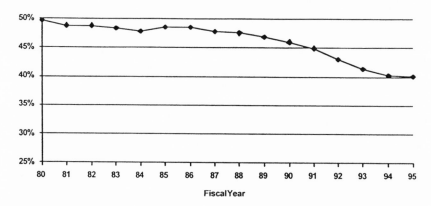

Figure 6.1B

State Funds As a Percentage of All Operating Revenues: Public Colleges and Universities FY 1980 to FY 1995.

Note: Excludes hospital-related revenues.

institution adopt systemwide uniform rates for the general-purpose tuition and fee charges. Institutions within the system, however, are often granted more local authority to establish unique rates for specialized fees (e.g., a campus recreation fee, a health services fee, etc.).

A major difference in budgeting practice across the states and their public university systems concerns who "owns" tuition and fee revenue. The owner-ship of tuition and fee revenue is a particular problem in those states where one or more of the institutions have significant proportions of nonresident students who are expected to pay significantly higher tuition than their in-state counter-parts. The concern is whether institutions may be receiving an inappropriate financial incentive to enroll nonresident students when these students gener-ate revenue from both by-the-state-appropriation and the tuition surcharge. Systems also vary from one another in terms of their treatment of general-pur-pose fees and more specialized charges to students.

In some states, the amounts collected from students are considered to be state revenues that must be deposited in the general state treasury for re-appro-priation back to the institutions. In other states, the institutions are allowed to "keep" their general-purpose tuition revenues but the estimated amount of such collections is deducted from the requirement for state appropriations, thereby eliminating inappropriate incentives.

The University of Wisconsin System plays an especially active role in the systemwide management of tuition and fee revenues. The UW System has created a systemwide pool comprised of a portion of the excess tuition collections from those campuses that exceed their tuition revenue targets. The primary purpose of this pool is to serve as an "insurance" program that provides supplemental support to those campuses that fail to meet their tuition revenue targets.

3. *Treatment of Other Non-State Revenues.* Beyond state appropriations and student tuition and fees, the typical system office usually does not play nearly as active a role. The system role with respect to budgets for auxiliary enterprises, contracts and grants, and similar activities is usually restricted to a limited staff review and perfunctory board approval. For instance, the typical system-level concern with the auxiliary enterprises budget is no more than to check that these activities continue to operate on a self-supporting basis.

Budgets derived from private giving, in particular, receive relatively little system-level attention. In some instances, in fact, university foundations are established as separate legal entities with separate boards of directors that are not under the jurisdiction of system boards and officials. Where systems are concerned with private giving, their role is largely supportive. For instance, several systems (including those in Florida and North Carolina) have policies to encourage private giving through provision of state matching funds to establish endowed chairs.

BUDGET REQUEST AND ALLOCATION MECHANISMS

Systems rely on a number of different practices and procedures to request and allocate the state appropriation. Systems in a majority of states rely on formula budgeting models for at least some aspect of the budget process. Proponents of funding formulas cite their advantages as being equitable, objective, and predictable.

The use of formulas is especially prevalent in the south, where Caruthers and Marks found that systems in each of the fifteen states that comprise the Southern Regional Education Board rely on formulas. National surveys typically show that 30–35 states report the use of higher education funding formulas (McKeown). In the remainder of the states, an incremental funding approach is most often employed.

Among the 30+ states that use formulas, a great variety of practices can be observed. In some systems, a formula is used in a "zero-based" setting. That is, the formula is used to calculate total funding requirements each year with each university assumed to have no funding entitlement except whatever their current workload variables generate through the formula. In other settings, the "base budget" is assumed to be in place, and the formula is used only to request new funding based on growth or other changes in workload.

States also differ greatly from one another in terms of the number of different formulas used and the proportion of the overall budget that is subject to formula calculations. The typical pattern, however, is to have separate formulas for each major expenditure function (i.e., instruction, research, public service, libraries and other academic support, student services, institutional support, and plant operations and maintenance). In some cases, a function may not be funded by formula (e.g., public service requirements may be handled incrementally) or two or more functions may be combined (e.g., student services and institutional support). Regardless of the exact format, the formulas attempt to demonstrate equity by providing the same funding rate per student in equivalent situations.

The typical funding formula for instruction is largely enrollment driven. Although the specific formats may differ across the states, each formula somehow can be reduced to a dollars per full time equivalent student enrolled format. Frequently, the funding rates vary according to the student's program and level. The influence of enrollment levels also can be seen in many of the support formulas, which often are expressed as a percentage of the enrollment-driven instructional formula or on a dollars per student basis.

Performance budgeting approaches are becoming more prevalent in many systems across the nation (Layzell and Caruthers). Under this concept, the allocation of dollars is based on levels of performance (e.g., retention rate, graduation rate, etc.) rather than the enrollment of students. The prevailing structure of performance funding models is used to provide an add-on to the traditional formula-determined amounts. A performance supplement in the 2–5 percent range is typical, but one state (South Carolina) is now attempting to transform their funding model into one that is totally based on performance.

BUDGET CONTROL AND FLEXIBILITY PRACTICES

Other than the ongoing debates about the equity of the allocation, the biggest source of continuing budget-related friction between system officers and campus personnel revolves around budget control and flexibility issues. Generally, most budget control procedures are dictated by the state government rather than by system boards. Controls frequently are in place that restrict the number of positions that can be created, limit the ability to transfer funds intended for one purpose to another (e.g., from library book acquisitions to faculty salaries), require that the planned purchase of goods and services receive prior approval before funds are committed, or require the reversion of unspent appropriations to the state treasury at year's end.

Some systems have undertaken major initiatives in recent years to gain more budget flexibility for their constituent institutions. In some cases, universities are now exempt from state personnel system procedures or have more flexibility in purchasing arrangements than other state agencies. Some systems grant differing levels of flexibility to individual institutions based on their demonstrated ability to manage their internal affairs (e.g., a consistent pattern of clean audits).

Perennial Budget-Related Issues for Systems

There are a number of budget-related issues that systems must deal with on a regular basis. This section deals with four in particular:

1. Interinstitutional funding equity;
2. Academic program planning and review;
3. Systemwide "utilities" (e.g., administrative and academic computing, library and information resources); and
4. Human resources/collective bargaining.

INTERINSTITUTIONAL FUNDING EQUITY

The concept of "equity" takes on a special level of importance—and complexity—for multicampus systems. This is because of the constant struggle to recognize and maintain a sense of "uniqueness" and distinctiveness of mission for each institution within the system while achieving the unstated goal of "strength through cohesiveness" that underlies the formation of all systems.

This is especially true of system budgets. Here, two types of equity are important: horizontal equity and vertical equity. Horizontal equity is defined as the equal treatment of equals, while vertical equity is defined as the unequal treatment of unequals. From a budgetary standpoint, horizontal equity is achieved when institutions of similar size and breadth of program have the same level of resources. Vertical equity is achieved when institutions with valid differences in size, scope, and mission are funded on an unequal (but appropriate) basis.

Obviously, the relative importance of achieving horizontal versus vertical equity depends on the type of system. For example, in segmented systems such as the Pennsylvania State System of Higher Education where institutions have generally similar missions, achieving horizontal equity is the central goal. On the other hand, consolidated systems such as SUNY or the University of Wisconsin System that include a wide range of institutional types (i.e., two-year campuses to major research universities) require a greater focus on vertical equity. However, given that mission differentiation is rarely a black and white issue within systems, it is necessary to be concerned with both types of equity.

As described earlier in this chapter, one of the major reasons behind the development and use of funding formulas by systems is the enhancement of funding equity. By definition, using a consistent set of funding rates achieves the goal of equitable funding outcomes. Many systems have also greatly enhanced the sophistication of their funding formulas by introducing factors that differentiate among academic disciplines, levels of enrollment, and/or type of institution in order to achieve vertical equity.

ACADEMIC PROGRAM PLANNING AND REVIEW

Given that the academic enterprise is the heart of higher education, academic program planning and program review are inextricably linked with institutional—and therefore system—budget matters. The need for new programs or enhancements of existing programs drive budget requests. Program reviews provide the rationale for continued resource allocations to specific academic programs, or conversely the rationale to shut down low quality or unproductive programs. In times of fiscal stringency, program reviews take on special importance in justifying the continued allocation of even scarcer resources among competing academic programs.

Program planning and review in system settings is different from that at single institutions because the entire system must be considered in these processes. One of the arguments in favor of systems is that financial resources can be deployed more efficiently and effectively among several institutions than at one institution to achieve the desired results. From an academic program standpoint this means that each institution can offer a different set of programs, thereby maximizing the systemwide program array without unnecessary duplication among institutions. As indicated by Eaton and Miyares, "it is as a system that institutions work to carry out statewide and regional goals to increase access to higher education. Systemwide program review has as its major objective an examination of issues associated with need and duplication" (69). Thus, both program planning and review activities must consider the impact on the systemwide program array.

The University of Maryland and University of Wisconsin systems provide two useful case examples of the essential linkages between academic program planning and review and budgeting at a system level. In response to severe resource constraints, the University of Maryland System evaluated several academic programs in 1992 to determine how the system might reallocate resources by "eliminating, downsizing, and consolidating many academic programs" (Eaton and Miyares, 74). Two groups of programs were analyzed: those that had low productivity (e.g., low degree production) and those that were high cost or not central to a specific institution's mission. As the result of this review, more than 60 academic programs were discontinued and many others were downsized or consolidated, freeing up over $10 million to be reallocated to key system priorities through 1997.

Also as part of the annual budget process, each institution in the University of Maryland System submits a "financial plan" requesting additional state funds to support new initiatives. Part of this plan includes an estimate of the reallocated funds that would be available to fund these new initiatives resulting from academic program reviews and from increases in administrative efficiency and productivity.

The University of Wisconsin System provides a related example of the link between academic program planning and resource allocation (see Sell, 23–39). During the 1970s and early 1980s, enrollment in the UW System grew significantly without proportional increases in state support, which led to widespread concerns about instructional quality. In response, the UW Board of Regents adopted a policy of systemwide enrollment management in 1986 with the goal of reducing enrollments while increasing financial support per student. Although this policy was successful, the UW System was also faced with the perennial problem of addressing faculty salary needs and unfunded academic program priorities. To resolve this problem, the university's 1991–93 biennial budget request included a commitment to use savings due to enrollment reductions to finance unfunded budget priorities related to improved instructional quality.

This initiative was referred to as the Quality Reinvestment Program (QRP) and its use extended into the mid-1990s. Approximately 48 percent of the QRP funding reallocated between 1992 and 1995 went to boost faculty salaries, while the remaining 52 percent went to improve instructional technology access, library needs, instructional laboratory modernization, program renewal, and other instructional needs. Many state legislators were accepting, if not actively supportive, of this initiative. However, many faculty and staff on the campuses saw this as a "dangerous" intrusion by the UW System Administration into the use of base budget funds for "generic purposes" (see Sell, 23–39). In the end, it was generally accepted that QRP reallocation was one of the few ways the UW System could improve faculty salaries and enhance academic programs during a period of state budget austerity.

SYSTEMWIDE UTILITIES

Systems will often choose to organize "utility" functions such as academic/administrative computing and library resources as a systemwide function in order to leverage these scarce resources to have the most effectiveness for the system as a whole. The organization of these functions can have budget-related implications for the system in both the planning/implementation and the operational phases.

Planning for and implementing both computing and library resources on a systemwide level adds complexity and changes the nature of resource requirements from those that are needed at the campus level. The issue that most often comes to the forefront in very short order is the question of technogical compatibility among campuses. For example, systems seeking to establish a systemwide administrative computing network will need to ensure that there is a basic level of compatibility among campus-based information systems before this can take place. This becomes even more problematic as institutions themselves are seeking to decentralize computing on campus. Likewise, systems seeking to establish a network among campus libraries will need to ensure that the necessary connections can be made among the libraries (e.g., cataloging systems). All of these activities will have resource requirements that systems will need to budget for, including funding for necessary equipment purchases to enhance compatibility as well as additional expenses for the inevitable systemwide planning committees and working groups that will be established.

An important question that will need to be addressed in the planning phase is where the "utility" operations will actually reside: at the system office or at the campus level. If it is at the campus level, it may be necessary to designate a lead institution to actually staff the operation. In any event, the mechanisms used to fund the system's operating budget will need to be adjusted to recognize the additional fixed costs of these utilities.

Once implemented, operating such systemwide utilities obviously has ongoing resource requirements as well. One strategy that systems use to fund these utilities is annual "user" fees levied on campuses that are based on such factors as institutional headcount, number of faculty and staff, or prior utilization patterns. Another strategy that some systems have used is a "revolving fund" that is dedicated to financing the specific function. Such revolving funds are specific pots of resources that are reallocated each year among campuses based on prior and projected utilization of the function. It should be realized that establishing such dedicated funding mechanisms often requires detailed and (sometimes) delicate negotiation with both campus personnel and state budget officials to ensure a proper level of understanding.

HUMAN RESOURCES AND COLLECTIVE BARGAINING

A final issue that will be covered in this section is the impact of human resources and collective bargaining on system budgets. Given that salaries and benefits represent the major portion of operating budgets in colleges and universities (typically ranging from 60 to 80 percent), these functions have significant implications for system budgets. It should be further noted that public institutions of higher education often operate under state personnel and/or civil service rules, which will also have an impact on how system and campus human resources functions are configured and operate.

One impact that the human resources function has on system budgets is in the area of salary and benefits administration. Depending on how the system human resources function is configured, this could involve a number of budget-related activities, including:

1. The establishment and revision of position pay ranges;

2. The determination of annual salary increase guidelines;

3. The allocation of annual salary increase dollars;

4. Payroll operations; and

5. The determination of annual employer health insurance and retirement contributions.

Depending on state requirements, some system human resource offices may also be assigned the "position control" function. This involves monitoring the number of positions filled at each campus to ensure that they do not exceed their authorized level. A variant on this activity in some states is the requirement to generate a certain level of "vacancy savings" during the budget development process (i.e., salary savings due to anticipated vacant positions). In these states, system human resource and budget offices may be required to monitor and calculate these vacancy savings.

A final related issue pertains to systems that have unionized faculty and/or staff and engage in collective bargaining. Again, all states have different procedures and regulations governing public employee bargaining, and some or none of the actual bargaining between management and labor representatives may be within the control of system or campus officials. For example, in some states, systemwide clerical and technical staff may be within a statewide bargaining unit with other state employees where a state agency takes full responsibility for collective bargaining while the system deals only with faculty bargaining (if applicable).

For those systems that do have the responsibility for negotiating and administering their labor agreements, both the systems and their campuses face an annual challenge in negotiating the major focus of most agreements: salary adjustments. In some instances, this negotiation may take place after the budget allocation from the state has been finalized and the system has a set pool of resources which the board is to allocate among employees. In other instances, the results of this negotiation feed into the budget process. In both cases, systems face the challenge of maintaining or enhancing systemwide salary equity and adequacy with the reality of very scarce resources.

Emerging Budget-Related Issues for Systems

The final section of this chapter evaluates several emerging budget-related issues that are or will shortly be impacting systems, including the following:

1. Accountability/Performance Measurement
2. Collaborative Programming
3. Instructional Technology/Distance Learning
4. Access
5. Articulation with other Educational Sectors

ACCOUNTABILITY/PERFORMANCE MEASUREMENT

State-level policymakers (e.g., legislators, governors) have been monitoring the performance of publicly funded institutions of higher education since the 1980s via a variety of accountability mechanisms. During the past few years, budgetary constraints paired with an ongoing interest in accountability and programmatic outcomes by policymakers have also brought about a renewed interest in the uses and implications of performance-based budgeting, i.e., allocating resources to institutions based on the extent to which they achieve previously established goals, objectives, and outcomes.

This is by no means a new concept in public budgeting, either in general or for higher education specifically. The federal government attempted to implement various forms of performance-based budgeting in the late 1960s and early 1970s (e.g., PPBS, zero-based budgeting), and the state of Tennessee has had an ongoing performance-based funding program for higher education in place since 1978. However, a primary difference between performance-based funding then and now is the comprehensive nature of some of it, currently under consideration by state policymakers, and the seriousness with which these initiatives are being considered.

Performance-based funding initiatives for higher education have had some success, most notably in Tennessee (Folger). Tennessee's incentive funding program and the additional funding received by institutions both directly and indirectly as the result of this program has been held up as the prime example of these benefits. Ashworth cautions, however, that fully implementing performance-based funding for higher education has two fundamental problems. First, "uniform agreements on the values that would have to be cranked into a formula do not exist, and data are not available within reason or within tolerable costs to feed such a formula system" (11). Secondly, it is conceivable that, if all funding were distributed on a performance basis, there could be significant redistribution of funds from year to year. This would adversely affect the ability to plan and execute at both a system and a campus level, ultimately defeating the purpose of performance budgeting. A related challenge for systems is the need to develop a credible set of performance indicators that measure the collective outcomes of institutions that may have very different missions and goals.

Despite these potential limitations, the concept of performance-based funding for higher education is alive and well in several states. A recent SHEEO (1997) study found that 22 states were using performance indicators as the basis for allocating resources to their institutions of higher education, either directly or indirectly. Of the 22 states reporting the use of performance indicators for allocating resources in 1997, seven reported that there was a direct linkage between the use of performance measures in resource allocation and 15 indicated that there was an indirect linkage. There is a subtle but significant difference between having a direct versus an indirect linkage in performance-based funding. Having a direct linkage means that the attainment or lack of attainment of an objective as measured by any performance indicator has a direct impact on the resources provided to the institution. For example, if an institution's funding were partially based on the attainment of a 60 percent graduation rate for all entering freshmen within six years, and the institution had only a 45 percent graduation rate, this would result in a negative impact on the resources provided to the institution.

On the other hand, having an indirect linkage in place provides for a much more subjective atmosphere of interpretation in applying performance indicators in the resource allocation process. That is, while performance indicators play a role in allocating resources to institutions under such a model, there are other factors considered as well. Thus, in our previous example of the six-year graduation rate, the institution would not *necessarily* be assured of a corresponding reduction in funding or other negative consequences.

The state of South Carolina presents an interesting case study regarding the future of performance-based funding for higher education. In 1996, the South Carolina General Assembly, prompted by a group of private business leaders in the state, enacted the most significant performance-based funding program to date. This program has since been implemented by the state Commission for

Higher Education and is based on institutional performance across 37 specific performance indicators which will be phased in through the year 2000. At that point 100 percent of state funding for public higher education will be allocated based on institutional performance as measured by these indicators. The significance of this particular program becomes quite clear when considering the fact that other state performance-based funding initiatives allocate from under one percent to four percent of state funding for higher education (Burke and Serban).

COLLABORATIVE PROGRAMMING

One of the primary benefits of multicampus systems is the ability to leverage resources at each institution with those from other system institutions. A primary example of this is the collaborative programming concept where institutions pool instructional resources (e.g., faculty, staff, technologies, facilities) to jointly offer academic programs among two or more institutions. This is especially useful in leveraging the resources of high cost programs such as engineering, allied health areas, and nursing. This concept is also becoming increasingly attractive to system boards and legislatures who are attempting to address the increased demand for high cost professional and technical programs with little or no additional resources.

One recent example of this approach is a collaborative nursing education program developed in the University of Wisconsin System among its five institutions that offer baccalaureate-level instruction in nursing. The target audience for this program is working nurses who have completed RN training and desire a BSN. This program involves a comprehensive series of courses taught both on-site in hospitals and at each institution through both distance learning technologies and classroom instruction. Students register at one of the five institutions, but take courses offered by faculty from all institutions.

The most positive aspect of this type of collaborative programming effort is the opportunity to pool instructional resources in a cost-effective manner. However, such collaborative programming efforts also require significant planning and ongoing coordination which require additional resources. The collaborative nursing program example cited earlier was greatly assisted by the presence of the systemwide continuing education extension function which already had an administrative mechanism in place for coordinating collaborative instructional efforts among UW System institutions. However, systems that do not have such mechanisms in place will need to invent them. Ultimately, then, systems may find that collaborative programming offers opportunities for both financial and instructional efficiencies in meeting instructional demand, but not for achieving cost savings.

DISTANCE LEARNING

One trend that is rapidly changing the character and structure of American higher education is the increased use of electronic technology in the delivery of instructional programs. To date, much of the financial planning and budgeting for so-called distance learning has been on an *ad hoc* basis. As such delivery approaches become more widespread, however, they are likely to require significant changes in system-level budgeting practices.

One obvious concern, so far, with funding for distance learning is the significant cost of investment in computer hardware and software. Although distance learning has been touted as an opportunity to realize significant cost savings in what has traditionally been a labor-intensive industry, early experience shows that instruction provided through distance learning often has a greater cost per unit than more traditional delivery methods. Due to the rate of technological change, any potential cost savings may continue to be offset by the ever-present need to update equipment.

Some states and their university systems have turned to innovative ways to finance the needed technological infrastructure. The State University System of Florida, for instance, is part of the Florida Distance Learning Network, which was created by the state legislature to bring together the state's telecommunications industry and educational systems to develop collaborative approaches for using technology to address educational needs.

Many of the traditional approaches for funding colleges and universities are based on geographical concepts. For instance, students from other states typically pay higher tuition rates than do in-state students. This differential is based on the concept that state residents are already subsidizing the cost of public higher education through state taxes and should thus pay a lower tuition rate than out-of-state students who have not directly contributed to state tax revenues. Likewise, funding formulas reimburse universities for credit hours produced on their respective campuses. Distance learning, however, may make such place-bound designations obsolete. Televised courses raise the issue of which institution is allowed to be reimbursed for the credit—the institution that broadcasts the course or the institution that registers the student and provides the classroom, counseling, and parking. For courses offered over the Internet, the geographic location of the student appears to have little importance.

Ultimately, issues surrounding the financing of distance learning will likely spill over to the overall issue of financing public higher education. This is due to the enhanced market competition for educational services that is being introduced by distance learning. Both private providers (e.g., the University of

Phoenix) and public institutions are finding geographical distinctions such as state boundaries increasingly irrelevant in offering courses and programs, resulting in increased competition for students. This competition, while theoretically beneficial to program quality, will also add a competitive dimension to pricing that will need to be recognized as institutions go from a limited number of "set prices" based on student level or place of residence to potentially dozens of different rates based on market demand and supply.

ACCESS

As advanced instruction becomes even more critical for maintaining and expanding job skills, the need for near-universal access to higher education is becoming a much more important issue to many university systems. Access issues usually have at least three dimensions—financial, geographic, and programmatic.

Financial access to a university system is measured in the relative charges for tuition and fees. In recent years, student charges have been rising rapidly to offset reduced rates of state appropriations. In many instances, a certain portion of the increased tuition revenue has been set aside to fund increased student financial aid. Nonetheless, public concern continues to escalate over college affordability. Financial access is likely to become an even greater issue over the next few years as enrollment growth from the "baby boom echo" generation further dilutes state appropriations per student.

When many public institutions were created, they were purposely located in rural areas. Small towns were thought to provide a safe environment where the state's youth could be sent to study away from home for several years. While this model still functions well for the traditional residential student, lack of geographic access is a significant problem for young adults who are trying to balance careers with part-time participation in higher education. Similarly, for traditional-aged students, who for financial reasons may need to live at home while attending college, geographic access is a critical concern.

A less visible yet equally significant access issue concerns the availability of specific programs. Through their academic planning and program review policies, most university systems have limited access to certain high cost programs. Such limits are especially noticed for programs at the graduate level (e.g., many institutions are not permitted to offer the doctorate) or in certain professions (medicine, law, engineering, etc.). In both cases, perhaps the primary rationale for limiting program access relates to the high cost of program delivery.

These three access issues (financial, geographic, and programmatic) are combining to place great pressure on system leaders to develop more cost-effective ways to meet the educational needs of their constituencies. Some systems are already responding through new approaches to delivering instructional programs, including distance learning and multi-institution centers. The attraction of these types of solutions is their presumed ability to overcome geographic or programmatic access barriers at reduced cost.

ARTICULATION WITH OTHER EDUCATIONAL SECTORS

A final issue to be discussed here is the need faced by systems to reach out to other educational sectors. Among other desired education reforms, governors, legislators, and other state policymakers are increasingly calling for a "seamless web" of education that removes barriers between K–12 education, community and technical colleges, and public universities. The most common manifestation of this to date has been the establishment of "articulation agreements" between community/technical colleges and public four-year institutions, in which community college students can transfer some or all of their coursework to the four-year institution with no loss of credit for the student. Just as importantly, the state avoids the cost of providing a similar educational experience to the same student twice. The development of a common course numbering system by a number of states has also enhanced the transfer function.

Increasingly, postsecondary education institutions are being called upon to reach out to K–12 systems to provide high school students with the opportunity to obtain college-level credit while still in high school. A variant on this is the "Tech Prep" concept being implemented in many states where high schools, community/technical colleges, and universities work together to provide both technical and academic training to high school juniors and seniors and to prepare them for the workforce.

These initiatives all have resource implications for participating systems. Sometimes funds are specifically appropriated for these activities by the state to cover some or all of the cost. In other instances, systems must either reallocate or charge a portion of the cost to the student.

Summary and Conclusion

Systems face different issues than single institutions in the realm of budgeting, ranging from the mechanics of the budget process to the policy goals to be achieved through the budget. While each system differs somewhat, there has generally been a clear division of labor between governing boards, system offices, and campuses in this arena. Boards set budget priorities/policy goals and monitor progress in achieving these goals; system offices focus on the acquisition, allocation, and management of state appropriations and the coordination of system resources; and campuses implement board policy and are responsible for ongoing financial management, including the acquisition of nonstate revenues.

In the growth period of higher education, systems were seen to be a rational approach to the efficient and effective management of a state's higher education efforts. However, the relative proportion of public institution budgets coming from state funds has steadily dwindled over time to well under half of the total operating revenues. While state funds still constitute a significant proportion of the total (40 percent on average), institutional revenues are clearly more diversified than they once were. Thus, some may question whether systems—whose primary charge has been the oversight of state appropriations—play a relevant budgetary/financial role, or *any* role, anymore.

All of this raises the basic question: are systems becoming irrelevant? We think not. Rather, we believe that systems are now undergoing a fundamental change from financial intermediary between state government and campus, to a much less regulatory entity which has the potential to serve as a facilitator for state higher education goals as well as a catalyst and advocate for campus-level initiatives. For example, as state governments become less of a financial "stakeholder" in public higher education, campuses will likely call (and are calling) for additional flexibilities in the use of the state funds received. At the same time, state legislatures are often loath to give up control over the use of any public funds absent any accountability mechanisms. Systems present an opportunity to meet both campus- and state-level goals through the design of appropriate accountability mechanisms. The performance-based funding initiatives, underway in several states that were discussed earlier, provide an opportunity to link the allocation of funds to specific policy goals.

Another example of how systems can be helpful in this changing environment is in the growing area of distance learning. As previously discussed, the advent of distance learning has added a new element of competition to the market for educational services that will have an impact on both the financing (including pricing) and delivery of these services. In addition to enabling efficiencies in the use of distance learning technologies, systems provide an opportunity for the constructive management of this competition through the establishment of financial incentives (and disincentives) and the encouragement of strategic alliances and program offerings among system institutions (i.e., the "virtual university").

In short, the changing financial environment for public higher education need not be viewed as a death knell for the viability of systems. Instead, we believe that there is an opportunity for systems to evolve into a positive and proactive force for helping both states and institutions achieve their goals.

7

INSTRUCTIONAL PRODUCTIVITY OF SYSTEMS

Michael F. Middaugh

American higher education, and the state systems that largely comprise it, now has at its disposal clear evidence that the enterprise is far more productive and teaching oriented than its critics claim. That evidence is highlighted in this chapter, and the author argues that the time has come for state systems to be proactive in using it.

Much has been written in recent years concerning the productivity of American institutions of higher education, little of which has been in a positive vein. The 1996 edition of *U.S. News'* "America's Best Colleges" argued that:

> The trouble is that higher education remains a labor-intensive service industry made up of thousands of stubbornly independent and mutually jealous units that must each support expensive and vastly underused facilities. It is a more than a $200 billion-a-year economic enterprise—many of whose leaders oddly disdain economic enterprise and often regard efficiency, productivity, and commercial opportunity with the same hauteur with which Victorian aristocrats viewed those in "trade." . . .The net result is a hideously inefficient system that, for all its tax advantages and public and private subsidies, still exacts a larger share of family income than almost anywhere else on the planet (91)

The article goes on to suggest that higher education officials are attempting to hide the campus causes of escalating tuition rates, i.e., "declining teaching loads, nonproductive research, ballooning administrative hierarchies, 'celebrity' salaries for professional stars, and inflated course offerings," and culminates with the following judgment: " If colleges and universities were rated on their overall financial acumen, most would be lucky to escape with a passing grade."

Such comments also capture the blanket negative indictments found in national polls against most large organizations in our society, such as university systems, big government, large industrial organizations, and "big" religion (Gaither, Nedwick, and Neal, citing National Opinion Research Center data).

As troubling as these blanket indictments might be—for surely they are read and accepted as gospel by millions of American parents and taxpayers—more troubling is the absence of convincing counterarguments from the higher education community. The clarion call for developing such evidence was heralded by Robert Zemsky, of the University of Pennsylvania, and William Massy, from Stanford University, in their 1990 definition of the "academic ratchet."

> The academic ratchet is a term to describe the steady, irreversible shift of faculty allegiance away from the goals of a given institution, toward those of an academic specialty. The ratchet denotes the advance of an independent, entrepreneurial spirit among faculty nationwide, leading to increased emphasis on research and publication, and on teaching one's specialty in favor of general introduction courses, often at the expense of coherence in an academic curriculum. Institutions seeking to enhance their own prestige may contribute to the ratchet by reducing faculty teaching and advising responsibilities across the board, thus enabling faculty to pursue their individual research and publication with fewer distractions. The academic ratchet raises an institution's costs and results in undergraduates paying more to attend institutions in which they receive less attention than in previous decades." (22)

Within the context of these different views of American faculty, this chapter addresses the issue of productivity in higher education systems. The three cornerstones upon which most institutional mission statements are constructed include teaching, research, and service. In this chapter, productivity will be subdivided into "instructional" (i.e., teaching) and "noninstructional" (i.e., research and service) categories. The discussion of higher education systems will focus largely on national level data, primarily extracted from the National Study of Instructional Costs and Productivity located at the University of Delaware. However, the findings and discussion are equally applicable to systems at the state level.

Developing Information on Productivity

The seminal question at the heart of this chapter is, "How productive are systems?" This is neither a trivial nor a simple question. American taxpayers invest billions of dollars in state higher education systems. Recent figures indicate higher education is America's thirteenth largest industry, with total costs approaching $120 billion annually. It is, therefore, both reasonable and prudent for tax payers to ask what return they are receiving on such a large investment. State systems of higher education, in particular, seem vulnerable, both because of their size and the amount of their budgets, and the lack of strong counterarguments against the impersonal and unproductive charges made by their critics.

Having said that, however, it is important to again underscore that the concept of "productivity" in higher education is a complex construct. It embraces productivity in the classroom—student credit hours and organized class sections taught. Faculty are hired, and ultimately tenured, in large measure with the expectation that they will teach. Is this in fact happening or is teaching being neglected for the sake of research, for example? At the same time, government, industry, and other external entities look to higher education to generate and transmit new knowledge and state-of-the-art technology, and, in turn, they support and back up that expectation with contracts, grants, and other funds. Are higher education institutions "producing" in regard to that expectation? Further, are the costs of instruction, research, and service measurable and consistent with institutional and system missions?

In examining productivity, the analytical tool of choice is the National Study of Instructional Costs and Productivity (NSICP), of which the author of this chapter is Director. NSICP was initiated at the University of Delaware in 1992, largely in response to a need for interinstitutional comparative data on cost and productivity measures at the academic discipline level. The University of Delaware, like a great many postsecondary institutions, had over the years developed a series of indicators for describing teaching and research productivity, and for measuring unit costs of instruction. During the late 1980s and early 1990s, these indicators proved particularly helpful in making resource allocation and reallocation decisions between and among academic departments, based on trend information with regard to productivity and cost (Middaugh and Hollowell, 61–75). A significant limitation of those indicators, however, was that they were institution specific. While it was possible to make comparisons between the history and political science departments or the physics and chemistry departments at the University of Delaware, there was no way to assess the relative productivity or costs for those disciplines compared with similar programs at other institutions. Out of this particular need the National Study of Instructional Costs and Productivity was born.

Now a mature data collection methodology embracing colleges and universities across the nation and still growing, NSICP's development was funded initially by a Cooperative Education Program Grant from Teachers Insurance and

Annuity Association/College Retirement Equities Fund (TIAA/CREF), and subsequently by a three-year grant from the Fund for Improvement of Post Secondary Education. This funding enabled a panel of measurement experts to meet annually to address appropriate strategies for collecting detailed data on teaching loads by faculty category, and expenditure data for instruction, research, and public service. Most important, the data are collected at the level of academic discipline (Exhibit 7.2). This is a particularly important concept because productivity—both instructional and non-instructional—and costs at an institution or in a system are shaped by the *mix* of academic disciplines as well as the *level* of course offerings. Thus, in discussing the productivity of a given institution, or of a total system, it is possible to better understand the drivers of productivity when one understands the disciplinary mix of the institution or system.

NSICP is designed to answer the question, "Who is teaching what to whom, and at what cost?" The study collects detailed teaching load data and examines student credit hours and organized class sections taught by four categories of faculty: tenured and tenure-track faculty, permanent nontenure-track faculty, temporary faculty, and graduate teaching assistants. Student credit hour and class section data are arrayed by level of instruction—lower division undergraduate, upper division undergraduate, and graduate—and by course type—regularly scheduled and individualized instruction.

Teaching Loads as a Measure of Productivity

The *U.S. News* and *Change* magazine's criticisms of higher education cited at the beginning of this chapter would have us believe that faculty on recurring contracts, particularly tenured and tenure-track faculty, in large impersonal systems with their research campuses, rarely teach undergraduates. One would get the distinct impression that these individuals, whose salaries constitute the majority of instructional expenditures at any college or university, do anything but teach and that instructional productivity is minimal, particularly at research institutions. The first part of this examination of productivity will concentrate on teaching productivity. It will address the issue of who is teaching what to whom, and will also examine how much teaching is being done.

Conventional wisdom would suggest that, within a system of higher education institutions, faculty at comprehensive institutions (i.e., those offering primarily the baccalaureate degree, with graduate programs in selected disciplines) would have heavier teaching loads than their colleagues at doctoral level universities, who in turn would teach more than faculty at research universities. To test this hypothesis, data from the 1995 NSICP were examined.

Teaching load data were collected from 32 research universities, 43 doctorate-granting universities, and 85 comprehensive colleges and universities. The data reflected workload information for 24 academic disciplines commonly found at most institutions of higher education:

Communications	Economics
Education	Geography
Foreign Languages & Literature	History
English Language & Literature	Political Science
Biological Sciences	Sociology
Philosophy	Theater and Stagecraft
Chemistry	Fine Arts and Art Studies
Geology	Music
Physics	Nursing
Psychology	Business Administration/Management
Anthropology	Financial Management Services
Engineering	Accounting

The data were collapsed into a single data set, reflecting the aggregate teaching activity at each of the three Carnegie institutional types, i.e., research universities, doctoral universities, and comprehensive colleges and universities. The findings were quite instructive and shatter many of the myths discussed earlier.

Table 7.1 summarizes the findings. On average, across the 24 disciplines, tenured and tenure-track faculty taught 55 percent of all lower division undergraduate student credit hours at research universities, 57 percent at doctoral institutions, and 74 percent at comprehensive colleges and universities. Contrary to external criticism, one in every two student credit hours generated in freshman and sophomore level courses at research and doctoral universities, and three of every four student credit hours at comprehensive institutions, are taught by tenured and tenure-track faculty. Lower division courses tend to be introductory in nature, and are not the esoteric variety which Zemsky and Massy (16–22) attributed to tenured and tenure-track faculty, "largely at the expense of coherence in an academic curriculum."

The results are even more impressive when one examines student credit hour generation in all undergraduate courses, both lower division and upper

Table 7.1   *Comparison of Selected Instructional Productivity and Cost Measures:*
1996 NSICP Data for Research, Doctoral, and Comprehensive Institutions
Summarized for 24 Academic Disciplines

	Research Universities	Doctoral Universities	Comprehensive Colleges/Universities
Proportion of Lower Division Student Credit Hours Taught By: Tenured/Tenure-track			
Faculty	55	57	74
All Permanent Faculty	67	66	81
Proportion of All Undergraduate Student Credit Hours Taught By: Tenured/Tenure-track			
Faculty	65	67	79
All Permanent Faculty	77	75	86
Proportion of Lower Division course Sections Taught By: Tenured/Tenure-track			
Faculty	41	49	72
All Permanent Faculty	51	58	79
Student Credit Hours per Total FTE Faculty	224	238	249
Organized Class Sections per Total FTE Faculty	2.4	2.8	3.5
Direct Instructional Expense per Student Credit Hour Taught	174	136	131
Sponsored Research/Service Expenditures per Tenured and Tenure-track FTE Faculty	30,063	7,419	987

division. Tenured and tenure-track faculty at research and doctoral institutions teach two of every three student credit hours on average across the 24 disciplines under examination, with four of five student credit hours taught by tenured and tenure-track faculty at comprehensive colleges and universities.

If the examining lens is expanded to include all regular faculty, i.e., tenured and tenure-track *and* permanent nontenured faculty, the proportion of undergraduate student credit hours taught by faculty with whom the institution has a recurring contractual arrangement was 77 percent at research universities, 75 percent at doctoral universities, and 86 percent at comprehensive institutions. Put another way, when a student or parent pays tuition, it is ostensibly to purchase instructional services from those permanent employees in whom the institution has invested professional responsibility for educating students. The dollar amount of tuition charged at an institution (i.e., full-time or part-time rate) is a function of the number of credit hours purchased. The data clearly demonstrate that the vast majority of those student credit hours are being delivered by permanent faculty, and in particular by tenured and tenure-track faculty. The customer is receiving the commodity which he/she is purchasing with the tuition dollar. The charge that universities, particularly research universities, are large, impersonal organizations where the teaching is largely conducted by teaching assistants does not withstand vigorous scrutiny.

How, then, can there be a lingering perception that a preponderance of other than regular faculty are in the classroom? In looking at the issue of teaching workload, NSICP goes beyond the student credit hour as a measure of teaching activity. The Study also examines organized class sections, i.e., those regularly scheduled meetings of a consistently constituted group of students throughout a term for the purpose of receiving instruction. However, the Study does not look solely at credit-bearing organized class sections. It also examines zero-credit organized class sections such as laboratories, discussions, and recitations which are appended to, or are prerequisites for, regularly scheduled credit-bearing sections, and which consume instructional resources and involve instructional activity.

When organized class sections were examined, on average, tenured and tenure-track faculty taught 41 percent of all lower division undergraduate class sections (compared with 55 percent of student credit hours) at research universities; 49 percent at doctoral universities (compared with 57 percent of student credit hours); and 72 percent at comprehensive colleges and universities (compared with 74 percent of student credit hours).

The proportion of all undergraduate organized class sections taught by tenured and tenure-track faculty at research universities is 56 percent; the proportion is 62 percent at doctoral universities and 78 percent at comprehensive institutions. When the faculty pool is expanded to include all permanent facul-ty—both tenured/tenure-track and nontenure-eligible—the proportion of undergraduate organized class sections taught by those faculty is 67 percent at research universities, 71 percent at doctoral universities, and 85 percent at com-prehensive colleges and universities. Clearly, those faculty in whom the insti-tution has the most invested, i.e., permanent employees, are in the classroom the majority of the time, regardless of Carnegie institutional type.

It is important to note that, while the data reported in this chapter reflect a national sample of postsecondary institutions, the data submitted by institu-tions within state systems of higher education mirror these same national pat-terns. Consequently the national generalizations concerning relative teaching loads by Carnegie institutional classification are fully applicable to university systems as well.

What of the disparity between student credit hours taught and organized class sections taught, particularly among tenured and tenure-track faculty, where the former proportion is consistently higher than the latter? The answer obviously rests with zero-credit organized class sections, which, at research and doctoral universities in particular, tend to be staffed by part-time faculty and teaching assistants. It is not at all unusual to have a tenured faculty member teach the lecture portion of an introductory physics class, with the laboratory and recitation sections being led by a graduate teaching assistant. The pattern is both common and pedagogically sound.

Higher education institutions must be more assertive on this issue. Instead of being on the defensive about teaching assistants leading organized class sec-tions, colleges and universities should use the data described in this chapter to underscore the following point. First, as noted earlier, the commodity for which tuition is the currency, i.e., the student credit hour, is largely delivered by per-manent faculty and tenured and tenure-track faculty in particular. Zero-credit laboratories, recitations, and discussion sections are designed to reinforce the materials presented in the credit-bearing portion of a course, and indeed enhance the prospect for student success. Parents and students are both familiar with and accepting of the practice of using student teachers in elementary and sec-ondary schools in an apprenticeship to full employment as a K–12 faculty mem-ber. The same principle applies in higher education, and it needs to be discussed openly. New college and university faculty will be better teachers if they are exposed to appropriate resources and experiences as graduate teaching assis-tants, with guidance from their faculty mentors. And finally, there is no body of research that argues that graduate teaching assistants are pedagogically unsound instructional resources.

Clearly, there is a substantial body of evidence regarding to instructional productivity among America's faculty, and the data are largely positive. How does this relate to the earlier criticisms of American higher education with regard to cost, and to the assertion that faculty engage in nonproductive non-instructional activity, particularly in the arena of research? The issues are inter-related, and the following data shed initial exploratory light.

Looking at the volume of teaching loads (as opposed to the proportion of student credit hours and organized class sections taught), tenured and tenure-track faculty at research universities teach the fewest student credit hours per FTE faculty, followed by those at doctorate granting universities, with the heaviest teaching loads found at comprehensive institutions. Organized class sections mirror this pattern. Cost data reflect the lighter teaching loads at research universities. The average direct instructional expenditure per student credit hour at research universities, for the 24 disciplines examined in this analysis, was $174. This compares with an average direct expenditure per student credit hour of $136 at doctoral universities, and $131 at comprehensive colleges and universities.

However, the teaching load and cost data should be viewed within the context of institutional mission. Research universities should reflect, in addition to teaching, what their name implies—research and public service. Separately budgeted research and service expenditures per FTE tenured and tenure-track faculty average $30,100 across the 24 disciplines at research universities, compared with $7,400 at doctorate granting universities, and $990 at comprehensive institutions.

Externally sponsored activity, as measured by direct expenditures, is important in looking at the overall notion of productivity in systems. Large public systems of higher education, such as those in New York, North Carolina, and Texas, embrace institutions that fall into the research, doctoral, and comprehensive institutional categories. The cost per delivered student credit hour of instruction mirrors the patterns previously described from the national data set. Yet the costs are not passed along to the consumer. The in-state tuition rates at research universities within a system are not all that different from those at comprehensive institutions. It is the heavy investment in externally sponsored activity that helps to offset the higher costs of instruction at research institutions, where the data also demonstrate that faculty still teach undergraduates despite their research and service obligations. As will be discussed shortly, the by–products of research and service activity also include current and state-of-the-art curricula. In sum, looking at the total package of data from the National Study of Instructional Costs and Productivity, there can be little doubt that the American system of higher education, and the state systems that comprise it, are productive and continue to be models for the rest of the world.

Noninstructional Productivity

Before getting into a discussion of the relative merits of pure and applied research at American colleges and universities, the academic and fiscal implications of university research should be considered. In fiscal year 1995, colleges and universities responding to the National Science Foundation Survey of R&D Expenditures in Science and Engineering reported a total of $21.6 billion in research and development contract and grant expenses for that year (National Science Board, Science and Engineering Indicators—1996). That research generated full support in the form of research assistantships for 87,900 full-time graduate students in science and engineering fields. This represents one in every four full-time graduate students enrolled in those programs, and relieves the institutions of over 25 percent of the cost of supporting graduate student funding. Put another way, the research productivity of American higher education made it possible for nearly 88,000 students to pursue advanced degrees without incurring significant debt—a remarkable outcome! These research assistantships—coupled with institutionally funded teaching assistantships in those fields—help to ensure a pool of Ph.D. candidates trained in state-of-the-art research techniques and capable of transmitting and adding to the most current body of knowledge in their chosen field. It would not be overstatement to say that graduate education, as we know it, in the United States would cease to exist were it not for the strong research activity of America's faculty.

While training graduate students is an important product of research activity, there continues to be persistent criticism that faculty do research at the expense of teaching. The 1993 National Study of Postsecondary Faculty, conducted by the National Center for Educational Statistics, examined the teaching and research activity of faculty. Nationally, all faculty report spending 54 percent of their time in teaching activity, 18 percent in research, 13 percent in administrative activity, and 15 percent in other activities. Clearly, teaching does not suffer at the expense of research. Some might argue that this is a skewed statistic because it includes all disciplines at all institutions, including two-year colleges where the primary mission is teaching. To respond to that concern, it is instructive to examine the same data base, focusing on the fields of science and engineering, where research is an expected component for promotion and tenure, and will therefore be quite prevalent.

1996 National Study of Instructional Costs and Productivity

Institution: _____

Academic Department/Discipline: _____

Associated CIP Identifier: _____

Which degrees are offered at your institution in this Department/Discipline?   (Circle all that apply.)

Associate   Bachelor's   Master's   Doctorate

A.   INSTRUCTIONAL WORKLOAD - *FALL SEMESTER, 1994*

Please complete the following matrix, displaying student credit hours and organized class sections taught, by type of faculty, and by level of instruction. *Be sure to consult definitions before proceeding.* While we would like all cells completed, shaded areas are optional, consistent with the directions below.

Classification	FTE Faculty			Student Credit Hours								Organized Class Sections				
	(A) TOTAL	(B) Buy-out	(C) Instructional (C=A-B)	(D) Lower Div. OC*	(E) Upper Div. OC*	(F) Undergrad. Indiv. Instruct.	(G) TOTAL Undergrad. Credit Hrs. (G=D+E+F)	(H) Graduate OC*	(I) Graduate Indiv. Instruct.	(J) TOTAL Graduate Credit Hrs. (J=H+I)	(K) TOTAL Student Credit Hours (K=G+J)	(L) Lab/ Discussion/ Recitation Sections	Other Section Types (Lecture, Seminar, etc.)			
													(M) Lower Division	(N) Upper Division	(O) Graduate	(P) TOTAL (P=L+M+N+O)
Regular Faculty:																
- Tenured/Tenure Eligible																
- Other Regular Faculty																
Supplemental Faculty																
Teaching Assistants																
- Credit Bearing Activity																
- Non-credit Bearing Activity																

Reminder: Use Fall 1994 Semester Data as of your official institutional census date.

   * OC = Organized Class

Is your Academic calendar:
_____ Semester
_____ Quarter

Exhibit 7.2

Important: *If you cannot differentiate between "Organized Class" and "Individualized Instruction" student credit hours, assign all credit hours to the "Organized Class" column. Similarly, if you cannot differentiate between "Lower Division" and "Upper Division" undergraduate student credit hours, report all those credit hours under "Total Undergraduate Credit Hours."*

Page 2

National Study of Instructional Costs and Productivity   Institution: _____

Academic Department/Discipline: _____   Associated CIP Identifier: _____

B.   COST DATA: *Academic and Fiscal Year 1994-95*

1.   Total student credit hours generated during Academic Year 1994-95, which were supported by the Department/Discipline instructional budget (NOTE: Semester calendar institutions will typically report fall and spring student credit hours; quarter calendar institutions will report fall and winter and spring student credit hours.)

   A.   Undergraduate   _____
   B.   Graduate   _____

2.   Total direct expenditures for instruction in Fiscal Year 1995.

   A.   Salaries   _____
   B.   Benefits   _____
   C.   Other than personnel expenditures   _____
   D.   Total (Sum of A thru C)   _____

3.   Total direct expenditures for separately budgeted research activities in Fiscal Year 1995.   _____

4.   Total direct expenditures for separately budgeted public service activities in Fiscal Year 1995.   _____

Exhibit 7.2 (continued)

Looking across the full spectrum of Carnegie institution types, faculty in science and engineering spend, on average, 44 percent of their time teaching and 32 percent of their time in research. The teaching activity averages two courses, primarily at the undergraduate level. At research universities, where science and engineering faculty report spending one third of their time teaching and 42 percent in research, with the typical teaching load slightly over four credit hours, the number of undergraduates taught was nearly double that for graduate students. Even faculty whose primary responsibility is research taught on average one course, with undergraduates comprising 60 percent of the enrollment in all courses taught by this group. The data do not support the assertion that teaching—and particularly undergraduate instruction—is compromised by research. Indeed, there seems to be a symbiotic relationship between the two areas, with students serving "apprenticeships" in connection with the two areas of activity.

Outcomes from university research are the subject of a whole other book. Suffice to say that technological advances, breakthroughs in pharmaceutical and biomedical research, innovations such as genetic engineering for agriculture, etc., are examples of the ways in which university-based research positively affects the quality of life. Spin-off industries from university research parks have clear economic impacts on the region immediately surrounding the institution. According to the National Science Board (1996), the number of patents awarded to academic institutions has skyrocketed. Approximately 300 to 400 patents were issued annually to institutions of higher education during the 1980s. That number has since quadrupled, with some 1,761 patents issued in 1994. University research is clearly about more than journal articles and presentations at professional meetings. There are real and tangible outcomes related to the noninstructional productivity of higher education faculty. This research, in turn, has a positive impact in the lifestyle of the average American.

Productivity in Systems

The national data examined throughout this paper are mirrored in every respect at the state and system level. How productive, then, are systems? Is an institution more or less productive if it is part of a system? The data reviewed throughout this chapter suggest that higher education institutions are extraordinarily productive. What can systems, which are among the sources of these data, say about the issue of productivity?

Obviously they can say a great deal. Higher education systems offer a myriad of choices and potential to consumers of its services. The parents of a college bound student can find an ideal fit for their child. If the student requires a great deal of personal attention and interaction with instructors, the data suggest that he/she will find it at a comprehensive institution. Indeed, colleges such as the State University of New York at New Paltz, the University of North Carolina at Ashville, Prairie View A&M University in Texas, or any of the schools in the California State University System have built their reputations on the teaching mission of their faculty. Promotion and tenure at these institutions is predicated on excellence in teaching, and the instructional output data described in this chapter demonstrate the productivity of tenured and tenure-track faculty. Research and service are also components of faculty activity at comprehensive institutions, but these schools are primarily characterized by teaching.

That is not to suggest that faculty at research and doctoral universities are not involved in teaching; the data described in this chapter demonstrate that most of the instruction in these institutions is carried out by tenured and tenure-track faculty. But theirs is a very different mission from comprehensive colleges and universities. Major research universities within higher education systems are expected to generate new knowledge and to impact the state and region. It is hard to imagine the Research Triangle Area in North Carolina, with its numerous research and development centers and spin-off industries, emerging without the University of North Carolina and North Carolina State University. America's reputation as the major agricultural producer of the world is due in no small way to the research and cooperative extension activity of the state flagship institutions in the National Association of State Universities and Land Grant Colleges.

It is hard for this author to envision the Delaware economy without the symbiotic relationship between the numerous chemical industries headquartered in the state such as the Dupont Corporation and Gore Industries and the University's Chemical Engineering Department, or without the College of Business and Economics and its interplay with MBNA and other major entities in the banking and credit industry. Clearly the research and service activities of universities impact the quality of life and the economies of the regions they serve.

Are systems productive? Obviously. If the tripartite mission—teaching, research, and service—of American higher education is complex, the systemic nature of higher education systems facilitates its realization. As research and doctoral universities add to the body of knowledge across disciplines through research and public service activity, they ensure a steady stream of highly trained faculty who will continue to populate not only those institutions, but also the comprehensive and two-year schools within the overall system of higher education. In the latter schools, faculty primarily teach as the data in this chapter clearly demonstrate. The strength of American higher education is precisely the diversity of the institutions which comprise it. The national system of higher education, and the state systems that comprise it, have never been more productive. Rather than respond apologetically to ill-founded criticisms of American higher education, colleges and universities must assume a more aggressive posture and use data such as those described in this chapter to educate legislators and taxpayers as to the substantial return that higher education provides for resources invested.

PART THREE

REPRESENTATIVE MULTICAMPUS SYSTEMS

Part III of this volume provides four case studies—two community college systems and two senior level systems—covering the modern multicampus university. We should emphasize here what it is that we hope to gain from such case studies of individual systems. In the review of large organizations (systems) and their individual units (campuses), as in the case of cultures and individual personalities, the in-depth investigation of a single case still remains the best means for investigating and revealing the wholeness of the system and the various processes in action. These case studies permit us to see how particular components—history, location, culture, organizational structure, personalities, problems, and opportunities—all participate in the development of the character of the total system, and how the distinctive parts fit into the pattern of interrelationships by the system. Generalized knowledge of these inner dynamics and their relations to outside forces also will help to form the basis for review and planned change in other comparable types of systems and academic environments. More than this, such case studies can help immediately to lift the reader to a higher level of realism and sophistication.

We follow, then, in this section with four in-depth chapters on different types of systems which we think are significant: (1) The segmented approach of the three California systems; (2) The University of Houston System, a prototype of the urban multicampus system; (3) The Miami-Dade Community College System; and (4) The Maricopa Community College District. Despite their differences, these systems are all interrelated, and yet all four do not cover the subject fully. The total volume will allow the reader to extrapolate a broader picture of multicampus systems, emphasizing the extent to which the great differences among, and the complexities within, the individual systems depend on the forces in their larger society and culture.

California's three sharply differentiated tiers, or system segments have—for all their weaknesses—arguably evolved into the nation's premier system of public higher education; however, certain reforms may be necessary if this state is to continue its tradition of educational excellence into the twenty-first century.

8

THE CALIFORNIA EXPERIENCE

The Segmented Approach

William H. Pickens

*California's three sharply differentiated tiers, or
system segments, for all their weaknesses, have
evolved arguably into the nation's premier systems of
public higher education; but certain reforms may be
necessary if this state is to continue its tradition of
excellence into the twenty-first century.*

The Segment Is Destiny

"Character is destiny" wrote Heraclitus, a Greek philosopher with firm convictions about what force most shaped human lives. Surely the force today that most shapes the destiny of American public colleges and universities is "the system," or, specifically, the way that campuses are defined and linked to one another.

California provides a striking example of how one approach to creating higher education systems can powerfully shape their destiny. This state organized all its public campuses into systems or, more accurately, into segmented tiers where institutional level is the most distinguishing and permanent feature. The original purpose was to promote order during the growth of higher education, to ensure student access by guaranteeing entry somewhere, and to foster clear expectations about who does what. In California, the concept of a higher education *system* is not nearly so significant for policy and institutional behavior as is *segment*—a sharply differentiated set of campuses joined together in some fashion.[1]

This chapter will describe how a multicampus approach to system building operates when its central organizing principle involves tiers of institutions organized within a very structured policy environment. While the focus is on California, the chapter's purpose is to identify lessons for any state or set of institutions that seek more orderly policies for growth or clearer definitions of mission. California serves well as a case study for the "segmented" approach because it has pursued this organizational direction as strongly as any state and firmly stands on one side of the spectrum.

California higher education consists of a public "sector" (the three public "systems": the University of California, the California State University, and the California Community Colleges) and an independent "sector" (those colleges and universities controlled by private organizations). Table 8.1 shows the magnitude of this educational enterprise: more than two million students and $23 billion of annual expenditures on education, research, public service, and innumerable other activities. Obviously, the sheer size of California higher education requires some well-defined, organizing framework for the institutions.

While quite powerful, California's three public segments have long operated within the confines of a Master Plan for Higher Education which defines their missions and general orientation. With a strongly segmented approach, the state predictably has a weak and diffuse coordinating structure (Richardson, 16–17, 50; CRMP, "Issue Papers" 235–48). "The California system was designed to maximize the influence of [educational] professionals and to minimize external intrusions," a recent study of systems in seven states concluded, "and it achieves that objective" (CHEPC, "State Structures" 17).

Because of their numbers, California campuses, like most others throughout the United States, were organized into larger clusters years ago. While the maturing of these clusters into systems seems almost inevitable, their evolution into such hardened entities as "segments" was not. The result has been that, in California, these clusters of institutions are different in fundamental ways, far beyond their distinctions of mission.

Table 8.1   *Higher Education in California at a Glance.*

Segment/Sector	Campuses	Credit Enrollment 1997	State General Funds in Billions	Total Spending in Billions
California Community Colleges	106	1,200,000	$3.2	$3.6
California State University	22	326,000	$1.9	$3.8
University of California	9	164,000	$2.3	$11.1
Independent Institutions*	72	231,000	$0.2	$6.5
TOTAL	209	1,921,000	$7.6	$25.0

*These are the members of the Association of Independent California Colleges and Universities, which represents institutions with the vast majority of students in nonpublic institutions and which provides reliable data. See AICCU, *The Uncertain Partnership.* Source: *Governor's Budget, 1998/99, 11.*

These differences have a universal presence in conversations about policy and practice. Californians seem incapable of talking about higher education without talking "segments." To suggest that the legislature combine systems, as occurred in Minnesota or Massachusetts, is unthinkable to policymakers. The reason for this iron grip of "segmental thinking" on the minds of Californians is easy to find: the arrangement appears to provide order, clarity, and efficiency to public higher education.[2]

This chapter will first describe the origin and evolution of these segments. Why start here? The reason is that the origins of these systems have stamped a seemingly permanent character and configuration on each. To understand where they started is crucial to working successfully with their governance and administration today.

The chapter will next describe California's famous "Master Plan for Higher Education" as it shaped public higher education.[3] The "Plan," however, is many things. In one sense, it was a coalition's report with fifty-nine recommendations published in 1960. In another sense, it is the legal codification of structure and function for California higher education (the Donahoe Act of 1961), along with various statutes of reform and mission statements adopted later. In perhaps the most important sense, the Master Plan represents a set of public understandings, enormously powerful in their ability to shape what Californians want from higher education: access, affordability, a source for social mobility, predictability about who can attend, collegiate institutions at once diverse but organized, and universities considered the best in the nation.

Finally, the chapter will identify the strengths and weaknesses of the "segmental approach" to system building and consider whether it is possible to retain the benefits of order, access, and balance while reducing the obvious defects of this approach.

Origins and Evolution

THE UNIVERSITY OF CALIFORNIA: CONSTITUTIONAL AUTONOMY AND A SINGLE VISION

Today, the University of California consists of one medical and eight general campuses which enroll 166,000 students, a University Extension service with five hundred thousand enrollments in continuing education, three U.S. Department of Energy laboratories, five teaching hospitals, and field stations and research centers throughout the state. In total, the university employs 132,000 faculty and staff (Atkinson, 1) and has an annual budget of more than $10 billion. While the university receives "only" $2 billion in state support for operations, its regular educational program depends heavily on state government.

Unique among public institutions, the University is established in California's Constitution as "a public trust." Its governing board is granted "full powers of organization and government, subject only to such legislative control" as to insure fiduciary responsibility (Article IX, Section 9). Over the years, this "constitutional autonomy" has provided the university with both an "arms length distance" from Sacramento and vastly more control over its internal affairs than is true for the rest of public higher education. These provisions, as elaborated in case law as well as tradition, have provided considerable autonomy for the University for its academic programs and its financial structure (for instance, the University of California system has its own treasurer and retirement system).

Even with its enormous size, UC is still considered a statewide "system" with a single governing entity, the Board of Regents, and a systemwide president whose office is responsible for legislative relations, system planning, and systemwide programs. While the board exercises authority over most fiscal, capital, and legal areas, it has delegated extensive authority to the university faculty in academic and other professional areas. The nine campuses of the university also enjoy considerable autonomy in managing their affairs, especially in determining expenditures, employment decisions, purchasing and contracting, and conducting collective bargaining. The systemwide office plays a major role only in general decisions about allocating state appropriations, systemwide programs, and broad matters of policy.[4]

Despite decentralization and campus autonomy, a remarkably singular vision about what it means to be a real UC campus pervades the system. Perhaps this vision comes from the fact that the university's campus in Berkeley, established in 1868, has been the founder and model for all other UC campuses. Only in the twentieth century did the university gradually expand: first to UCLA in the twenties, to Davis in the thirties, to Santa Barbara in the forties, and to three new general campuses in the fifties and sixties. The vision is that all should maintain or achieve standing as comprehensive graduate and research campuses, and that regularly matriculated students would attend classes full-time. Clark Kerr, UC President during the tumultuous sixties, worried about this vision: "I had seen the hatred that came about because of (Berkeley and UCLA) trying to be two peas in a pod, each one the same size and formation, and the dread [which I felt] to see that go on among eight (general) campuses" (Douglass, "Isomorphism" 38).

Obligatory rhetoric to the contrary, all eight general university campuses seem driven by this single vision of what constitutes a legitimate *university* approach to education and research, a vision that greatly increases the costs of undergraduate expansion and limits the system's flexibility. As the most prestigious among California's segments and with such international prominence, of course, the University of California has enjoyed the resources to operate as a diverse collection of campuses with a single, ambitious, and expensive vision.

THE CALIFORNIA STATE UNIVERSITY: FORGING INDEPENDENT COLLEGES INTO A SYSTEM

The California State University is the nation's largest four-year system of higher education, with twenty-two campuses which enroll 340,000 regular students and thousands more in continuing education. Despite this large and sprawling presence, the CSU maintains its unique identity among the segments: it alone emphasizes undergraduate academic education and concentrates its graduate-level enrollment in professional fields such as business, education, and engineering. This segment is much more accommodating of part-time students than is the University of California, and the CSU enrolls far larger numbers of community college transfer students (almost 60 percent of CSU baccalaureate holders have credits from California's two-year colleges).[5]

The state university is also a system with a single governing entity, the Board of Trustees, and a statewide "chancellor" whose office is responsible for legislative relations, system wide planning, information about all campuses, and other activities that represent collectively the twenty-three campuses. While the CSU faculty have not been delegated the extensive responsibilities assigned to the UC faculty, the CSU Academic Senate, consisting of elected representatives from campus senates, plays a major role in initiating and recommending academic policy. The board selects and evaluates the chancellor and campus presidents. Collective bargaining over contracts occurs on a statewide basis at the CSU, not campus-by-campus. This approach to bargaining has a profound influence on the internal decisions and priorities on CSU campuses.

The system's origins led to this present pattern. In 1960, the California state colleges were fourteen widely different and fiercely independent entities. The colleges consisted of former normal schools, polytechnic institutions in San Luis Obispo and Pomona, and nationally prominent campuses such as San Diego State and San Francisco State. The 1960 Master Plan extracted these colleges from under their coordinator, the public schools' Board of Education, and established them as a single system under their own Board of Trustees. The real work of consolidation and system formation, however, was conducted by the system's longest-tenured chancellor, Glenn Dumke, who served throughout the sixties and seventies.

The California State Colleges, as they were known then, sprang from no single model but were forged into a system through a top-down, bureaucratic, centralized approach. Within a decade of creation, the college system more resembled a state bureaucracy than a university. It had developed an elaborate and centrally controlled formula for generating resources from the state government and distributing them among campuses; the formula's complexity enhanced the authority of the handful of system administrators who understood it. "It is impossible to over-emphasize the complexity of the budget of the California State University," admitted these administrators in 1990 (CSU, "Resource Equity" 3).

In addition to the financial centralization, a civil service model determined personnel policies within CSU for most of its history, and a large central administration in Long Beach promulgated extensive regulations and distributed authority. System officials frequently adopted regulations for all campuses because of the suspicion, often well-founded, that one or two would get into trouble if left to their own devices. Sardonically, campus officials called this "the Rule of 19." Statewide collective bargaining and resulting contracts have also increased the tendency toward uniform approaches. All these internal tendencies toward centralization were increased by the fact that California state government exercised direct authority *only* over the state colleges (the University of California enjoyed constitutional autonomy and the junior colleges were local entities).

The system's third chancellor, Barry Munitz, implemented a much more decentralized and entrepreneurial approach to administration after arriving in 1991. Legislation has removed several of the more onerous state controls over purchasing, payment procedures, and personnel regulations (CSUs, "Statement" ACHE 26). The segment now faces the challenge of an appropriate balance between systemwide and campus authority. It is far from achieving this balance yet.

THE CALIFORNIA COMMUNITY COLLEGES: A DIVERSE AND FRACTIOUS CONFEDERATION

The California Community Colleges are the largest and most heterogeneous postsecondary institutions in the nation. The colleges enroll more than 1.4 million students in credit and noncredit programs consisting of university-level transfer courses, vocational programs, remedial instruction, continuing education, and basic survival skills instruction. Total expenditures among these colleges are about $3.7 billion annually, with the state appropriating roughly 80 percent, including property tax revenues and student charges.[6]

In terms of governance, the colleges more resemble a loosely coupled "confederation" than a "system." They are organized into a three-level structure: (i) a statewide chancellor's office and Board of Governors, (ii) regional districts governed by locally elected trustees, and (iii) individual campuses. Ultimate governance responsibility is vested in seventy-one district boards of trustees which control 107 campuses and hundreds of instructional locations off-campus. Statewide officials have statutory responsibility for some areas of regulation, monitoring, and planning but have only a slight impact on the day-to-day operations of campuses. In part, this weakness comes from the fact that the Board of Governors hires only the statewide chancellor and has no appointive authority over district personnel who are subject to the local boards. Further emphasizing where the real authority resides, collective bargaining occurs on a district-by-district basis. "In the case of community colleges," a national study of governance concluded, "it is not clear that the system office has the capacity to do anything other than monitor the statutory environment within which individual campuses do whatever they please" (Richardson, 14).

Although exempt from many of the state regulatory agencies, the statutory framework imposed on the community colleges is far more extensive than for two-year colleges in most other states. The Education Code imposes dozens of definitions, rules, and regulations on how colleges can conduct their business. Since Proposition 13 (1978), the community colleges have struggled with the anomaly of having a rigid, state-determined finance system imposed on locally governed institutions. Before Proposition 13, the districts were accountable to the property taxpayers within their boundaries since this was by far the largest source of community college revenues. The trustees themselves determined the tax rates. Now, the legislature distributes property tax revenues and the state funds flowing to districts, while considerable latitude for expenditure authority and contractual commitments remains with the trustees—a serious split of accountability.

Because of their political muscle, faculty unions dominate the elected boards in many districts, to their apparent benefit in the collective bargaining process (Healy, 20–21). All these structural tensions cause enormous frustration throughout the system, from the statewide Board of Governors to the district administrators through to faculty on the campuses themselves.

The California Master Plan—Access and Order

For almost four decades, California's Master Plan has influenced the structure, functions, and financing of higher education. The original document was a lengthy examination of the needs and ambitions of higher education, but its central recommendations on the structure, function, and governance were straightforward:

1. A space would be available somewhere in higher education for all quali-fied and motivated undergraduate students.

2. No tuition (payment for the cost of instruction) would be imposed on California residents, and students would be charged low fees only for "auxiliary services" (the Plan's term).

3. Each "level" of public higher education (or "segment" as they came to be known) would have different roles and functions.

   a. The University of California was to emphasize graduate and profes-sional programs with exclusive authority among public institutions to award the doctoral and advanced professional degrees (medicine, law, dentistry, and veterinary medicine). The Plan identified the university as the sole academic entity for "state-supported research." Little change in its mission has occurred since the Master Plan.

   b. The state colleges (now the California State University) were to emphasize undergraduate instruction and master's level work. The colleges were authorized to conduct research consistent with the instructional mission and to award the doctorate degree only in conjunction with UC or private institutions. Legislation in 1989 expanded the mission of CSU to include "broad responsibility to the public good and welfare of the state" and "programs of public service" for students and faculty. For the first time, the state com-mitted itself to finance research related to the institution's instruc-tion and public service missions, but few funds have actually flowed for this.

   c. The "junior" colleges—now community colleges—were to offer instruction up to but not beyond "the fourteenth grade level," specifi-cally courses for transfer to four-year institutions, vocational and tech-nical instruction, and general or liberal arts courses.

   d. Different admission pools were established for the UC and the state colleges, and these have not changed. The UC was to select students from the top eighth of the graduating seniors in public high schools in California, while the State Colleges were to draw students from the top third (these represented considerably smaller pools than earlier). This tightening of admissions and the increased transfers from junior colleges were supposed to result in a ratio of roughly 40 percent lower-division (freshmen/sophomores) and 60 percent upper-division students (juniors/seniors) by 1975.

e. Junior colleges were to play a larger and more formal role in the higher education system and extend their coverage throughout the state. These colleges would be expected to educate the large number of students who would be diverted from the four-year institutions during their freshman and sophomore years of college. The policy was considered good for the students (by having campuses closer to home and offering smaller classes) and good for the taxpayers (by avoiding the costs of constructing and operating more four-year campuses to accommodate lower-division students).

f. The state colleges were to be governed by a new Board of Trustees but the legislature did not attempt to give the new Board constitutional status, as the Plan recommended.

g. A statewide coordinating body, the Coordinating Council for Higher Education, was established with representatives from the public institutions and the private colleges and universities. This council was later reconfigured into the California Postsecondary Education Commission (CPEC), an independent state agency charged with long-term planning and analysis of higher education.

h. An expansion of the State's Scholarship Program (established in 1955) was recommended in order to increase the ability of students to choose private institutions. This is now called the "Cal Grant program," and is one of the nation's largest state, need-based systems of financial aid.

"[M]ore than anything else," observed an authority on California higher education, the 1960 Master Plan "was about broadening access in a disciplined way. . . . The goals of opportunity, access, and participation were the glue that held the California Master Plan together" (Callan, "Time" 86).

Strengths of California's Segmented Approach

NEAT AND ORDERLY

The California approach has fostered a more orderly growth of higher education than in most states. Once they were organized into segments and their missions defined by the Master Plan, campuses did not engage overtly in "turf wars" to expand their mission or become more comprehensive at public expense. This also discouraged efforts by powerful legislators to upgrade the campuses within their districts for local promotion, not statewide needs. As a result, California was not faced annually, as were so many states, with clamors for expansion and expensive aspirations for advanced degrees.

AN ENDURING FRAMEWORK FOR LONG-TERM STABILITY

Clear statements about role and mission, established in statute, are valuable in providing long-term direction for educational leaders and guidance to state officials. Without these statements, "mission creep," or the desire to expand institutional scope and capture more prestige, appear an irresistible compulsion (Knutsen, 44–45). The goals and expectations of the Master Plan were idealistic enough to be challenging but practical enough to be achieved, at least through the recession of the 1990s. California successfully constructed "a vast array of public colleges and universities and [continued] to support their operations with large annual appropriations of public funds," a blue-ribbon commission concluded in 1986 (CRMP, Issue Paper #3: 37).

SOLID EXPECTATIONS FOR THE PUBLIC

A statewide policy that a space at one of the campuses in each segment would be available for any resident student provided the public with solid expectations about admissions and an incentive to succeed in high school. Students understood that if they took college preparatory courses and performed at a certain level in high school or in community colleges, they were guaranteed a space in their baccalaureate-degree granting system of choice. They were told that this opportunity would not be snatched away by fiscal shortfalls or institutional whim. The guarantee, of course, is complicated by the difficulty of establishing which courses transfer for what kinds of credit and which are equivalent for general education, major prerequisites, and so on.

APPROPRIATE LEVELS OF RESOURCES

By establishing different missions and structures, state government has been able to concentrate resources on the particular kinds of institutions that public officials believed would best serve the Californians at the time. The needs of each segment are considered separately by the governor and legislature, with attention to the different kinds of missions. The institutions have had different approaches to setting the levels of student charges and expanding educational opportunities into underserved areas. Each segment is expected to be effective without seeking the resources to be "all things to all people," and the state has not succumbed in its appropriations policies to "leveling up or down," toward some indistinguishable middle.

THE RESEARCH UNIVERSITY ENHANCED

The segmented approach provided a monopoly among public institutions to the University of California over state-funded research and advanced graduate education. Without doubt, this has concentrated resources in a way that helped California to build the most prominent public university system in the United States. Although the university receives far more funding for research from the federal government and private sources than from the state, it acknowledges that "state funds are the core that attracts extramural funds so necessary for the conduct of major research projects" (UC, "Budget" 71).

BENEFITS TO PRIVATE INSTITUTIONS FROM SEGMENTING GRADUATE EDUCATION

By restricting doctoral degrees and advanced professional education among public institutions, the Master Plan ensured that California would have a relatively low public expenditure on post-baccalaureate education for a state of its size and advanced economy. As a result, independent institutions have a far larger share of graduate and professional education than is true in most states with large public systems. The policy of segmenting public support for graduate education has (a) resulted in a strong emphasis on graduate education at UC; (b) limited access to advanced graduate education that is publicly subsidized; (c) reduced taxpayer spending *per capita* for graduate education; and (d) assisted those independent institutions that grant doctoral degrees by reducing competition with the public sector.

BLENDING ELITISM AND POPULISM

With its widely different pools of college eligibility, the segmented approach sought to blend extensive access with the exclusiveness and the high standards of senior institutions. In the words of a prominent historian, the Master Plan "sustained and bolstered California's commitment to both an 'open door' and meritocractic system, allowing talented students to matriculate through a tiered set of public institutions without the burden of fees for instruction" (Douglass, "Balancing" 11). In the words of the Paris-based Organization for Economic Cooperation and Development, "the California higher education system is recognized throughout the OECD world as a bold blueprint for providing widespread post-secondary education while preserving the separate missions of the three types of public institutions.... It seeks to reconcile populist with elitist institutions, access with success, equality with excellence, and the market with the state.... The Master Plan represents the most advanced effort through state action to organize mass higher education ... while maintaining a quality of research and education at the top which was unsurpassed anywhere among OECD countries and probably in the world" (OECD, *Reviews*). Following such adulation, though, the report worried whether "the sum of these admirable ambitions may be greater than that of public willingness to vote their necessary funds" (OECD, *Reviews*; Pickens, 50).

Weaknesses of California's Segmented Approach

Too Strong a "Pecking Order." The California approach, which created such distinct tiers, predictably led to differences in prestige which remain firmly in place. The lines of prestige, drawn generally along segmental lines, may have little to do with the actual quality of education or the contributions of institutions to students or California as a whole. "California's educational system is truly equitable only if it offers a fair and plausible chance to persons of promise *wherever* in the system they find themselves," wrote a joint committee of the legislature concerned with this issue (JCRMP 60).

UNFAIR DISADVANTAGE

Certainly hierarchies in academia are common, even in states without segmentation. In California, more than elsewhere, the impression of a permanent hierarchy has discouraged many. This is felt most intensely at a personal level. Community college faculty report that "there is a sense of intellectual and social estrangement, of second-class academic citizenship, and very little chance to work collaboratively on intellectual or pedagogical issues" (JCRMP 107). Although the state university has expanded its curriculum and professional offerings since the 1960 Master Plan, many faculty believe their system is artificially truncated and placed at serious disadvantage in the competition for resources. "The Master Scam," complained one CSU professor, "is a politically mandated set of rules that allows those with the greatest power to grab the greatest share of resources and to maintain a monopoly of privilege" (Halpern, 43).

INSUFFICIENT INTEGRATION

A three-tiered, public system with increasingly limited access to the upper tiers is equitable and will work effectively only if each of the tiers is healthy and plays its role well. Most important, the links among the segments and with the high schools must be strong and active, and attitudes cooperative. These links have not been well achieved in California for the following reasons:

1. The decline of standards and college preparation among the public schools;

2. The long fiscal erosion of the community colleges starting with Proposition 13 (1978).

3. Many institutions have emphasized initial "access" more than carefully planned programs designed to challenge students and help them meet their educational objectives (California has one of the lowest baccalaureate-granting rates in the nation).

4. A reluctance for many years on the part of the University of California to establish transfer policies based on a "transfer core curriculum" or a set of uniform conditions. Frustrated with this attitude, the legislature mandated several policies during the late 1980s and a common course numbering approach in 1995. Recently, however, the University of California and the community colleges have signed an agreement to increase the number of transfers by 30 percent over the next seven years.

TENDENCY TO INVEST AT THE TOP

The segmental approach and the growing prestige of the University of California have inclined the state to invest its resources "at the top." Although UC suffered substantial cuts during the early 1990s, the community colleges have been underfunded for decades. The California State University also has not enjoyed the kind of state investment supplied to the University of California, for either facilities or operating revenues.

MUTUAL PROGRAMS AND JOINT FACILITIES ARE NOT ENCOURAGED

The segmented approach has reduced interest in joint programs between the segments and in closer collaboration to serve the needs of students who move among the institutions. Officials in systemwide offices have long understood that their chief responsibility was to campuses within their segment. Their mission, announced as "excellence within each segment," has been used to justify insularity. Frequently, system officials consider "intersegmental relations" as a distraction from the real business of managing their segment well. Very few administrators or faculty ever serve in more than one segment, so their outlooks are narrowed accordingly.

WEAKENED STATEWIDE COORDINATION

The segmented approach has limited the state government's ability to coordinate higher education and to shrewdly direct resources to accomplish public purposes. Each segment's budget is usually considered separately in budget hearings, and each has a different process for calculating needs and for receiving appropriations. To keep peace among the segments, capital outlay revenues from statewide bond initiatives are distributed equally to each, despite their different sizes. Segmentation has subtly undermined efforts to achieve a fuller sense of a common purpose throughout higher education.

A "GO IT BY YOURSELF" ATTITUDE DURING FISCAL CRISES

As is true in every state, periodic budget shortfalls have shaken California's higher education systems, sometimes severely. Some crises have arrived through voter initiatives (Proposition 13, the property tax limitation), but most have come from downturns in state revenues (1970–72; 1981–83; 1990–1994). During these times, the segmented approach has inclined state officials to respond by encouraging the institutions to do the best they can with the resources available (including large increases in student charges). Totally absent has been a response coordinated for all higher education. (CHEPC, "Financing the Plan" 14–21; CHEPC, "Policy Vacuum").

INSTITUTIONAL DISTINCTIONS SEEM MORE IMPORTANT THAN PUBLIC PURPOSES

In practice, the segmented approach emphasizes institutional roles more than the broad purposes of higher education. When California's recent recession weakened the state's ability to fund the full range of promises of the Master Plan, the mission-differentiated systems and their segmental structures remained firmly intact. While this is not necessarily negative, a legitimate concern is that these segmented distinctions will long outlive the important general purposes, such as access and affordability, which inspired such distinctions originally.

The Future: Lessons of the Segmented Approach

Surely it is possible to retain the obvious benefits of order, access, and balance offered by the segmented approach while reducing or eliminating the defects listed above. The following are some ideas about how to do this.

STATE GOVERNMENT SHOULD CREATE CENTRAL FUNDS OF
SUFFICIENT SIZE TO ENCOURAGE COLLABORATION

For all states, an important question is: how can incentives be provided to increase the status and opportunity for all institutions without expanding their mission or functions? If policies are constructed properly, these funds can be used competitively to encourage attention to public purposes beyond segmental distinctions.

THE STATE'S POLICY AND BUDGET PROCESS SHOULD BEGIN WITH THE
EDUCATIONAL NEEDS OF THE PUBLIC AS A WHOLE RATHER THAN
WITH SEGMENTAL ISSUES

A segment-by-segment process, which takes minimal account of the others and their needs, organizes public policy discussions into compartments. The policy process should proceed along broader lines than this.

A HIGH PRIORITY SHOULD BE PLACED ON "PERSONNEL SWAPS" AND
"INTERSEGMENTAL CROSS-TRAINING."

While much can be gained from a segmented system for definitions of the systems *as organizations*, nothing is gained—indeed much is lost—when these distinctions are imposed severely *on individuals* and personnel are segregated for their entire careers. Encouraging faculty and administrators to spend time working in another segment both widens their perspectives and brings fresh ideas into each segment.

STRONG REGIONAL ASSOCIATIONS SHOULD BE A BRIDGE
BETWEEN SEGMENTS

Formal associations that cluster campuses together, both within and among the segments, are in the public interest. Especially in large states, a major weakness of a statewide system is the gulf between "system" and "campus." Regional clusters of two-year, four-year, and graduate research campuses bridge that gulf and provide better services for students. These structures can encourage program coordination within the region, establish arrangements for sharing facilities and equipment, provide a central location for interinstitutional data, and generate information about institutions in the region. They use the strength of natural affinities offered by geographic proximity. Often, these regional organizations, such as the Oklahoma Regional Higher Education Center, require separate funding and incentives from state government. They are not natural outgrowths of a segmented approach to higher education.

OVER THE YEARS, A FEW CAMPUSES SHOULD BE "IN TRANSITION" BETWEEN THE SEGMENTS

Periodically, a few two-year colleges should be converted into four-year institutions and moved into the next segment, rather than building a campus from the ground up. A strong state college campus should gradually be converted into another university campus if its region has a compelling case for this need and other colleges are nearby to take up the slack.[7] While difficult and requiring long lead times, such transitions clearly serve a larger public interest, especially in lowering costs, when one segment needs to expand. The transitions should be based on statewide considerations rather than on campus or regional ambition alone, and they should be mutually acceptable to both systems. The state, however, should require attention to these intersegmental alternatives before considering other, more traditional, solutions to meeting increased demand.

Conclusions and Implications

California has reaped great benefit from its segmented approach to organizing public institutions and from its policy framework and expectations for higher education which are enshrined in its Master Plan for Higher Education. The limitations of such an approach, however, while evident from the beginning, are increasingly troublesome. The challenge for California, as for any state that follows "segmentation" as its organizing principle, is to maintain traditions of order, balance, and mission differentiation during times that call for more collaboration, broader perspectives, and cross-service.

NOTES

Bill Pickens is solely responsible for the contents of this chapter, and his opinions do not necessarily represent the policies or views of the Citizens Commission.

1. The best, most comprehensive sources for understanding the overall organization, financing, and characteristics of higher education in California are: CRMP, "Issue Papers: The Master Plan Renewed" (1987); Condren, "Preparing for the Twenty-First Century" (1988); JCRMP, "California Faces" (1988); CPEC, "The Challenge of the Century" (1995).

2. The power of mind-sets, or "mental models" as they are called, is well defined in Peter Senge's *The Fifth Discipline* (pp.174–204), one of this decade's best explanations about the role of ideas in organizational behavior.

3. See Liaison Committee, *A Master Plan* (1960). An excellent summary of the Master Plan's history and changes appears in CPEC, *Master Plan, Then and Now* (1993).

4. The university's history, structure, and regulatory framework have been chronicled by John A. Douglass, the most prominent authority on these matters and on the university's role under the Master Plan. See the References listing for his articles used in this section. Professor Douglass is Executive Director of the Santa Barbara Division of the UC Academic Senate. See also Stadtman, *The University*.

5. The CSU is best described in these recent publications: Munitz, *Compact II*; CSUs, "The Cornerstones Project" (1997).

6. The best sources for understanding the full range of governance and financing issues within the Community Colleges are CRMP, Background Papers for "The Challenge of Change" (1986); McCurdy, *Broken Promises* (1994); CCC Board of Governors, "Basic Agenda" (1996).

7. This is exactly the situation in California's San Joaquin Valley, where an expensive tenth campus is proposed for the University of California.

9

THE URBAN SYSTEM

The University of Houston

William P. Hobby
Saralee Tiede

*Never have urban systems been as valuable as they
will be in highly urbanized twenty-first century
America. This is a case study of a dynamic,
successful urban university system in troubled
times and the steps it took to address several
problems concerning its mission and identity.*

There are many ways of defining an urban university. Location, student population, and philosophy are all important (Elliott, 20). By all of these criteria, the University of Houston System (UHS) is a textbook example of an urban university system. UHS has four universities located in or near the nation's fourth largest city, Houston, on the Texas Gulf Coast. Houston has a population of 3 million within its extensive city limits. See Table 9.1.

Table 9.1 *The University of Houston Institutions.*

UNIVERSITY	LOCATION	FOUNDED	ENROLLMENT Fall 1997	BUDGET FY 1998 (Appropriated)
University of Houston	Central Houston	1927	31,602	$157,932,031
University of Houston-Downtown	Downtown Houston	1974	8,194	$21,894,756
University of Houston-Clear Lake	Southeast Houston	1973	6,947	$27,130,457
University of Houston-Victoria	150 miles southwest of Houston	1973	1,491	$7,213,332

Its links to a prosperous, dynamic city, its diverse academic offerings, its areas of excellence and emerging excellence, its strong and growing research centers, and its record of reaching a diverse student body in innovative ways make UHS one of the best-equipped institutions to meet the demands of the twenty-first century. Yet, in 1995, the University of Houston System was a troubled institution, beset by declining enrollment, diminishing tax support, and conflict over its role.

History and Structure of the System

The University of Houston, the oldest and by far the largest of the universities, was created in 1927 as a dynamic young city sought a way to provide postsecondary education for its high school graduates. Houston doubled in size between 1920 and 1930, fueled by cotton, lumber, trade, and the robust young offspring of the Spindletop oil strike—petroleum and petrochemicals.

The new institution was named Houston Junior College and was administered by the Houston Independent School District. Classes met from 4 to 9 p.m. in San Jacinto High School near downtown. (It is a beginning that has benefited and plagued the university, as it struggled hard to throw off the "Cougar High" nickname.) When classes began with 230 students, about two-thirds of the student body were employed full or part time. It is not that different today. About 40 percent of students attend part time and take longer to graduate—the mean is 6.2 years (Texas Higher Education Coordinating Board, 1996, Appendix A). Few of them live on campus.

At all the UH universities, the population is similar. Students are older than those in traditional residential universities. In 1996, only one-third of the 47,200 students were age 18 to 22. About 26 percent were over 30, and another 40 percent were over 23 (University of Houston System 20). Such a student profile is not uncommon to many urban colleges and systems.

The new college's goals were set out in a 1927 bulletin: "To give to Houston and vicinity an institution which shall serve to the very best advantage the needs of the citizens of this section of Texas under conditions which shall make it available to all, and organized and conducted on such a basis as to assure every student two years of high grade standard college training" (Nicholson, 45). Houston Junior College existed side by side with the Houston College for Negroes, operating out of Jack Yates Junior-Senior High School, which later became Texas Southern University in 1947 and today is located a few blocks east of UH.

JUNIOR COLLEGE TO UNIVERSITY

The junior college became the University of Houston, a four-year institution, in 1933. It offered arts and industries, science as applied to technical and vocational pursuits, liberal arts and culture, extension and adult education. It rapidly outgrew its high school environs, and in 1938, a new campus started to rise on 108 donated acres of blue gumbo mud and pine forest southeast of downtown. The new campus was made possible by the generosity of wildcatter Hugh Roy Cullen, who left school in the fifth grade to work in a candy factory. He was interested in UH "if it gives a chance for an education to youngsters whose fathers have to work for a living" (Nicholson, 112). Cullen contributed $335,000 for the liberal arts building, the foundation for tens of millions of dollars the Cullen family would contribute to their beloved university.

UH was officially separated from the school district in 1945 when a Board of Regents was created by the legislature. In 1947, it acquired its mascot, the cougar. In 1963 it became a state university. In 1971 its successful athletics program won it acceptance into the Southwest Conference. In 1996 it had 14 colleges, 281 degree programs, 30,000 students, and 1,927 faculty. It awards about 200 doctoral degrees annually and is ranked a Carnegie Research University II with sponsored research totaling $55 million.

In another era in another place, UH might have been an institution with a main campus and three or more branch campuses. But in fast-growing Texas after World War II, the custom was to create full-blown, freestanding universities. So UH-Downtown, UH-Clear Lake, and UH-Victoria were created by statute and have their own presidents, student bodies, logos, and school colors. Clear Lake and Victoria are upper-level institutions, partnered with community colleges. UH-Downtown is an open admissions institution, specializing in moving students from the barrio to the college classroom and in giving fully employed Houstonians a place to earn a degree by attending nights and weekends. Each university has a distinct, important identity and plays an important role in its community.

UH-DOWNTOWN

UH-Downtown was until 1997 the only Texas university limited to undergraduate programs. With a location in the middle of downtown Houston, a student body of 8,000 that is the most ethnically diverse in Texas, a complete weekend university and exemplary outreach programs for high school students, UH-Downtown is an urban university in the classic sense (Bartelt, 16). It started as South Texas Junior College and became a part of UH in 1974. UH had had a

Downtown School (that name still rankles faculty at UH-Downtown since it is rarely used in a complimentary way) since 1942. The troubled private junior college occupied a 613,000-square foot site at One Main Street, and the Downtown School was losing its lease at another location.

The junior college and its building were acquired in 1974, and the school became a college. It filled a number of needs: it maintained a downtown presence for UH; it satisfied the growing demand for an open enrollment institution so that UH could preserve its more rigorous admission standards; and it had potential, soon fulfilled, to expand service to the community. Partnerships, public and private, now reached through inner-city high schools and middle schools to elementary schools to prepare low-income, minority students for college. An urban teaching program, conducted almost entirely in inner-city schools, helps prepare students, some of them reared in the neighborhood, to teach in those schools.

In 1995, funding was the major challenge at UH-Downtown. Limited to undergraduate courses, which return less in state dollars than graduate courses, it was less well financed than comparable institutions. In FY 1995, it spent $5,436 per full-time student equivalent, compared to $10,156 at UH, $8,299 at Victoria, and $8,125 at Clear Lake. The state average was $9,806, according to the 1996 expenditure report by the Texas Higher Education Coordinating Board.

UH-CLEAR LAKE

UH-Clear Lake, located "between the ultimate technology of the LBJ Manned Spacecraft Center and the pristine quiet of Armand Bayou," is a suburban institution even though located within Houston city limits. Its programs are closely linked to its neighbor, now called the Johnson Space Center, Mission Control for many historic space missions. It was begun to offer "goal-directed professional training to a high level of skill" (Nicholson, 455) as well as a liberal education. Its student body is 62 percent female and has an average age of 32. This university pioneered in linking itself closely to the nine community colleges in its region, forging student contracts to ensure student success. An exemplary program called Gator-Bear reaches into elementary schools to find students likely to pursue teacher education. UH-Clear Lake was authorized in 1971. The university opened in 1973, with classes meeting in the Clear Lake Graduate Center. It enrolls 7,000 students and offers 72 degree programs.

UH-VICTORIA

UH-Victoria, 150 miles southwest in what is called the Golden Crescent area, is the youngest university; it was created when a group of education-hungry citizens and community leaders started lobbying for a university in 1969. Victoria, a trading center for an agricultural and petrochemical economy, had a junior college but no university. By 1973, the University of Houston had been given approval by the Coordinating Board, Texas College and University System, to create an off-campus center in Victoria. The student body consisted of 105 students.

Ten years later, in 1983, the Texas Legislature created the UH-Victoria. Today, it offers 28 bachelor's and master's degree programs in the arts and sciences, business administration, and education. Its student body numbers 1800. It has 91 faculty and an annual budget of $10.4 million. In 1995, the main concern was growth. The population curve in its 15-county region was flat, and UH-Victoria had responded with aggressive entrepreneurship. One of its efforts was to offer off-campus courses in fast-growing Fort Bend county just southwest of Houston.

System Culture and Evolution

By the mid-1960s it was clear, as Nicholson wrote, that a University of Houston System was "inevitable, given the dynamic energy of the Houston metroplex and the possibility of requests for educational services in areas historically and economically linked to the city." In that era of manifest destiny for higher education, expansion was a given. In 1968, the Coordinating Board recommended two branch campuses, one north and one south, for UH. The south institution became the upper-level UH-Clear Lake. The northern outpost was mired in political controversy and finally achieved reality only in 1997 as the University Center, a multi-institution teaching center in which UH and UH-Downtown participate with six other institutions.

The system administration to govern the four universities was created by statute in 1977, but the appropriation to finance the new administrative structure was vetoed by then Governor William Clements. Legislative language directed the universities to financially support the structure for services rendered, setting the stage for perpetual conflict over whether services were needed and reasonably priced.

Even before the system officially existed, there were differences of opinion over the future of the University of Houston. During a 1976 self-study, faculty charted a future for UH as a flagship campus, with enrollment limited to 30,000. The number of undergraduates would be reduced, support for research increased, and weak programs targeted for elimination or removal to one of the other universities.

In the same self-study, faculty expressed a concern that UH's future was threatened by new system components. The debate was framed when members of the Southern Association accrediting team questioned why faculty wanted to create "a watered-down MIT, Illinois or University of Southern California instead of a vigorous, independent-minded institution reflecting the unique needs, challenges, strengths and opportunities of Houston itself" (Nicholson, 459–460).

Nearly 20 years later, that debate had only intensified. One faction of UH faculty feared that the system administration and the other universities were draining resources that would have propelled UH to the coveted Carnegie Research I ranking. Though its budget (about $22 million) was modest by comparison with the University of Texas System and the Texas A&M University System, the cost of the system administration was a far more contentious issue than in those larger systems. The issues were difficult: the imbalance in size and dimensions between UH and its sister universities, the difficulty of dividing a diminishing pie, and the tension between those who saw UH as a unique urban institution and those who preferred that it follow a more traditional path to excellence.

Conflict was aggravated by pressure on resources. Enrollment had begun a decline in 1992 and had dropped nearly 3,000 by 1995. Part of this could be explained by the demographic curve. The number of traditional college-age students dipped as baby boomers aged, and their children were not yet college age. But the enrollment decline occurred as the population of Houston was rising and as enrollments were growing at other large Texas universities.

Meanwhile, the diminishing resources that plague all of higher education had an especially adverse impact on the UH System. In Texas, the state general revenue contribution per student declined 24 percent between 1985 and 1997. Shrinking revenue is a particularly difficult problem at urban institutions since their facilities, faculty, and staff must accommodate a larger number of students taking a lower number of credit hours. Interim UH President Glenn Goerke liked to say that when a full-time student at UH started his or her day, four students woke up. Urban institutions, as Peggy Gordon Elliott notes, were lean and mean before that phrase ever came to be the rallying cry of corporate America.

State funding for higher education is based on semester credit hours, so an enrollment decline could have been expected to cause a severe loss of revenue. Fortunately, UHS was insulated from serious damage by generous grants of state hold-harmless funds, but it was experiencing a drain on resources from its athletics program. A break-up of the Southwest Conference left UH in a new conference likely to reduce television revenue and crowd appeal. In 1996, UH was castigated by a legislative subcommittee for amassing the largest athletics deficit in the state.

Tension and other events resulted in turnover at top levels of administration. UH had three presidents in five years. In mid-1995, the system chancellor and presidents at UH and UH-Victoria resigned. Regents brought in administrators, including the authors of this chapter as chancellor (William P. Hobby) and deputy chancellor (Saralee Tiede) for two-year terms.

Strengths and Shortcomings

Strengths and shortcomings can be opposite sides of the same coin. That is often true in urban university systems. One of the great strengths of the UH system is location, location, location. This was apparent even in 1927, when a questionnaire answered by 218 students showed that most of the respondents attended because of its convenient location. Seventy students said they could work in the day and attend classes at night.

Location gives the universities a large pool of potential students, an attractive climate for faculty, eminent professionals willing to serve as adjunct professors, and great opportunity to interact with the community. But it can also be a drawback in attracting traditional students whose parents worry about crime, safety, and the many distractions of city life. Only about one-third of UH students come from outside Harris County.

The mission and future of the University of Houston System is closely linked to the city. The Houston culture and economy have shaped curricula just as the universities have contributed to the city's strength. Particularly strong programs, like the Health Law and Policy Institute, optometry, and pharmacy are related to the presence of the Texas Medical Center. The excellence of programs in creative writing, drama, music, and visual arts depend on the city's vibrant arts community, just as the colleges of law and architecture owe much to the city's professional communities. The Space Vacuum Epitaxy Center and the Partnership for Space Exploration would not exist without the Johnson Space Center, nor would UH-Downtown's innovative urban teaching program exist in a different setting.

Some faculty have been concerned that UH would be co-opted and corrupted by its relationship with the city's business and industry. The 1938 drive to raise private contributions for the new campus was the first evidence of the strong financial support Houstonians would give their university, but it also resulted in an unfortunate legacy—the sense that UH leaders were most concerned with producing a trained work force and educated managers for industry, with vocational courses rather than traditional curricula (Nicholson, 105).

There is considerable evidence that the symbiosis is limited. Houston is the energy capital of the world, the exporter of oilfield technology to the Middle East, the North Slope, and the North Sea, but UH is not particularly strong in geology or petroleum technology. Even though Houston's port leads the nation in tonnage and gives the city an international flavor, UH has not so far focused on international trade as part of its offerings.

Another strength of the universities is diversity. In the four universities combined, the student population is diverse, with 25,000 white, 5,950 African-American, 7,656 Hispanic, 5,900 Asian-American, and 2,680 international students in 1996 (UH, *Ethnicity* 20). When the Hopwood v. State of Texas decision, which proscribed the use of race or ethnicity in university admissions policies at the University of Texas at Austin Law School, left the University of Texas at Austin and Texas A&M University scrambling for ways to attract minority students, UH gained minority enrollment, based at least partly on its record as a welcoming, hospitable institution in a city proud of its diversity.

UH Regents, state leaders, and most national experts in education view increasing the educational achievement of African-American and Hispanic citizens as a critical challenge facing higher education. Yet diversity can hinder university recruiting efforts. It was an irony at UH that it was neither as black as many white residents thought, nor as white as many African-Americans believed. During the decade from 1976 to 1986, UH tracked other urban universities in losing ground, with its percentage of black students declining from 11.3 to 7.4 (Kinnick and Ricks, 27).

Another strength-shortcoming conundrum exists in the differing attitudes toward the universities' mission and future. Frank Newman, president of the Education Commission of the States, has said that urban institutions "are not yet sure of themselves. Their traditions are not so formed that they are barnacled, so that they have a great opportunity to chart a course that serves American society" (Elliott, 35). It was a common question when the UH System Vision Commission deliberated to ask which universities were to serve as models, when in fact UHS had a great opportunity to become the model itself.

It is not unusual for faculty at urban institutions to feel they are undervalued, (Elliott, 88). And UH's background as a junior college, as "Cougar High," was vexatious to faculty who saw their future connected to a prestigious research institution. Some remembered that the first effort to win state support for the University of Houston was won at the cost of a ban on state support of graduate courses. Others were concerned that some vestiges of the past, like the College of Technology, still remain.

The Transition

The task of the interregnum was to do as much as possible to solve the critical problems of declining enrollment and resources. The greater challenge was to change the culture from one of pessimism to optimism, from distrust to confidence, and from exclusion to inclusion.

A number of initiatives were begun between 1995 and 1997. The most important were expanding into Fort Bend County, restructuring the system of governance, creating a unified marketing effort, finding a shared vision, and increasing state funding for higher education.

THE UNIVERSITY OF HOUSTON SYSTEM AT FORT BEND

The UHS campus in Fort Bend county, southwest of Houston, is located in one of the fastest-growing counties in the nation and is a prime site for corporate locations. UH-Victoria had held classes there for several years, but the business and civic leadership wanted their own university. The state's only avenue for expansion at this time is through multi-institution teaching centers, through which several universities offer degree programs. At the first annual system leadership meeting we held in August 1995 (also the first to include faculty leaders), we decided to create a multiuniversity teaching center comprised of the four UHS universities, Wharton Junior College, and Houston Community College.

At that point only one multi-institution teaching center (in Dallas) had been approved in Texas. The University Center in north Harris County was still in planning stages and proceeding slowly. Through the Herculean efforts of staff and faculty, the UHS at Fort Bend teaching center was approved by the Texas Higher Education Coordinating Board in January 1996. Classes started that summer, and by fall 1997, enrollment had nearly doubled, reaching 930. In 1997, the legislature transferred 256 acres from the Texas Department of Transportation to UHS as a permanent home for the center. A substantial beginning has been made in raising money to start construction.

The initiative was important strategically because it sent a message to other university systems who looked yearningly at Houston as a rich area for expansion. It was also a positive move to halt enrollment decline. Perhaps most heartening was the cooperation it produced among provosts, admission officers, registrars, and faculty as they tried to create a student-friendly environment from the different admission policies, course structures, fees, and calendars at the four universities. In 1997, 20 percent of the courses were fully articulated, offering students the promise of a degree from one of the four UHS universities.

The speed with which the Fort Bend center was created obscures the immense difficulty of the task. There was no consensus that this was an appropriate direction for UHS. The old concern about misdirecting resources was alive and well. That it worked was due to superb leadership at all four universities as well as the tireless work and exceptional consensus building skills of Ed Hugetz, Fort Bend director.

RESTRUCTURING THE SYSTEM

By 1995, Regents were convinced that only a dramatic step would resolve conflict over governance. The system administration had become a flashpoint, blamed by a vocal faction at UH for maintaining a costly bureaucracy that made inappropriate demands on the universities. Generally, the smaller universities supported the *status quo.*

The Regents asked for an organizational review to identify administrative functions and where these functions were best performed. Three task forces, on academic affairs, administration and finance, and external affairs, had 60 days to present options. Each task force included regents, faculty, and administrators. The results were encouraging, not so much because they represented consensus on the best structure, but because they revealed a number of ways to improve operations.

For example, the task force on administration and finance determined that information resources and facilities planning needed review and improvement, regardless of structure. The external affairs task force identified several needs: consistent communication of a shared vision, rapid responsiveness to constituents, cost effectiveness, clear lines of communication and a constituent-centered approach.

On April 1, 1996, Regents decided to combine the offices of chancellor and UH president, effective when the search for a new leader was concluded. The new structure would not be in place for at least a year. For the transition period, we decided to increase faculty participation in the system operating structure. That structure consisted of councils of provosts, chief financial officers and external affairs officers, a Chancellors' Executive Council, and the University Faculties Executive Council. We added a faculty advisory committee to each council; faculty advisors met with that council once each month. The external affairs council also included alumni, student, and community advisors. The result was a better decision-making process.

A COMBINED MARKETING INITIATIVE

There are many ways to address enrollment declines, and marketing is always high on that list. Like most universities blessed with steady expansion, UH institutions had a philosophy best described as "open the doors and they will come." The problem was that they had stopped coming. Alumni skilled in marketing and public relations provided valuable advice. First, understand the problem, they counseled. They recommended that we discover, through market research, what barriers and perceptions impeded our efforts. They told us not to advertise for more students if the admissions staff was not answering their phones in a helpful, courteous way.

We commissioned a stakeholder survey in 1996. The objectives were to establish baseline measures of stakeholder satisfaction, to identify strengths and areas needing improvement, to increase enrollment and retention, and to generate additional support of the universities. More than 5,700 students, alumni, faculty, prospective students, parents, and community leaders responded. Generally, stakeholders agreed that:

1. The most important finding of the survey was that external stakeholders, community leaders, parents, employers, and alumni are more positive about the universities than internal communities such as faculty and staff. Overall, internal and external satisfaction was highest at UH-Clear Lake and UH-Victoria.

2. All four universities offer first-class education, have outstanding faculty, respect diversity, and contribute to the communities.

3. The universities need a clear mission and direction and links to the community.

4. Universities need more funded research, more nationally recognized programs, more alumni association membership, and more faculty and staff interaction with students and alumni.

However, a significant number of faculty were dissatisfied with pay, opportunity for input, internal communications, and the system administration.

The survey created guidelines for marketing and a clearer sense of problems that needed resolution. Meanwhile, all four universities pursued aggressive marketing programs, dedicating staff and resources to advertising and student recruitment. At UH, considerable effort went into creating a more user-friendly environment through such innovations as longer business hours for the financial aid office, graduate school counseling for juniors and seniors, retention programs for at-risk students, and contracts for community college students.

THE UNIVERSITY OF HOUSTON SYSTEM VISION COMMISSION

A two-year term is a short time in which to accomplish change and is too short to achieve many goals. It seemed best to attempt to construct a roadmap to guide us to those goals. We decided to appoint a Vision Commission comprised of national leaders in education, business, government, and culture. That 19 people of their stature were willing to devote such time and effort to this endeavor is a credit to the strength of this university system and the interest in crafting new directions for urban institutions.

The commission was successful because of these visionary people, but also because of the leadership of Dr. Kenneth L. Lay, whose understanding of vision has created one of the world's leading energy companies, Enron Corp. Dr. Lay, is a UH alumnus, a former regent, and one of Houston's business leaders. The next challenge was creating interaction with campus communities. That plan was developed by Dr. Peter C. Bishop, who chairs the UH-Clear Lake Studies of the Future program and skillfully served as facilitator for the Vision Commission. Each university community selected a team of campus leaders to work with the Vision Commission.

The commission meetings produced the most exciting, energetic discussion of the future of higher education we have been privileged to observe. Among the ideas that were expressed:

"It is powerful to be a major city. It is a powerful environment, and what raises the power is the preparation of students through urban life," Dr. Arturo Madrid, distinguished professor at Trinity University.

"Is the UH System going to define itself or let others define it? You can't imagine Houston without words like urban, international, Latin America, petrochemical, energy . . . these are the unique strengths to build on," Dr. C. Peter Magrath, president of the National Association of State Universities and Land-Grant Colleges.

"To be unique in profoundly different ways means freeing ourselves from the enormous grip of the past, and remember we're not the only ones. Your colleagues are deeply in the grip of that old model," Dr. Frank Newman, president of the Education Commission of the States.

"I do not believe we should condition our vision on the prior assent of the so-called stakeholder groups. It seems to me, particularly in educational institutions, that this is often prescription for paralysis," Dr. Chester E. Finn Jr., Fellow at the Hudson Institute.

"There is a growing disconnect on campuses between the internal priorities of people engaged in universities versus the external demands from students, employers and the community," Dr. Aims C. McGuinness Jr., senior associate of the National Center for Higher Education Management Systems.

"We seem preoccupied with housekeeping, maintaining endlessly, arranging and rearranging, defining and redefining, in hopes that we will uncover the right organizational structure, the right strategies, the right mission statement. But solutions built on ever changing circumstances will be just that—ever changing," Professor Angela Patton, former president, UH Faculty Senate.

"Our strengths lie in our ability to retain the learning lab quality of the university, the gathering place quality, the community of learning," Dr. Linda Gratch, former president, UH-Downtown Faculty Senate.

"The first person who says 'Harvard on the Bayou' is out of here," Dr. Frank Newman.

The product of this invigorating debate was this statement: The University of Houston System will become the preeminent metropolitan university system of the twenty-first century.

As we had hoped, the vision statement provided a roadmap to future greatness, but its real importance transcended that. It stimulated the sense of opportunity so obvious at these universities. It created a mechanism for future cooperation and guidelines for progress.

BACK TO BASICS

In 1995, UHS was not alone in watching its financial support diminish. Texas legislators followed the national trend in reducing support for state-funded institutions and shifting more of the burden to students and their parents. In 1995, chancellors of the Texas major university systems decided to create a unified, statewide effort to reverse the trend.

The consensus was that previous efforts had failed because they were self-serving and fragmented. The proposal for the 1997 legislative session was to look objectively at the needs of the state and the way that higher education could address those needs, given adequate resources. Staff task forces were created and started work in fall 1995. The resulting "Back to Basics" proposal owes much to a report, "Texas Challenged," done by Dr. Steve Murdock, Director of the Texas A&M University Department of Rural Sociology. The key findings were:

1. Texas' population is growing fastest among groups (African-Americans and Hispanics) in which educational attainment has been relatively low.

2. Texas lags the nation in production of college and university graduates.

3. Texas per capita income is below the national average.

4. If current trends continue, Texas' average household income will decline by $3,000 in constant dollars by 2030.

5. Support for public higher education in Texas has declined by 24 percent since 1985.

The proposal asked the legislature for $926 million to increase full-time faculty, to improve recruitment and retention efforts, to increase financial aid, to improve research and workforce preparation, and to produce more health professionals. The return on the investment was to be a 22 percent increase in the number of bachelor's degrees per year at the end of the phased-in program.

The Coalition for Higher Education included public and private universities, community colleges, and medical schools. We were fortunate that our efforts coincided with the efforts of Senator Bill Ratliff, chairman of the Senate Finance Committee, to change funding formulas for public universities. The legislature increased appropriations to higher education by $593 million, reversing a 12-year decline in general revenue appropriations. We did not achieve everything we had hoped, but ours was a multiyear effort.

The Future

When Philip G. Hoffman was inaugurated as president of the University of Houston on April 27, 1962, he said, "The University of Houston is not a great university. We believe, however, that it is a good university which has very much within its total situation the basic ingredients of greatness" (Nicholson, 417).

In 1997, the University of Houston System was once more on the march. The search for a new chancellor-president was successful. Dr. Arthur K. Smith, who had an impressive record of achievement at SUNY-Binghamton, the University of South Carolina, and the University of Utah, took office on April 1. His term promises to be rich in accomplishments.

For urban universities, and for UHS in particular, the future is bright. These universities are ideally positioned to address two of the most critical needs facing our society: the education of minority students and the demand for lifelong learning.

Texas and other states face dramatic demographic change. By 2030, Hispanics and African-Americans will be about 55 percent of Texas' population. The number of Anglo youths ages 5 to 17 will decline as the number of Hispanic youngsters increases rapidly. Historically in Texas and the nation, Hispanics and African-Americans have lagged behind Anglos in receiving bachelor's degrees, yet the part of the job market growing fastest requires a college education. It doesn't take a rocket scientist to see how grim our economic future will be if higher education cannot address this problem.

In Texas, our ability to do this was severely limited by the decision in Hopwood v. State of Texas, a Fifth Circuit ruling which found affirmative action programs in higher education to be unconstitutional. Interpreted by Attorney

General Dan Morales to apply to "all internal institutional policies, including admissions, financial aid, scholarships, fellowships, recruitment and retention, among others" (Office of the Attorney General, 24), this decision adversely affected minority enrollment at several Texas institutions.

The University of Houston and its siblings in the UH System continue to educate a disproportionate share of African-Americans, Hispanics, and Asian-Americans. About 42.5 percent of the UH student body is minority, including Asian-Americans (UH Office of Planning & Policy Analysis, *Ethnicity*). The population of UH-Downtown, where the student body had been about equally divided among Anglo, Hispanic, and African-American students, is tilting somewhat more toward Hispanic.

Location is one reason for the excellent record of these urban universities in providing access to historically undereducated populations. Houston is a diverse city—about 25 percent African-American, 30 percent Hispanic, and 5 percent Asian—and proud of it. In 1997, Houston voters upheld by a comfortable margin the city's affirmative action policy. Another reason is reasonable cost. Tuition at Texas public universities is among the lowest in the nation, and classes are scheduled so students can work while earning a degree. Less easy to quantify is the welcoming atmosphere, but it is definitely a factor.

The second important demand is for lifelong learning. When he spoke to the UHS Vision Commission, James Kollaer, president of the Greater Houston Partnership, said: "In 2015, my 12-year-old son will be 32, with an advanced degree. He will be in the second of his five careers (four of which have not yet been created), and he will be heading back to the third retraining of the 13 times he will be retrained for new tasks he faces on the job" (University of Houston System, *Beyond the Horizon*, 14).

Another study by Washington State University's Social and Economic Sciences Research Center shows that "college-educated Americans are keeping their edge in the workplace by making continued learning a high priority." Don A. Dillman, lead researcher on the survey, said that it has good news and bad news for higher education: "On the one hand, American colleges and universities have many more customers for educational services than is typically realized. On the other hand higher education institutions will have to change the way they do business if they are to service students. If higher education does not adapt to serve older working students, firms in the private sector will meet those needs."

The message from that study is that adults know they will need training and retraining on a continuing basis to meet the needs of a fast-changing workplace. The education they need must be affordable and convenient. The UH universities are ideally situated to meet this need. They have been meeting it for years, with convenient urban locations, graduate programs like the Executive Master's in Business Administration, continuing education, and distance education.

UH pioneered televised education with a public television station established in 1950, and UH still offers more televised courses than any other Texas institution, with 10 full degree programs available on Channel 8. Most of these are traditional taped lectures broadcast at night for students to record and replay. At UH-Clear Lake, the Center for Instructional Technology teaches faculty and students how to use distance education more creatively. UHS at Fort Bend has become a laboratory for distance education with four classrooms outfitted for interactive television and a number of courses offered through that medium. One course in organizational behavior combines interactive TV, the Internet, videotapes, CD-ROMs, and face-to-face instruction. Two Fort Bend courses are offered entirely on the Internet.

More ambitious is the effort to create a "Gulf Coast Knowledge Utility," which would link universities, community colleges, public schools, and hospitals in a distance learning network. That effort was sparked by creation of the state Telecommunications Infrastructure Fund, conceived as a $1.5 billion account financed by contributions from telephone and wireless telecommunications providers. Planning is underway to seek a grant for a collaborative application, but that effort is slowed by the different needs of the participants, according to UHS at Fort Bend Director Ed Hugetz.

"Those of us at the universities talk about instructional applications in math, reading and writing—in algebra, for example—it's the dropout killer and everyone agrees that we desperately need computer instruction," Hugetz said. "But the community colleges want to focus on workforce development courses, like web page design and technical support, and the public schools need equipment before they can do anything. We think collaboration will be very valuable, but we haven't yet agreed what our effort should be."

The need for urban institutions like UH and its sister universities is greater than ever, but significant challenges are ahead. In Texas, as in other states, the method of financing public universities does not recognize the unique needs of these institutions. With more part-time students, the demands for libraries, parking, counseling, and financial aid are higher. The situation is particularly painful at UH-Downtown, which operates with fewer dollars per student than most other state universities in Texas because its course offerings have been limited to low-funded undergraduate programs and because the state has recently cut back on reimbursement for remedial courses.

Enrollment at UHS has turned the corner with two successive years of increase systemwide. It is too soon to declare victory, but it is clear that a focused effort at better admission practices and higher retention can be successful. At UH, where the problem was most acute, increases occurred in the number of entering freshmen. Dr. Eduardo Apodaca, associate vice-president for enrollment, credits 26 measures including transfer agreements with community colleges, satellite outreach offices, field admissions, a summer program for high school teachers, a four-year graduation agreement, and expedited financial aid. Equally important and perhaps more cost-effective is the effort to retain students already enrolled. In fall 1996, 80.6 percent of all UH students who were enrolled in the spring semester returned. In fall 1997 the percentage was 83.3. The challenge facing UH will be maintaining the balance among white and minority students, as well as increasing the number of adequately prepared minority students. See Table 9.2, A B, C and D

Retention rates need improvement. As at other urban universities with large numbers of part-time students, UH and UH-Downtown have low graduation rates. A Coordinating Board study showed that only 37.4 percent of first-time entering freshmen in fall 1989 had earned a degree from UH six years later (although another 12.4 percent were still enrolled). At UH-Downtown, it was only 7.3 percent. Many of these students cannot carry a full course load and must take longer than the six years the state counts as a performance measure for baccalaureate degrees. However, there are also excellent programs, like the Scholars Community and Urban Experience, that help at-risk students stay in school. These programs are privately financed and limited by funds available.

UH, the flagship university, must continue its march toward excellence, as defined by traditional means: nationally ranked degree programs, award-winning faculty, National Merit scholars and other distinguished students, and more sponsored research leading to Carnegie Research I status. The means are there to accomplish this. The university added considerably to its endowment and to the number of endowed chairs in its recent $358 million fund drive. Aggressive recruiting is necessary to fill these chairs with the scholars who will attract research dollars and enhance the university's reputation.

Some encouraging events have already occurred. Thanks largely to the creative fundraising efforts of former Regent Chair Wilhemina "Beth" Morian, a granddaughter of UH benefactor Hugh Roy Cullen, the new Moores School of Music building has a ceiling painted by Frank Stella, a landmark in contemporary art. Entry into a new athletic conference produced a winning football season and a bowl game for the Cougars in 1996. The new governance system holds many challenges, but the prospects are good for less conflict and more cooperation.

The future for urban universities is bright with potential. The UH System has an ambitious vision of becoming the "preeminent metropolitan university

Table 9.2A: *A Profile of the University of Houston's Entering Freshman Class: Fall 1997.*

FALL 1997	HEADCOUNT	PERCENTAGE	GPA	CLASS RANK	SAT
White, Other	1001	35.4%	3.2	69.0%	1116
African-American	544	19.2%	3.1	72.0%	969
Hispanic	659	23.3%	3.2	73.7%	1003
Asian	613	21.7%	3.2	72.6%	1047
Native American	13	0.5%	3.2	64.4%	1104
Total	2830	100.0%	3.2	71.4%	1047

Table 9.2B: *A Profile of the University of Houston's Entering Freshmen Class: Fall 1996.*

FALL 1996	HEADCOUNT	PERCENTAGE	GPA	CLASS RANK	SAT
White, Other	909	38.1%	3.1	70.4%	1129
African American	456	19.1%	3.0	72.6%	985
Hispanic	494	20.7%	3.2	78.6%	1013
Asian	505	21.2%	3.2	74.7%	1075
Native American	21	0.9%	3.3	80.7%	1086
Total	2385	100.0%	3.1	73.6%	1066

Table 9.2C: *A Profile of the University of Houston's Entering Freshman Class: Fall 1995*

FALL 1995	HEADCOUNT	PERCENTAGE	GPA	CLASS RANK	SAT
White, Other	880	40.6%	3.0	72.6%	1124
African American	344	15.9%	2.9	73.4%	996
Hispanic	458	21.1%	3.1	78.3%	984
Asian	475	21.9%	3.2	76.6%	1066
Native American	11	0.5%	2.5	65.6%	1061
Total	2168	100.0%	3.0	74.8%	1068

Table 9.2D: *A Profile of the University of Houston's Entering Freshman Class: Fall 1994*

FALL 1994	HEADCOUNT	PERCENTAGE	GPA	CLASS RANK	SAT
White, Other	890	43.5%	3.0	72.0%	1122
African American	259	12.7%	2.9	73.8%	952
Hispanic	369	18.0%	3.0	77.7%	993
Asian	460	22.5%	3.3	78.5%	1072
Native American	17	0.8%	3.0	67.4%	1082
Total	2047	100.0%	3.1	74.7%	1080

system of the twenty-first century." That will require blazing a new path rather than seeking an institutional model to pursue.

One of the members of the Vision Commission, Aims C. McGuinness Jr., believes that this system will be judged by how it advances the capacity of modern society to address the educational, social, cultural, and economic problems of great metropolitan areas. "Because of vaguely defined missions, outdated policies and uncertain leadership, many systems are drifting in directions that contrast sharply with those toward which the UH System must move," McGuinness said (University of Houston System, *Beyond the Horizon* 24–25). A number of systems are characterized by:

1. Dominance of the traditional research university as the only respectable model for quality and prestige.

2. Closed governance processes and leadership styles that exclude key external stakeholders, such as employers and civic leaders, from decision-making.

3. An inwardly defined agenda determined by the priorities of constituent units and their faculties.

4. A "hunker-down" mentality that values competition and confrontation rather than collaboration and cooperation with other universities and education providers.

5. Low tolerance in faculty reward systems and system resource allocation for the priorities of teaching, application, and public service.

The Vision Commission saw a different system, one that achieves the highest prestige and respect because of its interconnectedness with one of the world's great metropolitan areas, and that serves as the highway through which the Houston community gains access to the latest advances in knowledge. It is that future we would hope for the four UH universities, each of them contributing in unique and important ways. It is a very bright future.

IO

MIAMI-DADE COMMUNITY COLLEGE

Unified Vision for a Multicampus System

Eduardo J. Padrón

The phenomenal growth of Miami-Dade
Community College led to a stagnant
confederation of independent, competitive
campuses before a tightly focused vision by new
leadership reworked its culture and tradition,
resulting in a reinvigorated unified system, now
greater than its parts.

Jeffery D. Lukenbill

Theodore Levitt

Founded in 1960, Miami-Dade Community College developed during its early years like many of the large urban colleges established in the 50's, 60's, and early 70's. Growth was phenomenal, far exceeding the expectations of the founding fathers. Curricula and support systems were almost afterthoughts, as attention by necessity was directed towards constructing facilities, hiring personnel, and establishing funding bases.

Miami-Dade is a good example of multicampus development in community colleges. From the concept of a single campus with a single building, the college evolved in a short fifteen years to a multicampus system of four distinct campuses. Paralleling the establishment of new campuses was the growth of a district administration to support the financial, personnel, and facilities functions of the college. Many collegewide functions were centralized with the goal of achieving greater efficiency and better coordination.

A by-product of this centralized administration, however, was increased tension between the campuses and the district office. The locus of decision-making, especially when those decisions affected students and learning, became a difficult issue. This is typical of many multicampus colleges and universities. To those on the campuses, the bureaucracy can seem inflexible, unresponsive, and detached from the realities of students and classrooms.

Miami-Dade's approach to the centralized-decentralized issue seemed to make a lot of sense as the College was expanding: centralize those collegewide functions that support students and the instructional program; decentralize instructional delivery and student support services. Campus administrations had the authority to organize the academic programs and instructional delivery in order to be as effective as possible. Thus, there were different organizations of academic divisions and departments, different arrangements of deans, associate deans, and chairpersons, different class schedules, different programs. And yet there was to be a single catalog and all courses and programs had to be approved by the centralized District Office of Education. Meanwhile, the budget, purchasing, construction, and personnel were supervised by District administrators.

A result of this management system for a multicampus college was a situation that now has become critical for the college's survival as a viable institution. A review of those early growth years reveals the development of an attitude within the college's campuses which was quite natural, and even encouraged. As new campuses were established, they were conceived as mirror images of the original campus. With the exception of the Medical Center, where all nursing and allied health programs were later consolidated, the other campuses had the same general education program, the same transfer programs, some of the same occupational programs, and similar continuing education offerings. As a result, geographical territories were staked out, recruiting areas were defined, and the campuses became more and more competitive.

Competition . . . so much a part of the American fabric, but so inherently dangerous for a multicampus college. How often has the faculty of one campus been pitted against the faculty of another campus? How often has there been an unhealthy competition for programs, finances, and students? How often have the personnel of one campus looked at the other's as inferior?

Miami-Dade experienced, and even fostered, that competition. As the newer campuses were established, they had their own athletic teams, their own school colors, their own mascots. The competition on the athletic fields was matched by the competition among the academic departments and the student support units. The greatest athletic rivalry was not with neighboring community colleges or other large urban colleges in the state, but among the campuses themselves. Likewise, the goal of an academic department was too often to be larger or better than the same departments on the other campuses. In their efforts to grow and be the largest (and consequently to have more of the resources, typically distributed on the basis of enrollment formulas), the campuses competed for the same students. Too often, a high school, a business, or an agency was approached by representatives of different Miami-Dade campuses trying to outdo one another in their efforts to get more students and more resources.

When the College, with its open admissions and low tuition, was the only game in town, it could get away with this competition. But the education world is different now. Just as the American manufacturers, busy competing with one another, were slow to respond to the competition from Asia, the College found itself slow to respond to the strong competition from the outside—proprietary schools, businesses and industries themselves, and even the local public and private universities. In some instances, those institutions took the community college's philosophy and practices and made them their own, while the college's campuses still competed with each other.

Add to the problems of competition additional changes being fashioned by the legislature, and a crisis was imminent. Suddenly, funding dried up, accountability standards were imposed, performance-based budgeting and funding became realities, tuition costs increased, and the costs of energy and technology skyrocketed. The community college was suddenly in real trouble.

A strong foundation for the College's growth was established by its first president, Peter Masiko. During the Robert McCabe era, Miami-Dade reached unprecedented heights of creativity and recognition. The 1986 University of Texas study of community colleges across the country affirmed Miami-Dade's place among the most forward-thinking institutions in the country. However, steadily declining state funding precipitated what came to be perceived within the College as perennial financial crises. Hiring, spending, and travel freezes were all too regular and, more importantly, new program initiatives too often were placed on hold for lack of available funds. In addition, the College was unable to keep pace with the incredible changes in technology.

The College's efforts to influence the state legislature seemed to fall on deaf ears. By 1995, Miami-Dade was receiving 12 percent less in real dollar state funding than it had 10 years prior, continuing an implausible 30 year/30 percent trend of loss to inflation. Despite a 2-year tax assessment approved overwhelmingly by Miami-Dade County voters in 1992, M-DCC continued to rank in the bottom 10 percent nationally in total funding. Meanwhile, the campuses continued to compete for academic programs, resources, and enrollments. The concept that what is good for one campus is good for the college as a whole was not understood.

Shortly after his appointment as District President in late 1995, Eduardo Padrón presented the College community with a thorough assessment of the College's financial state. Not only was the fiscal stability of the College in jeopardy, but now the continuing caliber of the institution's work was at stake. Years of stop-gap measures had failed and Dr. Padrón initiated the first of many steps to redirect the College's course. Miami-Dade would trade this war of attrition, which it was losing badly, for a far more decisive approach to fulfilling its mission.

Thus began the most comprehensive overhaul in the College's history and one of the most dramatic in all of higher education. Dr. Padrón's message was alarmist: the College's viability, even its survival, was in question. The possibility of even closing a campus was real. M-DCC would need to seriously redirect its resources to first shore up an exceedingly fragile College economy and deteriorating physical plant. At the same time, planning was initiated to reinvigorate academic programs and rethink the College's major operational systems.

The Revisioning Process

The Executive Committee (EC) of the College played a key role in establishing a renewed vision for Miami-Dade. At the time, the EC was comprised of five Campus Presidents (a sixth campus, InterAmerican, originally an outreach center, was established in 1997) and six District Vice Presidents. By late 1997, the number of vice presidents had been reduced to three. With the help of outside consultants, this group spent long hours articulating and prioritizing the College's long-range vision. The work produced a clearly idealistic declaration that also has provided a practical framework for projects as diverse as budgeting, organizational reengineering, and strategic planning. It read as follows:

> M-DCC's desired state: our vision of M-DCC in 3–5 years is to be the premier community college, renowned for its:

> 1. Satisfied, well-prepared students who, through their extraordinarily positive experience at M-DCC, have acquired the needed knowledge and skills to be successful in their ongoing academic and career pursuits;

> 2. Empowered employees, working within an environment that encourages creativity, risk-taking and accountability, who apply their individual and collective talents to fulfill the college's mission;

> 3. A highly supportive community that recognizes the significant impact of M-DCC's educational and training programs; and

> 4. Effective use of adequate resources to enable programs to flourish and the talents of people to emerge.

Commensurate with the Vision Statement, Dr. Padrón made public a work plan that served to focus the College's efforts for the first year of his administration. That plan emphasized building financial stability through a range of cost-saving measures and development of a strategic plan for building a more diverse funding base; the acceleration of the College's Education Review, a comprehensive reexamination of the Associate in Arts and Associate in Science core, development of occupational and technical programs to support Miami-Dade County's changing economy, and revamping of all student service functions for increased accessibility and responsiveness; development of a technology master plan, addressing administrative and academic computing as well as distance and virtual learning opportunities; and organizational reengineering, which would review and redesign the College's major administrative and support operations.

An enormous amount of work transpired in the ensuing two years. Participation was invited repeatedly as the only means not just to build consensus for the projected changes, but also to combat the inevitable anxiety that accompanied this level of change work. Well over 600 College employees participated in committee work in the major initiatives, with hundreds more attending town meetings and departmental screening of new proposals. With very few exceptions, work groups included representatives from each campus and sought to effect more consistent collegewide procedures and standards.

At times the College felt as if it would burst at the seams for the sheer volume of work in process. It was exciting, often difficult, sometimes tedious. It was embraced by some, resisted by others. The College altered its culture—one that had evolved very strong traditions over 35 years—in a remarkably short time frame. The following were the major thrusts of the reform effort, each of which has spawned implementation and/or follow-up projects which continue today.

Building Financial Stability

The College's financial crisis was the product of a number of converging factors. In early 1996, the Florida legislature was confronted with a revenue shortfall of nearly $1 billion and a constitutional prohibition against deficit spending. As it had for the past ten years, M-DCC's funding allocation again fell short of actual need. Plant maintenance appropriations, in particular, remained dismally below formula requirements, as they had been for several years. Full-Time Equivalent (FTE) funding was also in decline because of small but steady decreases in enrollment. Compounding the situation yet further, Welfare and Immigration reform legislation posed an enormous threat to the College's student base. Each bill proposed to eliminate financial aid to legal immigrants, who made up nearly one-third of the College's student population. Alone, those measures would have reduced revenues by over $30 million.

Some of the initial steps were familiar: hiring, spending, and travel were suspended with few exceptions. Additional steps, however, signaled the first break with tradition. A moratorium on new construction, a cherished staple for this heretofore growing institution, was enacted. The opening of new facilities at the Homestead and Wolfson Campuses also was delayed indefinitely to curtail operating costs.

REFOCUSING AT THE MEDICAL CENTER CAMPUS

The restraint on new construction included a proposed facility at the Medical Center Campus, for which $30 million had already been allocated in the upcoming budget. Since the facility was slated to house general education classrooms and faculty offices, with no space dedicated to Allied Health and Nursing, the broader question of the campus' function was raised. Again, a break with an established tradition ensued as the campus' focus was narrowed to its medical and biotechnical specialties. This was, in fact, the original intent of the campus. General education faculty were dispersed to the four full-service campuses and $30 million was made available for sorely needed renovations and repairs. The decision reflected a new integration of the campuses, surrendering an element of established campus identity at Medical Center Campus for a more unified approach.

RESTRUCTURING OF ATHLETIC PROGRAMS

In 1995, Miami-Dade was fielding 16 men's and women's teams, in many cases maintaining teams from the Kendall, North, and Wolfson campuses in a single sport. Each campus had amassed a record of excellence, winning numerous conference, state, and even national championships. Refocusing on the College's primary mission, however, dictated a change; the College instituted a "one sport/one team" concept. The number of intercollegiate teams was reduced to five, with each sport assigned to one of the three large campuses. Instead of athletic directors at each campus, one of the campus presidents was assigned overall responsibility, with one collegewide athletic director handling day-to-day responsibilities.

Economics was undeniably the driving force in the decision. With expenditures of almost $2 million per year and only 305 student athletes from nearly 60,000 credit students, the numbers simply did not support each other. While economics forced the decision, the make-up of the College ran counter to the extensive range of athletic programs. Sixty-seven percent of Miami-Dade students are part-time and many full-time students work, making athletic participation unlikely if not impossible. The state further

THE MIAMI-DADE COMMUNITY COLLEGE   *187*

compounded the situation by no longer affording graduation credit for physical education courses.

FUNDING THE VISION

In addition to the measures outlined above, the College took the painful step of
eliminating 119 administrative and support positions across the College in April
of 1996. It was another move that broke with precedent, not only at Miami-
Dade but no doubt at colleges and universities across the country. Consciously,
and often painstakingly, the focus of the institution was being honed to the educational mission. If resources and their use were at issue, then position support had to be evaluated in that light.

Budgets for academic years 1996–97 and 1997–98 reflected the College's
effort to tighten its collective belt and redirect resources to the vision prescribed
by the Executive Committee in early 1996. The sacrifices and redirections
inside were supplemented at the state level, where the long-standing decline
in funding was reversed in both the '96 and '97 legislative allocations. New
program development, technology, and student support received new infusions
and all had an invigorating effect on the College environment. Five new A.S.
and several short-term certificate programs emerged, with an additional 20
new programs by the fall of 1998. The programs highlighted technology, biomedical, and the entertainment industry, all among the highest priority needs
of the region's evolving economy. Many of the College's oldest buildings, worn
out from years of phenomenal growth, were refurbished and upgraded. Overall
compensation, lingering for years at the 25th percentile nationally, was upgraded via a new and vastly simplified salary schedule with higher minimums and
maximums.

Organizational Reengineering

In many ways, the term reengineering served as a lightning rod for the overarching change process at Miami-Dade. With its corporate roots and reputation for
downsizing, the introduction of the project generated controversy and anxiety. To
counter the expectations, project directors made extra effort to clarify the project's
intentions and approach as well as to solicit input on priority needs.

It was understood from the beginning that the Education Review would
address curriculum reforms and student services from a collegewide perspective. The curricula and instructional support systems had to be aligned.
This allowed reengineering to focus on operational systems. There was, in
fact, broad consensus that many of the College's practices were outdated and

unresponsive and perhaps, most important, inconsistent across the College. Through a series of campus town meetings, a collegewide survey, and constant updates and feedback between personnel and the project's leadership, a number of key areas emerged as most in need of attention. The first year of the project focused on the following:

1. Human Resource Development, including areas of training for all employees and specifically supervisory training; revamping the hiring process; evaluation/performance management; and an improved rewards system.

2. Budgeting and Planning, including building the College budget and allocating people and money equitably and effectively, which called for a review of the College's productivity and staffing formulas.

3. Maintenance, which addressed the need for a more consistent and effective means of identifying and responding to ongoing building and grounds needs.

Teams were carefully developed for each area of the work, ensuring that representation was afforded to each campus and each classification of employee: faculty, staff, and administrators. The teams also were a mixture of those with direct knowledge of the area's functioning (insiders), those who were most directly served by the procedures in question (customers), and still others who could be considered outsiders and added a more naive, fresh perspective to the discussions. The make-up of the teams served to reinforce the College's concern with being one college and not merely a confederation of independent, often competitive campuses. While there was avowed concern for maintaining the character of each campus, there was an even stronger motivation to generate universal procedures where they were warranted. The above areas and procedures certainly invited that treatment.

Reengineering town meetings were held on a monthly basis. Preliminary recommendations were aired here as well as in specific departments most affected by the recommendations. Eventually, the recommendations made their way through the Executive Committee, the President's Council (comprised of Deans, Presidents of Support Staff Councils and Faculty Senates, Student Government representatives, District Vice Presidents, and Campus Presidents), and the College's Board of Trustees.

The process forced fresh thinking on all fronts. Long-standing assumptions and taken-for-granted attitudes came under review. Clearly, the College's lack of uniformity was uncovered as a problem that gave rise to inequities in the quality of various work processes as well as the treatment of people across the College. Uniformity in procedure, however, did not imply centralization of authority, but simply better coordination and cooperation. Hiring's key procedures were decentralized to individual hiring departments, but uniform training was required for handling of documents and relations with applicants; technology added uniformity and speeded up the process; training recommendations also called for campus-based centers with a coordinated, equitable menu of learning opportunities; evaluation, performance management and rewards would be characterized by collegewide standards. The Maintenance recommendations centralized a previously campus-based operations structure but ensured that campuses would have local, ready response teams.

Recommendations were handed over to new implementation teams, again providing cross-college and cross-functional representation. It was expected that the new procedures would be in place during the winter term of 1998.

The Education Review: Planning for Student Success

In 1978, Miami-Dade produced a general education curriculum that gave much needed structure to what the College offered and how students would proceed in their academic pursuits. A modest review in 1991 only reinforced the principles and practices asserted in *General Education in a Changing Society* (Lukenbill and McCabe), and, in fact, the Miami-Dade approach emerged as a model for community colleges across the country.

But societies continue to change, and in 1995 Miami-Dade was confronted by a state legislature intent on outcome-based funding and workforce requirements that demanded a review of the education program at the College. The project's stated aim was to reassess the rationale, goals, and objectives of the transfer and occupational tracks as well as to redesign the all-important student flow process for each.

The curriculum areas to be addressed were comprehensive, including College and Vocational Preparatory, General Education, and Occupational Education (including A.S., Post-Secondary Adult Vocational (PSAV), and Supplemental courses and programs). The student support functions included recruitment, admission and registration, advisement and counseling, financial aid, entry-level assessment, retention, transfer, and job placement.

The leadership of the College left no doubt that it regarded the Education Review as the centerpiece of the College's reform effort. Great care was again exercised in assembling collegewide task forces to address the various elements of the review. Campuses could no longer address curricula and instructional delivery issues from a single campus viewpoint. Faculty were joined by support staff and administrators, with strong participation of the latter two on the student flow task force. As with the reengineering initiative, regular progress reports were circulated and open forums convened to solicit feedback from the College community.

The project was divided into a three-phase Assessment, Planning, and Restructuring and Implementation approach. From the outset, critical differences in service delivery and course interpretation were apparent across the College. As expected, no aspect of Miami-Dade's reforms generated more impassioned, often territorial, debate. There are no more essential topics for educators than what should be taught and how it should be delivered. The autonomy granted Miami-Dade's campuses had a significant effect on educational delivery, and the pros and cons came streaming forth as the Education Review proceeded. In the end, however, the most serious influence was exerted by two sources that commanded everyone's attention: first, legislative and funding mandates that limited credits and forced compression of the core, and second, business and university input which detailed prevailing skill needs and pointed unmistakably to weaknesses in Miami-Dade's graduates.

The latter input was collected through an extensive series of DACUMS (Designing a Curriculum), structured data gathering exercises which brought together well over 30 different groups commenting on the effectiveness of the College's program offerings. The range of panels included graduates, noncompleters, active students, faculty, representatives from 22 workforce realms, and university representatives.

Themes emerged that were eventually manifested in the revised core curriculum. All contributors recommended improved communication skills, both oral and written. Employers emphasized the ability to think critically for the purpose of problem solving, decision-making, and self-management on the job, as well as human relations skills. Essentially, employers wanted basic aptitudes in a given occupational area which they could further cultivate, but they stressed the need for general knowledge and skills which were transferable to a broad range of new endeavors.

The new Miami-Dade core course recommendation included a course in critical thinking, an oral communications component, as well as a required competency in technology. After extensive debate, the core retained a level of flexibility. Workforce and legislative requirements spoke specifically to what this large, urban educational system should do to respond to economic realities; educators, particularly in the social sciences and humanities, urged their colleagues to preserve a diverse, culturally sensitive general education menu.

Both viewpoints were included in the resulting compromise.

The Student Flow recommendations effected a far greater level of uniformity of approach than the College had ever demonstrated. With time-to-degree constraints, renewed emphasis was placed on career assessment, advisement, and informed decision-making about educational paths. More extensive faculty participation in all aspects of the student flow process was viewed as essential to student success. Simplicity and ease of access via electronic enrollment and one-stop processing catered to the realities of a part-time, older, working student body. Once again, the discussions pointed out how a large institution's procedures can become layered in complexity, losing sight of the most basic service requirements. The recommendations refocused all participants on point-of-service responsiveness to the College's most important constituency, the students.

PROGRAM CLUSTERS

A very significant approach to the curricular work for a multicampus college was the development of the concept of "program cluster" for occupational programs. In an organizational structure where the campuses actually competed for occupational and training programs, serious flaws resulted. Most important, consistent quality service was not being provided to all parts of the service area. Those living in the extreme end of the service area might have to travel as much as fifty miles to access a program that was offered only at another site. Even worse, campuses protected their programs, often not allowing courses to be offered at another campus; conversely, the host campus might relegate another campus' offerings to the most undesirable days and times.

The "cluster" concept groups similar programs under the administrative responsibility of a single administrator, with a primary goal of providing program courses to students at all campuses at time when they can best be served. In this approach, program growth benefits the faculty and departments at all campuses, competition among campuses no longer makes sense, and the reward system (distribution of resources) is collegeo based, not campus-based. Mutual support, no competition, becomes the driving force.

The Master Plan for Technology

Just after his appointment as District President, Dr. Padrón established the position of Vice President and CIO for Information Systems and Educational Technology and charged the new VP with developing a Collegewide Master Plan for Technology within the next year, or by the end of 1996. At the outset, the internal consensus was that the College was lagging dangerously behind in technology, a big ticket item that had been easily victimized in yearly funding deliberations. With a restatement of priorities, technology development, no matter the cost, was to be viewed as an absolute necessity.

The Master Plan was structured around the work of six major subcommittees: Academic Programs, including Technology and Student Support and Distance Education; Administrative Technology; Funding for Technology; Information Systems; Technical Standards; and Policies and Procedures. Over 200 people volunteered to participate on the above committees with an additional 200+, including students, joining associated work groups. The Network Administrators Group and the Florida Community College Software Consortium Steering Committee (FCCSC), the latter a very important component in the College's administrative technology development, also contributed to the Master Plan.

A set of simple assumptions guided the work of the subcommittees, highlighted by the recognition that students needed technology skills to be productive and competitive, and that faculty likewise needed those same skills to be able to empower students. Lifelong learning with respect to technology was included as a prevailing assumption, as was the recognition that the College now existed in a competitive environment requiring first rate technological acumen to remain viable.

Behind the assumptions and guiding principles, the teams produced an exceedingly practical and honest document. It reported, in each of the subcommittee areas, existing strengths and challenges, and the goals, objectives, and strategies required to elevate the College's capacity. The Master Plan was a year's worth of research, needs assessment, creative discussion and planning that has provided a long-term blueprint for the College's technological growth.

The implementation of this blueprint is essential, of course, to support the college's efforts in distance education. There was no question about this being a multicampus effort. There was, however, a basic theoretical question to be answered: would the distance education curricula be administered in a separate unit (akin to a separate campus) or as a collective effort involving all of the campuses? The former approach may be simpler and easier to coordinate, but the latter has a much greater chance of integrating distance education into the instructional fabric of the institution. In its goal of integrating the instructional program among the campuses, the college has chosen the latter approach. There will be a need for overall coordination of distance education, but responsibility for this coordination will be assigned to a particular campus, rather than to the District Office of Education. Again, this model reflects the need for overall coordination without added central administration. The effectiveness of the distance education program will be measured by how well it supports all campus programs and instructional activities.

The FCCSC, now known as the Odyssey Project, is a joint venture of eight Florida community colleges, originally spurred by the need to be more technologically in synch with the state's reporting systems and software. It is a massive project that will radically upgrade the College's systems for student information and tracking, payroll and personnel records, finance, and facilities management. It is one more major element of change directly impacting employees at every level of College functioning. Hundreds of administrative and support personnel throughout the system are scheduled for training, without which they will be unable to conduct their work. No less important than the Education Review or the Reengineering Project, the Odyssey Project requires constant communication updates. The value of effective information, conveyed in a variety of formats and groups, cannot be overestimated.

The Strategic Plan

The Miami-Dade strategic plan is a unique document, if for no other reason than the timing of its development—in the midst of profound change at the institution. At the heart of the planning process are the College's Mission and Vision Statements, the latter espousing a desired state that the College seeks to achieve in the ensuing three to five year period. A set of strategic goals has been drawn from these two statements, highlighting aspects of Miami-Dade's desired state that will be actively addressed during that time.

With these goals providing a focus, planners from the College's Department of Institutional Research conducted an environmental scan to identify trends that might enhance or impede the College's ability to realize the stated mission and vision. Both internal and external forces were identified in the scan, and in each case the plan suggested implications for Miami-Dade's progress.

The process then focused on the major projects in motion at the College: the Education Review, Organizational Reengineering, and the Collegewide Technology initiatives. The recommended goals and objectives, along with the implications of the environmental scan, were matched with the appropriate strategic goals, producing a set of relevant objectives for each.

Finally, the planners developed a set of measures to monitor the College's progress toward achieving the strategic goals. Chief among the measures were State Accountability Standards and additional measures that assess progress in generating performance-based funding.

Conclusion

Every large organization struggles to reconcile its size and complexity with the need for direct, quality communication and management. The polarities of autonomy, which invites more intimate interaction and innovation, and centralization, which has the advantages of precise standards of performance, are additional elements to conciliate for multicampus institutions. Miami-Dade recognized that it was time to thoroughly rethink its approach, beginning at the core mission and extending into its long-term vision and the practical applications of its work. The operative traditions, which had encouraged autonomy and competition among the campuses, clearly have given way to a more consolidated and unified understanding. To be sure, understanding is the foundation for practice, and as those core activities take new shape, new understanding must be cultivated.

What is occurring beyond the walls of the institution demand that we change to meet the challenges. We can no longer afford the internal competition and duplication of energy that characterized past efforts. We must discover a means of being one institution, more consolidated and efficient, and cultivate the necessary autonomy and diversity of thought and practice. To do so requires a more precise and, ultimately, practical appreciation of the purpose and direction of the College, shared throughout the institution. Leadership has a critical role to play but the understanding is important to everyone. It is a subtle but critical reworking of the College's culture and tradition. For Miami-Dade this effort has been dramatic and undoubtedly will continue to evolve as we adjust to the demands of a new time. Recognizing the need and staying the course provide extraordinary opportunities for the institution and its people.

II

THE MARICOPA COMMUNITY COLLEGE DISTRICT

A Culture of Deliberate Transformation

Linda M. Thor
Donna J. Schober
Laura Helminski

The Maricopa Community College District,
under the extended tenure and leadership of a
visionary chancellor and his management team,
fosters a culture of innovation and deliberately
transforms itself to meet the changing needs of its
communities.

The Maricopa Community College District (MCCD), serving the greater met-ropolitan area of Phoenix, Arizona, is committed to providing quality educa-tion to its communities. This, of course, is true for many fine institutions of higher education. These institutions are successful for many reasons includ-ing tradition, competitive edge, leadership, and faculty expertise. The MCCD, however, is unique in its success as a multicollege system because it has devel-oped a dominant culture of innovation and deliberate transformation.

The organizational culture of MCCD has a set of key characteristics and a shared meaning that distinguish it from other organizations. The key charac-teristics that the organization values and supports are a shared vision for inno-vation and learning, and the deliberate pursuit of transformation and growth. This culture has influenced our attitudes, behaviors, policies, and structures in the past and will continue to do so.

This chapter identifies factors contributing to the system's growth, evolu-tion, and high level of success during its thirty-five-year history as a multicollege district. Many of the opinions and conclusions expressed herein are based par-tially on an October 1997 study that comprised nine focus groups and was con-ducted by O'Neil Associates, Inc., of Tempe, Arizona. The populations recruited for the research included: two groups of alumni, two staff groups, three facul-ty groups, one group of non-MCCD educators, and one business group.

History and Structure of the System

Since its establishment as a district in 1962, the system has grown to be among the largest multicollege districts in the nation. It is the largest single provider of higher education in Arizona, with more than two million students having attended to date.

Today's MCCD grew, from one junior college that in 1920 enrolled fifteen students, to ten individually accredited colleges, a skill center, and numerous satellite education centers now, with more to come. It now serves more than 200,000 students annually, who average thirty years of age. More than 40 percent of the adults in Maricopa County have attended a Maricopa community college.

Maricopa County is larger geographically than Connecticut, Delaware, Hawaii, Massachusetts, New Jersey, or Rhode Island (*Milestones*, "Serving A Market Place Larger Than Six States"). The county's population, currently more than two million, is expected to grow to three million by the year 2000 and to 3.5 million by 2010 (Maricopa Community College District, *From Adobe Walls*).

The District's ten colleges are:

1. Chandler-Gilbert Community College
2. Estrella Mountain Community College
3. GateWay Community College
4. Glendale Community College
5. Mesa Community College
6. Paradise Valley Community College
7. Phoenix College
8. Rio Salado College
9. Scottsdale Community College
10. South Mountain Community College

Of the 6,400 credit courses offered, one-third are academic and two-thirds are occupational. Some programs are designed to prepare a student directly for a specific job. Others prepare students for transfer to a university. Still others enhance a student's ability to function more effectively in society. Degrees offered include Associate of Arts (AA), Associate of Applied Science (AAS), and Associate of General Studies (AGS). Additionally, thousands of occupational program certificates of completion are awarded each year (*Milestones*, "More Than 6,000 Courses").

Apart from the Maricopa Community Colleges, Maricopa County is served by three campuses of Arizona State University (ASU) and by a few other new but growing independent institutions of higher education.

The colleges' guiding force is the MCCD Governing Board. These five publicly elected officials— dedicated to their positions and to the prosperity of the educational system they influence—serve six-year terms with no compensation.

Even though some of its revenue comes from the state (16.7 percent) and from Maricopa County property taxes (56.9 percent), the District is a governmental entity of its own, separate from Maricopa County government. State oversight and coordination is provided by the Board of Directors for Community Colleges of Arizona. This body of fifteen members is comprised of one representative from each of the state's counties, each appointed by the governor for a seven-year term. A representative of the Board of Regents and the Superintendent of Public Instruction (or designee) complete the membership.

For the past twenty years, in many ways the MCCD Board's mentor has been Chancellor Paul A. Elsner, whose executive council includes each of the ten college presidents and four vice-chancellors. This innovative team, along with the faculty and staff, has gained substantial national recognition for its efforts and has garnered a generous number of awards. Indeed, this system illustrates the powerful and positive influence of a visionary personality and his management team on the development and direction of a community college system and its culture of innovation and transformation.

"It's rare when you go to a national conference and people see your badge and don't say, 'Oh, you're with Maricopa; I'd love to go there,'" reported one O'Neil study participant (O'Neil, "The Maricopa Community Colleges: Mission, Culture, Seminal Events and Challenges." 28).

The following diverse awards represent the District's success in meeting educational needs in its community, and the many specific contributions of Chancellor Elsner:

1. **1974**: The Maricopa Skill Center was recognized as one of the top five skill centers in the nation.

2. **1986**: Glendale Community College received an award from General Motors for its work with industry and its automotive training program.

3. **1987**: The Reverend Jesse Jackson, representing the District's Black Education Task Force, congratulated Elsner for his "outstanding contribution to cultural diversity and exceptional efforts in addressing the needs of minority communities."

4. **1990**: Elsner was named the nation's most innovative leader by the Association of Community College Trustees, receiving the Marie Y. Martin Chief Executive Officer Award.

5. **1992**: *U.S. News & World Report* featured the MCCD in its special edition of "America's Best Colleges."

6. **1992**: The Phoenix Think Tank won the coveted Anderson Medal from the Business-Higher Education Forum for addressing issues of at-risk students in grades K–12.

7. **1993**: The MCCD received the CAUSE Award for outstanding efforts in computer networking that had significant positive impact on teaching and learning. CAUSE is a national association devoted to promoting the use of information technology to improve the administration and delivery of higher education.

8. **1993**: Rio Salado College received the Pioneer Award, the Arizona Governor's Award for Quality.

9. **1994**: Elsner was honored with the Valley Leadership Visionary Award for positive and long-term active community involvement, significant contributions to the Phoenix Valley, and strong leadership qualities.

10. **1996**: Elsner was one of three educators in the nation to receive the Leadership Award of the American Association of Community Colleges for his long-standing commitment to community college goals.

11. **1996**: The Institute of Higher Education of the University of Florida honored the MCCD's "Strategic Conversations" concept with its Bellwether Award, recognizing outstanding and innovative practices successfully leading community colleges into the twenty-first century.

12. **1997**: The National Alliance of Business (NAB) selected the MCCD as "Community College of the Year" for its ongoing success in forging partnerships with business and industry (this was the first time NAB chose a community college system for this award).

13. **1998**: Elsner was named one of the nation's "Senior Leaders Inside Academe" by *Change* magazine.

14. **1998**: Elsner received the Lifetime Achievement Award for his major contributions to the national community college movement, and the MCCD received the David Pierce Organizational Leadership Award for its focus on becoming a Learning College. Both awards were presented

by North Carolina State University's National Initiative for Leadership and Institutional Effectiveness.

System Culture and Evolution

As a system, the MCCD has a strong organizational culture. External observers see common characteristics and widely held values. Internally, for instance, there is shared meaning with regard to innovation and transformation. This has become a cause and effect loop; that is, the MCCD leadership encourages innovation and growth, and innovators and risk-takers choose to come to the MCCD. Therefore, the dominant culture has a powerful influence on the behaviors and expectations of its members, who, in turn, influence the subcultures of the individual colleges.

Before reviewing each of the characteristics of the MCCD organizational culture, it is important to understand two pivotal driving forces behind the MCCD: its Vision, Mission, and Values; and Chancellor Elsner.

Vision, Mission, and Values

The MCCD has created a strong, open-system culture in which employees embrace the Governing Board's vision, mission, and values statements.

VISION

The MCCD vision is "to exceed the changing expectations of our many communities for effective, innovative, student-centered, flexible and lifelong educational opportunities. Our employees are committed to respecting diversity, continuous quality improvement, and the efficient use of resources. We are a learning organization guided by our shared values" ("Vision," Policy Governance Policies, July 22, 1997, motion no. 8673).

MISSION

The MCCD strives "to create and continuously improve affordable, accessible and effective learning environments for the lifelong educational needs of the diverse communities we serve" ("Mission," Policy Governance Policies, January 28, 1997, motion no. 8626).

VALUES

A powerful environmental influence in the MCCD culture is the values statement adopted by the Board and endorsed by the District's internal populations: "We accept the responsibility to respond to the needs of the people in our communities who desire to fulfill their potential in life. Therefore, we operate on the basis of openness and trust, to nurture an environment where all can be heard." . . . "We commit to living according to the following basic values . . . vital to maintaining the integrity and vitality of our community of learners. [We] value education, students, employees, excellence, diversity, honesty and integrity, freedom, fairness, responsibility, and public trust" ("Values," Policy Governance Policies, January 28, 1997, motion no. 8626).

MCCD constituents widely understand the vision and mission, according to the 1997 research. They unanimously view the MCCD mission as meaning "to provide universal access to higher education" (O'Neil, 2).

The Vision, Mission, and Values statements—deliberately formulated to direct and transform the District—underpin the MCCD culture and the philosophy of its chancellor.

CHANCELLOR ELSNER

Focus group members believe that the primary pivotal event in the college system's history was the appointment of Elsner as chancellor twenty years ago. He is credited with building the system into one of the largest, most respected, and visible community college systems in the nation. "If Elsner hadn't arrived here, we would not have ten campuses. We would have five or six . . . and a smaller enrollment. He said we are here to provide leadership for the country, not just for the [Phoenix] Valley," one focus group member explained (O'Neil, 23).

A visionary, Elsner has left a legacy that includes establishing a "college without walls," focusing on technology, germinating the "Continuous Quality Improvement" (CQI) initiative, decentralizing the system, developing strong leadership and college autonomy, and creating a culture in which most individuals feel that they can take creative risks.

Elsner is considered the "ultimate environmental scanner." In pursuing an eclectic set of interests, his hand lies on the pulse of change in education, technology, business, community, government, arts and entertainment, and many other areas influencing the MCCD. His special gift is the ability to synthesize what is happening locally and nationally, make connections, and then put forth remarkable ideas for others to act upon.

Table 11.1: *Seven Primary Characteristics of an Organizational Culture.*

1. **Innovation and risk taking**. The degree to which employees are encouraged to be innovative and take risks.

2. **Attention to detail**. The degree to which employees are expected to exhibit precision, analysis, and attention to detail.

3. **Outcome orientation**. The degree to which management focuses on results or outcomes rather than on the techniques and processes used to achieve these outcomes.

4. **People orientation**. The degree to which management decisions take into consideration the effect of outcomes on people within the organization.

5. **Team orientation**. The degree to which work activities are organized around teams rather than individuals.

6. **Aggressiveness**. The degree to which people are aggressive and competitive rather than easygoing.

7. **Stability**. The degree to which organizational activities emphasize maintaining the status quo in contrast to growth.

—Stephen Robbins
Organizational Behavior

Characteristics of Organizational Culture

It is the macro view of the MCCD that best shows the distinct personality of the District. Maricopa's culture is the shared perceptions of its employees, and an examination of their behavioral characteristics can indicate the essence of this culture.

In *Organizational Behavior*, Stephen Robbins notes that "recent research suggests that there are seven primary characteristics that, in aggregate, capture the essence of an organization's culture" (See Table 11.1.) In the following pages, each of Robbins' seven characteristics is examined as it is found in the MCCD culture.

1. INNOVATION AND RISK TAKING
The degree to which employees are encouraged to be innovative and take risks.

This is an area of great strength for the MCCD. From Elsner on throughout the system, innovation and risk-taking are very much encouraged. Obviously, in a multicollege system, there is more leadership brainpower, and more leadership diversity, leading to higher levels of creativity and success throughout the system than in a single college. Because innovation is valued and rewarded in the District, it has spawned wonderful ideas such as the "Ocotillo" initiative, in which faculty influenced the use of technology in instruction, and the dynamic "college without walls."

A pervasive innovation for which the MCCD is well known is its technology agenda; one of the most powerful deliberate transformations in the MCCD evolution. In the early 1980s, long before most higher education institutions even dreamed about the world of educational technology, Chancellor Elsner's vision was of a computer on every desk, and of the MCCD as a leader in the educational use of technology. Today with the strong support of the Governing Board, the MCCD has made it possible for students to access information from around the world through electronic networking. Faculty members teach with the aid of multimedia technology. A digital television network allows students to "attend" classes simultaneously on multiple campuses. Rapid communications are achieved by means of a microwave network linking all the colleges—a vital element in efficient management of an organization involving great geographic diversity and a year-round enrollment of nearly 200,000 students.

More than 12,000 computers are housed at MCCD, including many in computer centers that are readily accessible to all MCCD students. In addition to supplying hardware and software, the MCCD also strongly supports training for faculty and staff so that the District's computers can be utilized fully.

With great success, the MCCD has also adopted teaching and educational management techniques that are at the cutting edge of today's technology, and the District continues to undergo massive technological change. Currently, the MCCD is changing every one of its administrative computing systems through a massive, multiyear project called "Apollo." What is particularly important about this effort is that the purely technological changes are also being accompanied by people, process, and organizational changes in order to maximize the project's potential benefits. The most striking innovation to come from this effort promises to be the "Learner-Centered System"—a student information system placing learners at the center of the MCCD.

Another deliberate innovation involved a change in organizational philosophy. In the early 1990s, the MCCD leadership explored Continuous Quality Improvement as a foundation for structured problem solving, and for examining and improving its processes. This effort was identified as "Quantum Quality," again Maricopa's own distinct approach. Deliberate efforts to open our thinking about customer service and employee empowerment have surfaced throughout the system.

The "Quantum Quality" initiative precipitated organizational change, which evolved further to incorporate the principles described by Peter Senge as the disciplines of the "Learning Organization." "A Learning Organization is a place where people continually expand their capacity to create its future, where adaptive learning is joined by generative learning" (*The Fifth Discipline*). The MCCD leadership used the "Quantum Quality" directive as a foundation on which to build a Learning Organization. Now the culture embraces the five disciplines of a Learning Organization as intentional strategies for change: Personal Mastery, Shared Vision, Mental Models, Team Learning, and Systems Thinking. MCCD employees are encouraged to learn and are given the resources to do so through expanded opportunities in professional growth, staff development, access to technology, and employee renewal. Change is expected, deliberate, and supported.

2. ATTENTION TO DETAIL
The degree to which employees are expected to exhibit precision, analysis, and attention to detail.

This is not an area of great emphasis in the MCCD. In fact, one of the most common phrases heard around the District is "Let's not over-manage this." This statement is representative of the belief that time is better spent on the big picture.

Additionally, the MCCD is proud that it operates from a mere "inch" of board rules, compared to the "mile" of mandates demanded in many other multicollege systems. This leaves the day-to-day administrative decisions to the faculty and staff, opening the door for innovation and constant change so each college can effectively address its own community's needs.

3. OUTCOME ORIENTATION
The degree to which management focuses on results or outcomes rather than on the techniques and processes used to achieve these outcomes.

This was not an area of major emphasis until October 1996, when the MCCD board adopted policy governance following three years of study and extensive discussion with its internal and external constituencies. "Policy governance" is the model of board governance espoused by John Carver. Under policy governance, the board focuses on the future and on the development of policies (guidelines, limitations, and ends or outcomes) rather than on the administration (day-to-day operation) of the system. The MCCD board recognizes that to be truly in control, to own and direct change, all of the constituents in the multicollege system must understand the vision and mission of the system and contribute to achieving established outcomes.

This emphasis on outcomes and shared vision focuses the MCCD leaders on high-level issues to ensure progress. For instance, this orientation allowed the MCCD leadership to foresee years in advance the need to buy land for brick and mortar facilities to be built later; to recognize the value of new learning paradigms and the advantages of emerging technologies; and to see the importance of creating community partnerships.

4. PEOPLE ORIENTATION
The degree to which management decisions take into consideration the effect of outcomes on people within the organization.

Through the processes of initiating Continuous Quality Improvement and evolving into a Learning Organization, the role of the people in the MCCD has been reemphasized and reinforced. According to Senge's first discipline of a Learning Organization, Personal Mastery, people learn to expand their personal capacity to create desired results and to create a culture that helps all members develop and reach their goals. The MCCD staff has readily adopted this discipline. One focus group participant explained, "Expectations are very high. We don't want anything that is mediocre" (O'Neil, 15).

The MCCD leaders long ago realized that salaries and benefits directly affect the quality of candidates attracted to the system and the District's ability to retain them. Offering faculty salaries on par with the state universities and staff salaries in the upper quartile of comparable jobs in the community, MCCD can compete with the local universities for the best teaching faculty and with the private sector for support staff.

One of the significant ways the board learns and understands the views of the people in the MCCD is through a concept developed by the board and staff called "Strategic Conversations"—the 1996 Bellwether Award winner in the category of Planning, Governance, and Finance. A Strategic Conversation is an informal but structured discussion of an issue of strategic importance to the MCCD. Everyone is invited to attend and is encouraged to participate. "No rank in the room" is an important ground rule guiding participation. The meetings examine directions and assumptions and can serve as the basis for future board decisions. These sessions serve as an important foundation for the Learning Organization. They help the MCCD remain flexible and open to change by positioning it to learn from its own people and experiences.

5. TEAM ORIENTATION
The degree to which work activities are organized around teams rather than individuals.

Teamwork is an integral part of an organization committed to Continuous Quality Improvement. Strategies for working successfully in teams are part of CQI training. Teamwork is valued, as evidenced by the fact that a number of years ago, at the request of the MCCD, the League for Innovation's "Innovator of the Year Award" was changed to "Innovation of the Year Award," to emphasize teams instead of individuals.

One type of teamwork is reflected in the partnerships developed with the community—another deliberate transformation. These partnerships, with businesses, governments, students, and even other local educational institutions, help the District keep abreast of continually evolving needs. Essentially, "community relations" at the MCCD translates into "shared support and resources."

For instance, in recent years, the MCCD training contracts have included such well-known companies as BFGoodrich Corporation, Chase Manhattan Bank, Del Webb Hospital, Honeywell, Intel, McDonnell Douglas, Nissan Motor Corporation, Sears, Talley Industries, and TRW (Milestones, "Recruiting, Hiring, Training"). Perhaps most noteworthy is MCCD's partnership with Motorola. MCCD operates an entire facility, called Motorola University-West, devoted to upgrading the skills of some 21,000 Motorola employees in the Phoenix area.

The MCCD also develops customized degrees with public and private employers—another type of teamwork. An example is the seven-year-old partnership with the Arizona Law Enforcement Academy, which annually trains some 900 officers for major police agencies. The MCCD is also a partner in the region's economic development activities. Ioanna Morfessis, former director of the Greater Phoenix Economic Council, credits MCCD with "luring several businesses to the area by offering to train new employees and devising bargain-rate retraining programs" (*U.S. News & World Report* reprint).

Similarly, the MCCD teams up with other segments of the educational structure. An example is the Phoenix Think Tank. Originally designed to help reduce student failure in the Phoenix Union High School District, today's Think Tank energies are directed toward systemic change with the potential for long-range effects on procedures, curriculum, instruction, policies, and resource allocation to ensure successful students.

Think Tank members include leaders from thirteen K–12 school districts, the MCCD, ASU, the Department of Economic Security, the City of Phoenix, and several local businesses and community organizations. Benefits from this collaboration include a reborn focus on the achievement and transfer needs of urban students within the thirteen inner-city school districts; stronger articulation programs to ease student transfer between high school and community colleges and between community colleges and universities; and greater numbers of graduating high school students (currently 70 percent) entering Maricopa community colleges. In addition, the percentage of minority students at four-year universities is increasing and community organizations, school districts, and government agency leaders have become staunch community college advocates.

On the other hand, operating against teamwork are the effects of "FTSE." The Full-Time Student Equivalent, or "Footsie," is a unit of measure used in state funding; the more FTSE a college attracts, the more money it receives. This incentive has driven the colleges to create programs meeting the needs of a wide range of students and employers in the community. "Shaping college system policies to serve FTSE has also shaped the overall culture of the college system," observed one focus group participant (O'Neil, 20).

Although the drive for FTSE is an innate element of the MCCD culture, some people think that it produces a system rewarding enrollment rather than outcomes, and that it encourages competition between colleges rather than cooperation. That is, they think that the colleges are somewhat cautious regarding cooperation with each other for fear the venture might result in a higher enrollment for one compared with another.

Research participants point out that while students view the colleges as one system and enroll in courses at several campuses, there are barriers to doing so. "There is . . . no centralized registration procedure and students are . . . required to apply for admission to a college even if they have been admitted to another college in the [same] system" (O'Neil, 21).

Because of FTSE, some perceive that the colleges also "wage fierce turf battles over occupational programs . . . [making] certain job-training courses unavailable in selected geographical areas" (O'Neil, 22). Finally, FTSE provides the same dollars to support a high-cost nursing course as a lower-cost course like history. This might drive individual colleges to concentrate on providing the least expensive classes while still fulfilling the employment and educational needs in the community.

6. AGGRESSIVENESS
The degree to which people are aggressive and competitive rather than easygoing.

Autonomy is highly valued in the MCCD and is another example of deliberate transformation. Autonomy is reflected, at the most basic level, in the individual accreditation of each college (through the North Central Association of

Colleges and Schools), but its value goes much deeper into the culture and community. Colleges are largely free to determine their own staffing patterns, budget priorities, curricular directions, and enrollment strategies.

Most faculty members are pleased with this level of autonomy at MCCD. One focus group participant said, "Maricopa schools are better in terms of empowerment, openness, a nonthreatening, nonpunishing environment where you can explore and experiment and try new things" (O'Neil, 10). Another participant added, "I have advised student newspapers at three college systems. I've been waiting for something to happen that would create a problem between the newspaper and the administration. It finally sank in to me that it wouldn't be the case here, that life went on. This is the most open place, perhaps in the most open time of my teaching life" (O'Neil, 11). This level of autonomy, however, fosters internal competition, which also can enhance innovation. But on another level, it can also hinder cooperation.

O'Neil study participants felt some things might be more effectively centralized at the District level. The example most frequently mentioned had to do with marketing and advertising practices. Participants thought that it might be better to conduct Districtwide radio advertising rather than having one college in the West Valley pay for a radio spot that reaches students in all areas of the county (O'Neil, 30).

7. STABILITY
The degree to which organizational activities emphasize maintaining the status quo in contrast to growth.

In the MCCD, stability is not necessarily valued. Growth is valued. Thus, in the MCCD, growth *is* stability.Overall, the District has experienced phenomenal innovative, deliberate growth. Of course many factors contributed to its ongoing expansion, but most people would agree that the ultimate driving factors behind the growth of the system are Chancellor Elsner, a forward-thinking board, a booming county, and the funding tied to FTSE.

Within the MCCD, colleges that try to attract more students cultivate innovation. This spurs new programs and services as well as partnerships with business, industry, education, and government. It is this innovation within the MCCD structure that has encouraged colleges to turn to their individual communities for ideas on how to provide more accessible educational opportunities. And the natural result of meeting a community's needs is growth.

Significantly, the community has supported this growth. In a 1994 bond election, passed by almost a two-to-one margin, Maricopa County voters approved a capital development program for the colleges, to be paid with general obligation bonds totaling $385.8 million. "Backing came from approximately fifty organizations, chambers of commerce, professional groups, taxpayer associations, school districts and community-based organizations. . . . Over a seven-year period starting in 1995, bond money will be used to fund [a] major expansion of classrooms and laboratory space, to renovate or remodel aging buildings, implement security and energy-conservation measures, upgrade equipment, open a West Valley Skill Center, add four education centers, build a new campus in the East Valley, and purchase land for a future site in north Scottsdale. Eventually, all campuses will increase classroom space by about 40 percent" (Milestones, "Voters Provide Key For Future").

Other MCCD Strengths

Other strengths worth mentioning in an examination of the MCCD are its accessibility and its cooperative relationships.

ACCESSIBILITY

An important strength of the MCCD is its accessibility to students in terms of geographic location, flexible learning opportunities, economic value, and personal attention.

- **Location**. The colleges are strategically located throughout Maricopa County, with each of the ten colleges drawing students mostly from within six miles of its campus location. Students also can study from home through distance learning, and can attend classes in local churches, high schools, or other community facilities, including some worksites.

- **Convenience**. The flexibility in course offerings in terms of time, location, and delivery method fits the needs of the busiest of students. The sheer number of classes and the wide range of degrees and certifications offered are designed to meet the needs of individuals and local employers alike.

- **Cost**. Another major benefit to students is the cost of tuition, which remains much lower than at local universities. For example, both resident and nonresident annual tuition fees at MCCD colleges are as much as 45% less expensive than at ASU.

- **Faculty**. Research participants perceive MCCD faculty as being more accessible than university professors. They are more likely to provide personalized instruction due to a low faculty-to-student ratio and smaller class sizes, and they routinely provide home telephone numbers to their students (O'Neil, 8).

COOPERATIVE RELATIONSHIPS

Another significant strength of the MCCD is its emphasis on building positive, cooperative relationships with all of its constituencies. "Overall, the college system enjoys widespread community support and is highly respected nationally. [Its] many strengths are universally understood by all stakeholders" (O'Neil, 28).

An example of community support for the MCCD comes in the form of grants and contributions from individuals, groups, and organizations to the MCCD Foundation. The Foundation's current campaign involves raising $12 million in scholarship funds from local donors.

The District also shares a healthy relationship with the local state university, ASU. Among other things, the educational institutions share student information databases. In addition, MCCD provides a much-needed service in relation to the universities. According to one focus group member, "A high school education doesn't mean much anymore and the costs of going four years to a university will be out of reach for a lot of people. So, as time goes by, our system will be called on more . . . as more people take those first two years in our system" (O'Neil, 8).

The Future

To ensure a prosperous future, the MCCD leaders must address several pressing issues revolving around leadership, growth, and external forces.

LEADERSHIP

Probably the most momentous change on the horizon for the MCCD is the looming retirement of Chancellor Elsner in the summer of 1999. His absence and the development of a new administration under the next chancellor, could drastically alter the District's culture in the next millennium. MCCD has enjoyed so much growth and prosperity in its development that it might well be challenged to handle such significant change gracefully. Elsner's departure will offer a strong challenge to the culture of innovation and transformation that he and his management team established over his nearly twenty-two year tenure.

Moreover, even without a radical change in philosophy under a new chancellor, the MCCD will likely experience the exodus of a substantial percentage of its leaders and faculty because many are eligible for retirement at around the time of Elsner's expected retirement. Further, they represent and personify the culture and values of a leader soon to depart. The dominant question is how the departure of a visionary leader will affect the culture and values of the system in the twenty-first century.

Given that when one part of a system changes all other parts of the system are affected, these significant modifications in the leadership of the MCCD could have various effects. In a best-case scenario, the District could thrive—given adequate funding, adequate flexibility, further *deliberate* transformation, and a new chancellor who is in tune with the dominant MCCD culture.

In the worst case, the departure of Chancellor Elsner could cause a paralyzing sense of loss and a resistance to any changes that are attempted by a new chancellor, particularly if he or she is not yet fully sensitive to the current culture. However, even with a major change in leadership style, this scenario could be avoided or minimized and a level of continuity maintained, given strong direction from the Governing Board, leadership from the college presidents, and continued market-driven innovative action by the colleges. Several issues face the new chancellor and the governing board, as described below.

GROWTH

Under Elsner's leadership, the watchword has been expansion. The District has become used to adding colleges and educational centers year after year, and its constituents believe that growth is important. But the leadership needs to continue to look carefully at planned systematic growth and to ask questions. Is growth in one area happening at the expense of another part of the system? Is the planned expansion truly needed? Does technology provide sufficient access that brick and mortar facilities are unnecessary, or are such facilities too expensive to justify? Or is the technology too expensive to pursue?

EXTERNAL FORCES

Technology and other external forces might well lead to a redefinition of a "multicollege system," not only for the MCCD but nationwide. Multicollege systems of the future may not be close geographically, but rather united by mutual needs and strengths.

- Technology. Increased and broader uses for technology mean increased competition, not only among the MCCD colleges but also from public and private educational entities and businesses locally and nationally. MCCD colleges need to redefine the competition to account for external players, not *only* each other.

- Meeting Employer Needs. According to the O'Neil research, the District must continue to develop "training programs to meet the needs of Valley employers. . . . It is of key importance, regardless of the training area, to match the curriculum to the job market. Clearly, even closer coordination with industry through advisory councils or other mechanisms is called for . . . to keep the college system current in this area" (O'Neil, 32).

- Scope. Maricopa Community Colleges could be called upon to provide more certifications or even applied baccalaureate degrees, depending on their communities' needs. This could expand the definition of a community college. "The college system stakeholders," according to the O'Neil research, "envision a broadening of the mission by pushing the envelope even further, in . . . providing open-door, universal access for just about anyone who wants any kind of education at any time for any purpose" (O'Neil, 5).

Conclusions and Implications

Other multicollege systems can profit from the experiences of deliberate transformation by recognizing four important lessons learned by the MCCD.

1. **Recognize the power of shared vision, mission, and values**. Developed with the broad participation and understanding of stakeholders, a shared vision, mission, and values can be powerful driving forces in a complex multicollege system:

2. **Pay Attention to Culture**. The dominant culture of a multicollege system is an expression of the core values shared by a majority of its employees. The extent to which various characteristics of the culture are emphasized greatly influences how things get done and how employees behave.

3. **Don't Over-Manage**. One important choice leaders can make to build a foundation for success in any multicollege system is not to over-manage. Top-level leaders must not get mired in the intricate details of running the system. Their job is leadership: looking at the system's major issues, identifying significant trends, and setting outcomes as well as limitations.

4. **Learn**. Multicollege systems that wish to manage change better or to transform their culture can use the MCCD structure and experience as

a starting point, but they should also look for other successful leaders and institutional models from which to learn. Using a network of resources, asking questions, reading, and filtering the data pertinent to their particular needs can unearth the appropriate elements to help them thrive.

PART FOUR

CHALLENGES TO FUTURE DEVELOPMENT: FUTURE TRENDS AND IMPEDIMENTS

This concluding section of the monograph—let it be confessed—demands a certain amount of prescience. The aim of this section is to present an outlook about the future role and direction of multicampus systems, and thus give a future context in which the problems and processes treated in the earlier chapters may be viewed.

The earlier contributors have also addressed how some of the key elements surrounding multicampus systems—the new electronic technologies, in particular; different student constituencies, entrepreneurial competitors such as the University of Phoenix; and, of course, funding—will impact these bodies. Chancellor Donald Langenberg in the concluding chapter sees the multicampus system of the future as a "learning organization," and offers a visionary and articulate discussion of tomorrow's system. Reading Don Langenberg's chapter brings to mind the futuristic observations of Frederick Balderston:

> The university [system] is the "information and learning organization" par excellence, society's main repository of systematic knowledge and its main contributor to tomorrow's scientific and humanistic understanding. The university [system] is designed precisely for that mission. I venture the guess that the few years remaining of this century, and all of the next, will see information and learning organizations dominant in the advanced countries and be important in transitional societies as well. Other types of enterprises and institutions may therefore need to pay special attention to

the [system] as the archetype of the organization where discovery and trans-mission of knowledge are both the reasons for existence and the occasion for enduring satisfaction. (Balderston, *Managing Today's University*, xvi)

However, an historical perspective may also be instructive as prologue here. As Frank Bowen and Eugene Lee remind us in their introductory remarks, the postwar multicampus system they observed has changed less than the world surrounding it. Clark Kerr made the salient observations that universities are one of the most impervious institutions to change, and that "they helped to change the world but have themselves been much less changed than most of the rest of the world" (Kerr, "Critical Age" 184). If Kerr's observation that "every-thing else changes but the university [system] mostly endures" is correct, we must, therefore, give heed and take warning about system intransigence. Whatever the shape of things to come, it is important that the multicampus system does not have its role imposed on it by society. It must take a position of leadership, making new values for a new millenium and responding to changes that will be so pervasive they will touch the level of each of us in ways that we were not aware.

12

ON THE HORIZON
The Learning System

Donald N. Langenberg

The university system, already an ubiquitous
feature of the higher education landscape, is
destined to evolve into new and unusual forms
in the twenty-first century.

The university system and the multicampus university have become the dominant (if sometimes controversial) organizational structures in public higher education in the United States. The reasons for this are explored elsewhere in this volume. This chapter presents some ideas about the likely nature of their evolution through the early years of the twenty-first century.

Past and Present

Forecasting the future is a perilous enterprise. Success at the macroscopic level is possible, but rare. Failure at the microscopic level is almost certain. If one must enter a realm more thickly populated by fools than by angels, however, it is helpful to begin by stepping back a few paces to gain a panoramic view of what now is and what has gone before.

The fundamental unit of teaching and learning is composed of one teacher and one student. The classic example is Aristotle and a young student who became known as Alexander the Great. But even before this glorious pair came together, several such fundamental units had been organized into a community of teachers and learners dedicated to the study of philosophy. Aristotle's mentor, Plato, founded the Academy of Athens early in the fourth century BC. Later endowed, the Academy flourished for more than nine centuries, until it was finally closed by the Byzantine emperor Justinian. Thus lived and died the first known college in the western world, the first organizational *system* designed to foster higher learning.

The Dark Ages that followed the fall of Rome stifled further evolution in higher education for half a millennium, but the notion of a *collegium* or college survived in monasteries across Europe. There what remained of recorded classical scholarship was preserved, copied, and circulated.

As the Dark Ages gave way to the Middle Ages, higher learning emerged from the monasteries. In Bologna a college of law was founded late in the ninth century. Several centuries later, it was joined with colleges of medicine and theology in what is generally recognized as the first university in Europe, the University of Bologna. (The Arab University of Al-Azhar in Cairo preceded Bologna by more than a century.)

The organizational pattern established in the earliest universities persists today. A university is an assemblage of schools or colleges, most focused on a single broad area of study, with the whole designed to offer a comprehensive array of educational opportunities. A university is in effect a system of subsystems.

In their early centuries European universities dedicated themselves to fostering and developing the basic learned professions: law, theology, and medicine. Then, during the Renaissance, they became engaged in the revival of classical learning and thus created the area of scholarship (and, of course, the college) we now label "liberal arts" or "arts and sciences." During the Renaissance there also began a fundamental change in the purposes of universities. Originally, they had focussed on the essentially medieval purposes of preserving and transmitting existing knowledge. Now, to these was added the creation of new knowledge (thereby, in a sense, returning them to the tradition of Plato's Academy).

Over the ensuing centuries the resulting inexorable expansion of knowledge led to repeated subdivisions of areas of knowledge. Natural philosophy, for example, fragmented into astronomy, physics, chemistry, biology, geology, etc. And then, with terrifying inevitability, universities and colleges fragmented into ever-more-specialized academic departments representing specialty areas within subdisciplines within disciplines. Sub-subsystems within subsystems within systems! The modern university has come to resemble a huge family of nested Russian dolls.

Some believe that this modern university represents the pinnacle, the endpoint of academic organizational evolution. They expect (and desire) no further significant change, apparently assuming that the forces that drove the previous twenty-four centuries of evolution have ceased to operate. The facts suggest that nothing could be further from the truth.

In the United States, the Morrill Act of 1862 provided enormous impetus to the development of state-supported universities intended to provide higher education to many, ultimately most, American citizens. After World War II, the G.I. Bill reinforced and accelerated the trend to mass higher education. A consequence has been the creation in each state of many public universities and community colleges—in larger states as many as fifty or sixty altogether. From the standpoint of state political and educational authorities, the prospect of that many tax-supported institutions pursuing independent paths in the time-honored tradition of academic autonomy is an invitation to chaos. It is therefore not surprising that in the twentieth century new supra-university organizational schemes developed in the United States. They occurred in every state and in bewildering variety. According to McGuinness ("Perspectives"), who provides a useful taxonomy, "Multi-campus higher education systems are now the dominant form of governance of public colleges and universities in the U.S."

My purpose in presenting the foregoing historical recitation is to explain and support the following assertion: For the last twenty-four centuries humankind has met its growing need for higher learning through institutions of ever-increasing scale, span, and complexity. None of the forces that drove this evolution in the past have vanished. Indeed, new ones have appeared. Therefore, we can expect to see continuing organizational evolution of educational institutions in the future, and should not be surprised by the appearance of organizational systems quite unlike any existing ones.

My assertion that there are new evolutionary forces at work requires some explanation. But first, let us explore the notion of "system," both in general and as it applies to higher education.

What's a System?

Even the most unobservant citizen must have noticed that the world is becoming more complex, that increasingly everything seems to be connected with everything else. The three-foot snowdrift blocking my driveway is apparently connected with something called El Niño in the Pacific off South America. The unpleasant sudden drop in my net worth yesterday seems to be connected with some financial shenanigans in Bangkok. E-mail contact with my daughter has been cut off because some computer in Brussels crashed.

This trend toward increasing complexity and interconnectedness is as applicable to higher education as it is to the systems behind the examples above. (Each of the examples reflects the underlying presence of a system whose components are strongly interacting.) Such phenomena are the objects of study in the discipline of systems engineering. Here follow some basic definitions and concepts from the first chapter of a textbook entitled *Systems Engineering and Analysis*, by Blanchard and Fabrycky. I think the reader will find them useful aids in thinking about university systems.

> A system is a set of interrelated components working together toward some common objective. The set of components has the following properties:
>
> 1. The properties and behavior of each component of the set has an effect on the properties and behavior of the set as a whole.
> 2. The properties and behavior of each component of the set depends upon the properties and behavior of at least one other component in the set.
> 3. Each possible subset of components has the two properties listed above; the components cannot be divided into independent subsets.
>
> The properties given above ensure that the set of components composing a system always has some characteristic or behavior pattern that cannot be exhibited by any of its subsets. A system is much more than the sum of its component parts. However, the components of a system may themselves be systems, and every system may be part of a larger system in a hierarchy.
>
> Everything that remains outside the boundaries of the system is considered to be the environment. However, no system is completely isolated from its environment. A closed system is one that does not interact significantly with its environment. The environment only provides a context for the system. Closed systems exhibit the characteristic of equilibrium resulting from internal rigidity that maintains the system in spite of influences from the environment.

(Was there ever a better description of the ideal ivory-tower university?)

> An open system allows information, energy, and matter to cross its boundaries. Open systems interact with their environment, examples being plants, ecological systems, and business organizations. They exhibit the characteristics of steady state, wherein a dynamic interaction of system elements adjusts to changes in the environment. Because of this steady state, open systems are self-regulatory and often self-adaptive (Blanchard and Fabrycky, 2).

Why a University System?

What, then, is the purpose of organizing universities into university systems (or, for that matter, faculty into departments, departments into colleges, and colleges into universities)? The answer lies in the system definitions and concepts above. A properly designed and managed system can be far more than the sum of its components, and can provide benefits none of its components could provide alone.

Elsewhere (Langenberg , "Why" 8–9) I have described some of these benefits. They include (with quotes from the indicated reference):

- **Synergy**. "For the states, it means the ability to tap easily into the combined brainpower of multiple institutions to address economic, environmental, health care, and other public service needs." A recent example is the rapid and comprehensive response of the University System of Maryland in the summer of 1997 to an economic, environmental, and health-care crisis triggered by the eruption of a toxic single-cell organism (Pfiesteria) in tributaries of the Chesapeake Bay.

- **Strategy**. This benefit goes to the heart of the very definition of a system stated in the previous section. It depends on the strength of a crucial function of system management, leadership.

- **Efficiency**. The cost savings that can be achieved through collaborative efforts among several universities could in principle occur without a system. In practice, however, without a system leadership to encourage or, when necessary, force such efforts, they are quite unlikely to occur.

- **Accountability**. A system can ensure global accountability at the statewide level while adapting accountability requirements at the institutional level to the particular mission and circumstances of each institution.

- **Integrity**. "Like Janus, the central administration for a university system must keep watch both internally and externally. The internal watch ensures accountability, while the external watch ensures institutional integrity." The latter requires buffering the system's institutions from undue and inappropriate external intrusion.

Like all benefits, these come at some cost. The need to respect and take into account the needs of sister institutions within a system is viewed by some members as cumbersome and burdensome. No doubt living among siblings is more complicated than being an only child, but there are compensations.

Among other costs often cited by critics of systems are inefficiency due to added bureaucracy and a tendency to homogenize or "level down" the system's institutions. These are clearly spurious claims. The first would have us believe that a dozen governing boards and a dozen board staffs are more efficient than just one of each. The second ignores the fact that system leadership can provide an important countervailing force to the homogenizing influence of every institution's natural desire to "keep up with the Joneses." All in all, the benefits of a university system can far outweigh any costs, real or imagined.

It is worth noting that the benefits I have claimed for university systems have long been claimed by academic departments, colleges, and universities. Interestingly, the benefits of these subsystems are rarely questioned. Perhaps that's simply because departments, colleges, and universities have been around a lot longer than university systems, and we've come to take them for granted. Perhaps it is a general rule that, when a system becomes taken for granted, it becomes a subsystem and the next level of complexity evolves. Now let us turn to the forces currently driving the further evolution of university systems.

Evolutionary Forces

INFORMATION TECHNOLOGY

It is by now abundantly clear that the flowering of information technology is changing almost every aspect of our lives. In no area is that more true than in education, higher education in particular. That is so because the fundamental purpose of education is to transform information into knowledge, understanding, and, sometimes, wisdom. That requires that we generate, store, process, and disseminate information effectively and efficiently. Any new tool that radically changes and enhances our ability to do those things must inevitably and radically change and enhance the organizational systems we use in teaching and learning.

Universities' initial applications of information technology followed a pattern familiar in the initial stages of earlier new technologies. Faculty and staff simply used the new tools to do better what they were already doing. Telephones expanded and speeded communications previously conducted face-to-face or in writing. University scientists used computers to carry out computations on a scale impractical with older technologies. University libraries computerized their card catalogs and administrative offices computerized their accounting systems.

More recently, however, higher education has begun to recognize the profound implications of the merger of telecommunications technology with computer technology. We have begun to experiment with the heretofore impossible and unthinkable. Researchers located on different continents have learned to conduct team research as if they worked in the same laboratory. Students in different states take the same courses and receive their degrees at commencements on campuses they have never previously visited. The "virtual university" is rapidly moving from concept to reality.

Technological revolutions have occurred before, of course, but this one is different in pace. When Karl Benz replaced a horse with an internal combustion engine in 1885, the result, though revolutionary, continued to resemble and be called a "horseless carriage" for decades. More than half a century passed before the true nature and consequences of the resulting automotive transportation system became evident: a car (or two or three) in every garage, interstate highways, shopping malls, suburban sprawl, dying city centers, etc.

The information technology revolution is proceeding much faster. Moore's Law (which states that the power of integrated circuits on silicon chips doubles every eighteen months and their price halves) seems likely to continue to be valid for the forseeable future. The World Wide Web has mutated from an esoteric tool used only by a couple of thousand elementary-particle physicists to a common household utility in just a few years. As we in higher education come to grips with this revolution, scrambling toward the forefront while trying to escape being run over, we had better abandon our traditional academic caution and move a good deal more smartly. In what direction is not entirely clear, but move we must!

Demographic Diversification

The facts about our country's future high school graduates are now familiar. For most of the next decade they will steadily increase in number as a result of the "baby boom echo," and their ethnic and racial composition will steadily diversify. The portion of each high school graduating class that seeks immediate entry into a higher education institution will also steadily increase. The result for higher education will be larger entering freshman classes of far greater diversity. At least one state (California) is swiftly approaching the moment when the undergraduate student bodies of its colleges and universities will be one hundred percent minority. That is, *no* ethnic or racial group will be in the majority.

These quantitative and qualitative dimensions of demographic diversification certainly pose challenges for our university systems. But there is another less well-recognized dimension of the student population that has even greater potential to induce substantial structural changes in universities and university systems. That is the age diversification of their student clientele.

Over the past decade, despite tight university budgets and the tail end of a period of decline in the number of high school graduates, the population of American college and university students in the 18–24 year age range has been increasing slowly, at about one percent per year. During that same period the number of students 25 years old and older has been increasing nearly four times as fast. As this trend continues, there's obviously going to be a crossover some day. In fact, it's coming sooner than one might suppose, somewhere around the turn of the century. Beginning very early in the twenty-first century, the majority of American college and university students will be 25 and older!

That easily predictable event will have profound consequences for colleges, universities, and university systems. (Most of us have heard about the Year-Two-Thousand [Y2K] Problem, the prospective mass failure of computer systems unable to cope with the last two digits of the year rolling over from 99 to 00. But for higher education institutions, the accession to majority status of older students is the *real* Y2K problem.) This trend represents a problem simply because these students aren't the ones institutions are used to. They are working adults, they are parents, they are very serious—if part-time—students, and they are citizens who actually vote. As long as it was possible to marginalize them as "night-school" or "continuing-education" or "nontraditional" students, most institutions didn't have to pay much attention to how or how well they served these students' educational needs. Perhaps traditional private colleges and universities can continue to ignore these students, but public colleges, universities, and university systems cannot. They must learn how to serve these adults in adult ways, on their terms. This means delivering top-quality academic programs to them, tailored to their special needs, wherever and whenever they want them. With great historical serendipity, the technology to make these new educational services possible is arriving on the scene just in time.

The challenge and opportunity here may be even greater than simple projections of current circumstances would suggest. One of the principal reasons we are seeing such growth in adult students is that our nation is successfully negotiating the transition from an industrial economy based on natural resources and manufacturing to a postindustrial, knowledge-based service economy based on brain power. In such an economy education is a primary resource, perhaps *the* primary resource.

Part of a good college education, the part that teaches one how to think and learn and provides a basic kit of knowledge, is pretty durable. That is the part usually called "general education" or a "liberal education," and it can last a lifetime. But the part that teaches one how to apply thinking to a task somebody else will pay to have done is pretty evanescent. In our rapidly changing knowledge-based economy, that evanescence is increasing in pace and frequency. Consequently, more and more adults are discovering that they must continue to educate themselves if they want better jobs, or perhaps even to keep the jobs they already have. Jobs these days have a tendency to turn into different jobs very rapidly; the sign on your office door may soon read "Keep up or keep out!"

Estimates of the steady-state continuing education needs of America's twenty-first century work force suggest that 10–20 million workers will need to be engaged in formal postsecondary education and/or training at any given time. Compare that with the current total enrollment in our nation's colleges and universities, about 15 million. That this is not an entirely ridiculous estimate is suggested by the fact that, even today, total annual expenditures by American businesses on their post-secondary education and/or training programs are comparable with the total budgets of all American colleges and universities. Most of this enormous postsecondary enterprise is invisible from the viewpoint of higher education (with notable exceptions such as Motorola University), but it exists nevertheless.

One can of course argue interminably about the appropriate balance and relative value of education and training in our nation's total post-secondary education and training enterprise. My point here is simply that this enterprise is already enormous and is destined to grow substantially in the twenty-first century. (If one considers that similar forces are operating in all highly developed economies worldwide, the numbers become even more impressive.) This huge potential education market has not escaped the attention of the global business community, or of a few higher education institutions, here and abroad. American colleges and universities now have a market share in the United States somewhere around fifty percent, and it may be shrinking. Their market share abroad is negligible. The question is, what are they going to do about all this?

Creeping Systemization

I suggested above that our world is growing more complex, and that no enterprise is wholly autonomous or unrelated to other enterprises. For better or worse, I believe our world in general and higher education in particular are undergoing what might be called "creeping systemization." I also believe that this is happening for one or another of three very good reasons.

The first is that, as we learn more about how our world works, we discover new relationships and linkages. That is, we discover systems and system behaviors that may always have existed but previously went undetected. Environmental and ecological systems are examples. So are those that exhibit the phenomena studied in the new science of "chaos," in which tiny changes in stimuli can lead to huge and essentially unpredictable differences in outcome, even in very simple systems. (Consider the now standard example of the Chinese butterfly whose gently flapping wings can in principle induce a sequence of atmospheric events that culminates in a hurricane that devastates the East Coast of the United States.)

The second reason for creeping systemization in higher education in particular is that the nature of many existing university systems is changing. To understand how, it is helpful to return to the definitions given above of closed and open systems. We are used to thinking of universities as closed systems. Yet even some traditional universities are better characterized as open assemblies of closed systems. In these, the constituent components—departments and colleges—interact relatively weakly. Harvard, with its "every tub on its own bottom" philosophy, is an example.

More generally, most universities seem to be moving toward becoming open systems, in several different ways. It is increasingly common to hear of activist governing boards and intrusive legislatures that bring societal pressures for reform and accountability to bear directly on universities. Universities themselves are becoming more sensitive and responsive to their many clienteles—their students, their alumni, and their business communities, for example.

Furthermore, in their efforts to cope with the consequences of severely constrained financial resources, many universities are adopting new operating modes. Large public universities have traditionally operated as closed, nearly self-sufficient communities that provide to themselves—and often to others—a comprehensive array of services. They operate publishing houses, hotels, restaurants, apartment houses, and police forces. They sell everything from parking spaces to popular entertainment to brain surgery. (One is reminded of the trans-Atlantic luxury ships of yore—the Titanic perhaps.)

Now, however, "out-sourcing" and "privatization" have become watchwords. The rationale for these new operational approaches is that a university ought to focus on its basic academic functions of teaching and research, and leave the operation of the necessary support functions to those who can provide them more efficiently and cost-effectively. Following are examples of initiatives of this kind, some recent and some of long standing:

- Operation of campus food services (the "restaurants") is contracted out to commercial firms, including fast-food chains.
- Operation of campus bookstores is contracted out to national bookstore chains.

- Operation of student residences (the "hotels") is turned over to private landlords and property management companies.

- Delivery of clinical care by health professional faculty is organized in faculty practice organizations that operate semi-independently of the university.

- University hospitals are spun off as free-standing enterprises, either not-for-profit or for-profit, and become parts of expanding managed care organizations.

- Universities (e.g., the University of Maryland, College Park) explore privatization of their entire utility infrastructures.

- Universities (e.g., the University of Pennsylvania) contract out the management and operation of their entire physical plant and real estate organizations.

- Universities (e.g., the California State University system) seek to outsource their entire information technology infrastructure to consortia of vendors.

Even more unusual and less traditional systemic higher education initiatives are emerging. For example, in a few states (including Maryland), university systems are joining with state departments of education and state higher-education coordinating agencies in "K–16 Partnerships." These partnerships have as their initial objective the fostering of standards- and performance-based reform of their states' elementary and secondary schools. A fundamental premise of these partnerships is that elementary, secondary, and postsecondary educational institutions ought to be viewed as a single strongly interacting system, one that ought to be (though now is not) seamless. It follows from that premise that reforms in the elementary and secondary schools must necessarily be accompanied by related reforms in the universities, e.g., in their teacher education and in standards- and performance-based admissions and graduation.

The Western Governors University (née Western Virtual University) is another example of the formation of new levels and types of open systemic interactions. Familiar university systems are intra-state entities. Here we have a new system of universities spanning fifteen states and one territory, established for a particular purpose—bringing educational programs from all the universities in the participating states to the burgeoning population of adult learners.

The reader will recognize that all of these initiatives have the effect of pushing universities away from being closed systems and toward being very open systems. Alternatively, if one insists on thinking of "proper" systems as closed systems that interact only weakly with their environments, then the above initiatives must be seen as creating ever larger systems in which traditional universities are but one component, and in which the other components may not be universities.

It is important to recognize, however, that none of these new systems fits the industrial-age hierarchical model that underlies the thinking of those who are most fond of "system bashing." As noted above, critics of university systems commonly charge them with adding unnecessary layers of bureaucracy and homogenizing their components. These charges are presumably intended to call up an image like the early Ford Motor Company, mass-producing Model T's, each one identical to the next, with Henry himself controlling everything from the top. But today's emerging systems bear little organizational resemblance to Ford's early days or to the General Motors that Alfred P. Sloan Jr. created. Industrial-age organization charts simply cannot accommodate the emerging organizational realities of the information age and the twenty-first century. In these times, the key concepts are no longer "authority" and "control," but "partnerships," "collaboration," "cooperation"—and perhaps even "creative chaos."

Further support for this view can be found in the recent history of two competing businesses, Apple and Microsoft. Both developed early computer operating systems. Apple opted for a closed system in order to maintain tight control over its development and use. Microsoft opted for an open system. One consequence is that Microsoft's headquarters facility in Redmond, Washington is remarkably modest in size considering the scale of the corporate behemoth it houses. It disguises the fact that the *real* Microsoft enterprise comprises thousands of "independent" collaborating software developers spread across the globe. Another consequence is that Microsoft dominates its industry (not to mention our lives), while Apple is struggling.

The third good reason for creeping systemization is that totally new types of systems are appearing. An example of profound import and fundamental importance for higher education is the Internet.

A university has been aptly defined as a community of scholars gathered around a great library. That definition has been valid for twenty-three centuries, since the founding of the Great Library of Alexandria, around which developed what was arguably the world's first university. (The city of Alexandria, of course, was founded by Alexander the Great, student of Aristotle, whose mentor Plato founded the Academy of Athens. As they say, what goes around comes around!)

The definition was reinforced and made widely applicable by Gutenberg's fifteenth-century reinvention in the west of printing with moveable type.

The products of Gutenberg's technology are physical artifacts called books and journals. They are portable, relatively inexpensive, long lasting, and easy to use. To make them readily accessible to users it is necessary to collect them together and protect them from the elements in a building. After five centuries of printing, the collected mass of important and relevant books and journals is huge. A respectable university library must contain millions of volumes. Consequently, the library building must be very large, and the library's users must be assisted by, and the library managed by, professional information technologists called librarians.

Such a library is now to be found near the center of every university campus. The rest of the campus typically consists of an assemblage of classrooms, laboratories, offices, dining halls, student residences, athletic facilities, etc., all designed to support the community of scholars, faculty, and students gathered about the library. This is what most people think of when they think of a university.

It is important to understand that the campus exists because the library is there, because the library is the heart of the university's information infrastructure. It is also important to understand that the library takes its traditional form and function from the intrinsic nature of Gutenberg's technology.

Enter now the Internet, a creature of the information technology revolution. It represents a totally different technology supporting a radically new kind of information infrastructure. That information infrastructure is globally distributed rather than localized. It is interactive rather than immutably fixed; the user can change what is being used. The information it carries can take many forms, including moving and malleable images and sound, in addition to serial text. It can speak, and will soon be able to understand and respond "intelligently" to speech. Though it does operate under standards and protocols, the Internet exhibits few other signs of conventional organization. It appears to have no controlling management, no central headquarters. Who owns it? Everybody and nobody.

The Internet is surely a precursor of the ultimate open system. In my view, it will be the driving force behind the transformation of the very institutions that played a central role in its creation, our universities. That is why the visionary management guru, Peter Drucker, has said (Lenzner and Johnson, 122), "Thirty years from now the big university campuses will be relics. Universities won't survive. It's as large a change as when we first got the printed book."

Twenty-First Century, Here We Come

Now comes the hard part, figuring out what all this means for university systems in the twenty-first century. That task must and will be the principal preoccupation of many higher education, political, and societal leaders for the foreseeable future. I can only offer some personal speculations about what might happen.

First, university systems will become even more necessary and important than they now are—but not necessarily in the forms they now take. McGuinness ("Model") has written, "Despite all the challenges and a few successful, radical changes, multicampus systems are likely to be even more a characteristic of American public higher education in 2015 as they are in 1995. What will change most dramatically is what constitutes a 'system'; changes will be made in how systems are led and how they function, both internally and in relationship to multiple external stakeholders." I concur.

An example of what might change appears in Lee and Bowen's seminal book, *The Multicampus University*. They assert that a "defining characteristic" of a multicampus university is the existence of a geographically distinct community. That was true in 1971 and remains essentially true today. Most higher education institutions now define their characters and their missions partly in terms of their geographical locations and service areas. They see themselves as national universities, statewide universities, regional universities and colleges, or community colleges, for example. But the information technology revolution is now in the process of pulling the rug out from under this "defining characteristic." In a world where any institution with the will and the technology can deliver academic programs to anyone on the face of the Earth, anywhere, any time, will it really matter where that institution is "located"? Where will the virtual university be found? Will it have adequate parking?

I would also expect to see a continuation of the "unbundling" of university functions that is now under way. Many universities and university systems might well become holding companies that act as prime contractors with their various clients (including students) to provide integrated education or research services that actually are provided by subcontractors. Such subcontractors might provide police and security services, marketing and student recruitment, financial management, alumni management, or any of the other functions cited in the out-sourcing/privatization list above. Even instruction might be out-sourced (about which more below).

Still other examples lead us into the realm of "things unmentionable in polite academic company." Many would argue that the most important core functions of a university include quality assurance and performance certification. These are evidenced in the awarding of degrees, with qualifiers such as Summa Cum Laude, and in the added value commonly perceived to be inherent in statements such as, "I am a Yale graduate." One of the most important unanswered questions about the brave new world of the virtual university is how these essential functions are to be provided.

I have argued elsewhere ("Degrees" A64) that degrees and diplomas are obsolescent, and that new kinds of finer-grained and more informative learner performance evaluation and certification mechanisms need to be developed. If twenty-first century learners obtain their educations from a variety of institutions in many different modes over the courses of their lives, or even at the same time, then it seems obvious that there ought to be some sort of common currency representing the value added by education, wherever or however it is obtained. Currently we are in a situation analogous to the era when many banks and local jurisdictions issued their own monetary currency. The value of a currency unit depended on its source, and interchangeability was problematic. In higher education, similarly, the value of a Princeton degree is generally thought to be higher than one from the University of Southern North Dakota, and every transfer student knows the difficulty of cashing in credits from one institution at another.

Developing a common academic currency will not be easy—witness the difficulty our European friends are having with the Euro. But I think it's a goal worth pursuing, and I believe it might well be done by some independent organization established to serve us all. Some elements of this proposal are already present in the accreditation services provided by the regional accreditation associations and the performance evaluation services provided by the Educational Testing Service and the American College Testing Service.

Then there's that curious and fascinating university function called intercollegiate athletics. Steve Muller, former president of The Johns Hopkins University, has suggested that universities ought to sell their athletic teams to their alumni. I think a more rational and potentially profitable form of privatization here, for the few major athletic powers at least, would be to contract for the management and operation of their major revenue sports with the professional athletic leagues for which they already serve as farm teams.

Let me return to the notion of instructional subcontractors by returning to ancient precedent, as academics are wont to do. Many of the earliest universities patterned themselves on the University of Paris. That university was originally a corporation of its teachers. They collected fees from the students and determined the policies of the corporate body, the university. Though the governance of the corporation eventually passed into other hands at Paris and elsewhere, its original form survives today in the minds of our faculties as an ideal that might be termed the "University of Nirvana." Faculties generally believe that in the ideal university, in any *real* university, it is the faculty who propose and dispose in all matters of fundamental importance.

In a curious way, it may be that information technology offers at least some university faculty members a means of returning to the twelfth century. I think it not beyond the realm of possibility that groups of professors might incorporate themselves in order to provide instructional services to many universities simultaneously. There is an obvious market. Twigg has noted that in large comprehensive universities or community colleges offering many hundreds, even thousands, of undergraduate courses, close to half of the credit-hour "production" is typically in about twenty-five courses. These are precisely the courses too often delegated to junior faculty and graduate teaching assistants. Might not a really powerful group of professors using the best technology substantially enhance the quality of these courses with great benefit to the students and considerable profit to themselves?

Other early universities followed an alternate model, the University of Bologna. Bologna was a corporation of its students, who hired their own teachers and determined the policies of the corporation. Here again, one can imagine a twenty-first century revival of this ancient model. The possibilities inherent in the notion of a national (or international) student corporation contracting with universities or university systems—or faculty corporations—for educational services of the highest quality at the best prices are fascinating to contemplate. I happily leave that to the reader.

Before passing on to my conclusion, I feel bound to address the perennial question: "What does all this mean for tenure?" My answer is simple: If the evolution of higher education in the twenty-first century proceeds as I envision it might, I think tenure may eventually drown in its own irrelevance.

In this chapter I have tried to describe trends and influences that have brought universities and university systems to the threshold of the next century, beginning twenty-four centuries ago. These thoughts then led me to some speculations about the nature of multicampus (and, indeed, no-campus) university systems in the twenty-first century. My speculations are almost certainly wrong in detail and quite possibly misguided in general. But, to borrow and adapt a line from Shakespeare, all the world's a system! If my colleagues will keep that thought in mind as they help fashion higher education's future, then we may together succeed in creating a true learning system.

Almanacs, The Chronicle of Higher Education Almanac Issues, 1993–97. Washington, DC: The Chronicle of Higher Education, 1993–97.

Ashworth, K. H. "Performance Based Funding in Higher Education: The Texas Case Study." *Change* (Nov./Dec. 1994): 8–15.

Assembly Committee on Higher Education (ACHE). "The Master Plan for Higher Education in Focus." Sacramento: The Assembly, April 1993.

Association of Independent California Colleges and Universities (AICCU). *The Uncertain Partnership.* Sacramento: AICCU, May 1995.

Atkinson, R. C. "UC and California's Futures." San Francisco: Commonwealth Club, 2 May 1996.

Balderston, Frederick E. *Managing Today's University: Strategics for Viability, Change, and Excellence.* 2d ed. San Francisco: Jossey-Bass, 1995.

Bartelt, David W. "The University and Community Development: A Common Cause." *Metropolitan Universities* 6.3 (1995): 15–27.

Benjamin, Roger. "Looming Deficits: Courses, Consequences, and Cures." *Change* 30.2 (Mar./Apr. 1998): 12-17.

Blanchard, Benjamin S., and Wolter J. Fabrycky. *Systems Engineering and Analysis.* Englewood Cliffs, NJ: Prentice Hall, 1990.

Board of Regents. "A Study of the UW System in the 21st Century: A Final Report by the Board of Regents." Madison: Board of Regents, June 1996.

Boot, M. "Redefining Higher Education." *Christian Science Monitor.* 16 Nov. 1992.

Bowen, Frank M., et al. *State Structures for the Governance of Higher Education: A Comparative Study*. San Jose: The California Higher Education Policy Center, 1996.

Bracco, K. R. *State Structures for the Governance of Higher Education: An Annotated Bibliography*. San Jose: The California Higher Education Policy Center, 1997.

Bracco, K. R., and Y. Sanchez-Penley. "New York: Politics and the Funding of Higher Education." In Patrick Callan and J. E. Finney, eds. *Public and Private Financing of Higher Education: Shaping Public Policy for the Future*. Phoenix: Oryx Press, 1997.

Burke, Joseph C. *New Perspectives on System and Campus Roles in a Public Multicampus System*. Albany: State University of New York, 1994.

———. "Preserving Quality While Enhancing Productivity." *Studies in Public Higher Education* 4. Albany: State University of New York, 1993.

———. "Unity and Diversity: SUNY's Challenge Not Its Choice." In *New Perspectives on System and Campus Roles in a Public Multicampus System. Studies in Higher Education* 5. Albany: State University of New York, 1994.

Burke, Joseph C., and A. M. Serban. *Performance Funding and Budgeting for Public Higher Education: Current Status and Future Prospects*. Albany: Rockefeller Institute of Government, 1997.

California Citizens Commission on Higher Education (CCCHE). "Promises to Keep and Miles to Go: A Summary of the Joint Meeting Between the Citizens Commission and the California Education Roundtable on January 23, 1997." Los Angeles: The Commission, 1997.

California Community Colleges (CCC). Board of Governors. "Basic Agenda for the California Community Colleges." Sacramento: The Board, 1996.

California Higher Education Policy Center (CHEPC). "Financing the Plan: California's Master Plan for Higher Education, 1960 to 1994." San Jose: The Center, May 1995.

———. "State Structures for the Governance of Higher Education: A Comparative Study." San Jose: The Center, Spring 1997.

———. "California Higher Education Policy Vacuum: The Example of Student Fees." San Jose: The Center, April 1993.

California Postsecondary Education Commission (CPEC). "The Challenge of the Century: Planning for Record Student Enrollment & Improved Outcomes in California Postsecondary Education." *Commission Report 95-3*. Sacramento: The Commission, April 1995.

———. *The Master Plan, Then and Now: Policies of "A Master Plan for Higher Education 1960–1975" In Light of 1993 Realities*. Sacramento: The Commission, 1993.

California State University (CSU). Division of Business Affairs. "Resource Equity in the CSU." Long Beach: The System, November 1990.

California State University System (CSUS). "The Cornerstones Project: Strategic Planning at the California State University." Long Beach: The System, 1997.

————. "Statement of Rationale for an Increase in Administrative and Financial Authority of the California State University." Long Beach: The System, June 1992.

Callan, Patrick M. "The Gauntlet for Multicampus Systems." *Trusteeship* (May/June 1994): 16–19.

————. "Introduction." In J. McCurdy and W. Trombley, eds. *On the Brink: The Impact of Budget Cuts on California's Public Universities.* San Jose: California Higher Education Policy Center, May 1993.

————. "Multicampus Systems: Questions for the 1990s." Unpublished draft paper, 24 Feb. 1994.

————. "Perspectives on the Current Status and Emerging Policy Issues for State Coordinating Boards. *AGB Occasional Paper No. 2.* Washington DC: Association of Governing Boards of Colleges and Universities, 1991.

————. "Time for Decision: California's Legacy and the Future of Higher Education." In B. Goldstein, ed. *California's Master Plan for Higher Education in the Twenty-First Century.* San Francisco: American Association for the Advancement of Science, 1996: 85–92.

Caruthers, J .K., and J .L. Marks. *Funding Methods for Public Higher Education in the SREB States.* Atlanta: Southern Regional Education Board, 1994.

City University of New York. "Progress Report On Academic Program And Other Planning Activities." New York: City UP, 1 Dec. 1995.

Commission for the Review of the Master Plan for Higher Education (CRMP). "Issue Papers: The Master Plan Renewed." Sacramento: The Commission, August 1987.

————. Background Papers for "The Challenge of Change: A Reassessment of the California Community Colleges." Sacramento: The Commission, March 1986.

Commission on National Investment in Higher Education. *Breaking the Social Contract: The Fiscal Crisis in Higher Education.* Santa Monica, California: Council for Aid to Education (1997): 12. The Council is an independent subsidiary of RAND, a nonprofit organization, and the report is based on studies by RAND.

Condren, C. P. "Preparing for the Twenty-First Century: A Report on Higher Education in California Requested by the Organization for Economic Cooperation and Development." Sacramento: CPEC, 1988.

"Coordinating Boards." *AGB Occasional Paper No. 2.* Washington, DC: Association of Governing Boards of Colleges and Universities, 1991.

Creswell, J. W. "A Typology of Multicampus Systems." *Journal of Higher Education* (Jan./Feb. 1985): 26–37.

Daniel, John S. *Mega-Universities and Knowledge Media: Technology Strategies for Higher Education.* London: Kogan-Page, 1996.

————. "Why Universities Need Technology Strategies." *Change* 29 (Jul./Aug. 1997): 10–17.

Davies, Gordon K. "Higher Education Systems as Cartels: The End is Near." *Chronicle of Higher Education* (3 Oct. 1997): A68.

————. *Twenty Years of Higher Education in Virginia.* Richmond: State of Virginia Council of Higher Education, 1997: 26–27.

Douglass, John A. "Balancing Access with Quality: Creating California's Tripartite Higher Education System." Paper Presented at the Meeting of the National Academy of Education, University of Stockholm. 23 Sept. 1994.

————. "Isomorphism and the Quest for UCB's Raison d'être." *Viewpoint, in Coastlines: From USB.* Winter, 1993: 37–39.

————. "Major Transitions in the History of UC: A Summary for the Planning Retreat," Fall 1993.

Drucker, Peter. *Managing The Non-Profit Organization.* New York: Harper-Collins, 1990: 59.

————. *Management Tasks, Responsibilities and Practices.* New York: Harper-Row, 1973: 125.

Duderstadt, James. "Revolutionary Changes: Understanding the Challenges and the Possibilities." *Business Officer* 31 (July 1997): 32–39.

Duryea, E. D. "Evolution of University Organizations." In J. A. Perkins, ed. *The University as an Organization.* New York: McGraw-Hill, 1973.

Eaton, G. M., and J. Miyares. "Integrating Program Review in Planning and Budgeting: A Systemwide Perspective." In Using Program Review, *New Directions for Institutional Research* 86. San Francisco: Jossey-Bass, 1995: 69–79.

Edwards, M. "The Need to Understand the Conservative Identity." *Chronicle of Higher Education.* (5 Sept. 1997).

El-Khawas, Elaine. *Campus Trends 1994.* Washington DC: American Council of Higher Education, 1994.

Elliott, Peggy Gordon. *The Urban Campus: Educating the New Majority for the New Century.* Phoenix: Oryx Press, 1994.

Elsner, Paul. "Reinventing Governance: Maricopa Conducts Strategic Conversations." (April 15, 1996). Remarks delivered to the American Association of Community Colleges Annual Convention, Atlanta, Georgia, 15 April 1996.

Fisher, James L. "The Failure of Statewide Coordination." *Chronicle of Higher Education* 16 (June 1995): A48.

Folger, J. "Designing State Incentive Programs that Work." Paper presented at National Center for Postsecondary Education Governance and Finance Conference on State Fiscal Incentives, Denver, CO, Nov. 1988.

Foster, R. "Speaking of Leadership: Defining and Developing Institutional Leadership for the 21st Century." *Kellogg Leadership Forum on Institutional Change Report.* Austin, TX, Mar. 30–April 1, 1998.

Gade, Marian L. *Four Multicampus Systems: Some Policies and Practices that Work.* Washington, DC: Association of Governing Boards of Colleges and Universities, 1993.

Gaither, G., B. Nedwick, and J. Neal. "Measuring Up: The Promises and Pitfalls of Performance Indicators in Higher Education." *ASHE-ERIC Higher Education Report*

No. 5. Washington, DC: George Washington University Press, Graduate School of Education and Human Development, 1994.

Giamatti, A. Bartlett. *A Free and Ordered Space: The Real World of the University.* New York: W.W. Norton, 1988.

Gold, Steven, ed. *The Fiscal Crisis of the States: Lessons for the Future.* Washington DC: George Washington UP, 1995.

Graham, H. D. "Structure and Governance in American Higher Education: Historical and Comparative Analysis in State Policy." *Journal of Policy History* 1.1 (1989): 80–107.

Green, Kenneth C. "Money, Technology and Distance Education." *On the Horizon* (Nov./Dec. 1997): 1–3.

Greiner, W. R. "What SUNY Should Do: Promote General Strength by Supporting Individual Strengths." In *New Perspectives on System and Campus Roles In a Public Multi-Campus System. Studies in Higher Education* 5. Albany: State University of New York, 1994.

Halpern, D. F. "California's Master Scam." In B. Goldstein, ed. *California's Master Plan for Higher Education in the Twenty-first Century.* San Francisco: American Association for the Advancement of Science, 1996: 43–6.

Halstead, K. "State Profiles: Financing Public Higher Education: 1978 to 1997." *Trend Data.* Washington DC: Research Associates of Washington, 1997.

Hamel, Gary. "Killer Strategies that Make Shareholders Rich." *Fortune* 135 (23 June 1997): 70–84.

———. "Strategy as Revolution." *Harvard Business Review* 74 (Jul./Aug. 1996): 69–82.

Healy, Patrick. "Leaders of California's 2-Year College System Say Governance Structure Is at Breaking Point." *Chronicle of Higher Education* XLIV, 17 (19 Dec. 1997): 20–21.

Hines, E. R. *State Higher Education Appropriations 1988–89 Through 1996–97.* Denver: State Higher Education Executive Officers, 1989–1997.

Hooker, M. "Letter to the University Community." 1 Feb. 1995. In "Moving Toward the 21st Century: The President's Action Plan for the Year 2000." Amherst: University of Massachusetts Press, 1995.

Hopwood v. State of Texas. 78F.3rd 932. 5th Cir. 1996.

Jaschik, S. "1% Decline in State Support for Colleges Thought to be First 2-Year Drop Ever." *Chronicle of Higher Education* (21 Oct. 1992): 21.

Johnstone, D. Bruce. "Budget Options for SUNY in the Face of Additional Major Cuts in General Fund Appropriations" and "Explorations of Campus Closures in Response to Further Deep and Seemingly Permanent Cuts in Tax Support." *Studies in Public Higher Education* 2. Albany: State University of New York Press, Nov./Dec. 1991.

———. "Central Administration of Public Multicampus College and University Systems." Albany: State University of New York Press, 1992.

———. "Chancellor's Letter." *SUNY 2000: A Vision for The New Century.* Albany: State University of New York Press, Sept. 1991.

———. "Patterns of Finance: Revolution, Evolution, or More of the Same?" *The Review of Higher Education*. Mar. 1998 (forthcoming).

———. *Public Multicampus College and University Systems: Structures, Functions, and Rationale*. Washington DC: The National Association of System Heads [affiliated with the American Association of State Colleges and Universities and The National Association of State Universities and Land Grant Colleges], 1993.

Johnstone, Sally M., and Dennis Jones. "New Higher Education Trends Reflected in the Design of the Western Governors University." *On the Horizon*. (Nov./Dec. 1997): 8–11.

Joint Committee for Review of the Master Plan for Higher Education (JCRMP). "California Faces . . . California's Future: Education for Citizenship in a Multicultural Democracy." Sacramento: The Assembly, 1988.

Kauffman, Joseph F. "Supporting the President and Assessing the Presidency." In Richard T. Ingram and Associates *Governing Public Colleges and Universities: A Handbook for Trustees, Chief Executives, and Other Campus Leaders*. San Francisco: Jossey-Bass, 1993: 128.

Kerr, Clark. "Comments to CPEC." *California Postsecondary Education Commission, Report 93–21*, Oct. 1993.

———. "Comparative Effectiveness of Systems, Unknown and Unknowable." In Clark Kerr, et al. *12 Systems of Higher Education: 6 Decisive Issues*. New York: International Council for Educational Development, 1978.

———. " A Critical Age in the University World: Accumulated Heritage versus Modern Imperatives." *European Journal of Education* 22.2 (1987): 183–193.

———. "Foreword." In Eugene C. Lee and Frank M. Bowen *The Multicampus University: A Study of Academic Governance*. . New York: McGraw-Hill, 1971.

———. *The Great Transformation of Higher Education*. Albany: State University of New York, 1991.

Kerr, Clark, and Marian Gade. *The Guardians: Boards of Trustees of American Colleges and Universities: What They Do and How Will They Do It*. Washington DC: Association of Governing Boards of Universities and Colleges, 1989: 115-118.

Kinnick, Mary K., and Mary F. Ricks. "The Urban Public University in the United States: An Analysis of Change, 1977–1987." *Research in Higher Education* 31.1 (1990): 27.

Knutsen, K. "Beyond Business as Usual: A Framework and Options for Improving Quality and Containing Costs in California Higher Education." *An Occasional Paper from the California Research Bureau*. California State Library. 6 May 1993.

Langenberg, Donald N. "Degrees and Diplomas are Obsolescent." *Chronicle of Higher Education* (12 Sept. 1997): A64.

———. "Why a System? Understanding the Costs and Benefits of Joining Together." *Change* (Mar./Apr. 1994): 8–9.

Layzell, D. T., and J. K. Caruthers. "Performance Funding at the State Level: Trends and Prospects." Paper presented at 1995 Association for the Study of Higher Education Annual Meeting, Orlando, FL. Nov. 1995.

Leavitt, Michael O. "The Western Governors' University: A Learning Enterprise for the CyberCentury." In D. G. Oblinger and S. C. Rush, eds. *The Learning Revolution: The Challenge of Information Technology in the Academy*. Boston: Anker Publishing, 1997.

Lee, Eugene C., and Frank M. Bowen. *Managing Multicampus Systems*. [A Report for the Carnegie Council on Policy Studies in Higher Education.] San Francisco: Jossey Bass, 1975.

———. *The Multicampus University: A Study of Academic Governance*. New York: McGraw-Hill, 1971.

———. *The University of London: An American Perspective*. Berkeley: The Institute for Governmental Studies, 1989.

Lenzner, Robert, and Stephen S. Johnson. "Seeing Things as They Really Are." *Forbes* 10 (Mar. 1997): 122.

Liaison Committee of the State Board of Education and the Regents of the University of California. *A Master Plan for Higher Education in California 1960–1975*. Berkeley: University of California Press, 1960.

Lively, K. "Recovering From Recession." *Chronicle of Higher Education* (20 Jul. 1994): 17.

Lukenbill, Jeffrey D., and Robert H. McCabe. General Education in a Changing Society. Dubuque, IA: Kendall/Hunt, 1978

Lyall, Katharine C. "The Role of Governance in Systems." *Journal for Higher Education Management* 11.2 (Winter/Spring, 1996): 39–46.

MacTaggert, Terrence J., and Associates. *Restructuring Higher Education: What Works and What Doesn't in Reorganizing Governing Systems*. San Francisco: Jossey Bass, 1996.

Maricopa Community College District. *From Adobe Walls*, slide presentation, 1988.

Martinez, M. C., and T. Nodine. "California: Financing Higher Education Amid Policy." In Patrick Callan and J. E. Finney, eds. *Public and Private Financing of Higher Education: Shaping Public Policy for the Future*. Phoenix: Oryx Press, 1997.

Massachusetts Task Force. "Stabilizing The Commonwealth's Investment: Toward a Five-Year Financing Plan for Higher Education: A Report of the Massachusetts Task Force on Fair Share Funding for Higher Education." Boston, 15 Jun. 1994.

Mathews, J. "Ms. Machiavelli: City University of New York's Controversial Chairwoman." *National CROSSTALK: A Publication of the Higher Education Policy Institute* 5.3 (Fall 1997): 1, 15–16.

McCurdy, J. *Broken Promises: The Impact of Budget Cuts and Fee Increases on the California Community Colleges*. San Jose: CHEPC. Oct. 1994.

McGrath, C. P. *Governing the Public Multicampus University*. Washington, DC: Association of Governing Boards of Colleges and Universities, 1990.

McGuinness, Aims. C., Jr. "A Model for Successful Restructuring." In Terrence J. MacTaggart, ed. *Restructuring Higher Education: What Works and What Doesn't in Reorganizing Governing Systems*. San Francisco: Jossey-Bass, 1996.

———. "Perspectives on the Current Status of and Emerging Policy Issues for Public

Multicampus Higher Education Systems." *AGB Occasional Paper No. 3*. Washington, DC: Association of Governing Boards of Colleges and Universities, 1991.

McGuinness, Aims C., Jr., R. M. Epper, and S. Arredono. *State Postsecondary Education Structures Handbook*. Denver: Education Commission of the States, 1994.

McKeown, M. *State Funding Formulas for Public Four-Year Institutions*. Denver: State Higher Education Executive Officers, 1996.

Merron, Kenneth A. "Creating CQI Organizations." *QualityProgress* (Jan. 1994): 51–54.

Miami-Dade Community College, "Master Plan for Technology," as compiled by the Office of the Vice President and CIO for Information Systems and Educational Technology and the Collegewide Technology Committee, Florida: UP, n. d.

———"Recommendations of the Reengineering Teams for 1) Human Resource Development, 2) Facilities, and 3) Budget and Planning." Florida: UP, n. d.

———"Strategic Plan," as compiled by the Office of the Vice President for Planning & Development and the Department of Institutional Research, Florida: UP, n. d.

Middaugh, M. F. "Closing in on Faculty Productivity Measures." *In Planning for Higher Education* 24 (Winter 1995–96): 1–12.

———. "Instructional Costs and Productivity, by Academic Discipline: A National Study Revisited." A paper presented at the Annual Meeting of the Society for College and University Planning, Washington DC, July 1996.

Middaugh, Michael F., and David E. Hollowell. "Examining Academic and Administrative Productivity Measures." *New Directions for Institutional Research* 75 v19 no.3 (Fall 1992): 61–75.

Milestones. Prepared by the Marketing and Public Relations Department of the Maricopa Community Colleges. Phoenix, Maricopa Community Colleges, 1996.

Mingle, James R. "The Case for Coordinated Systems of Higher Education." Denver: State Higher Education Executive Officers, Sept. 1995.

Mingle, James R., and Rhonda Martin Epper. "State Coordination and Planning in an Age of Entrepreneurship." Unpublished paper, n.d. (1996 prox).

Munitz, B. *Compact II for Tidal Wave 2: Restoring the California Promise*. Long Beach: The California State University System, 1997.

Murdock, Steve. *Texas Challenged: An Assessment of the Implications of Population Change for Public Service Demand and Costs in Texas*. Department of Rural Sociology. College Station: Texas A&M University Press, 1996.

Newman, Frank. *Choosing Quality: Reducing Conflict Between the State and the University*. Denver: Education Commission of the States, 1987.

Nicholson, Patrick J. *In Time: An Anecdotal History of the First 50 Years of the University of Houston*. Houston: Pacesetter Press, 1977.

Norris, Donald M. *Revolutionary Strategy for the Knowledge Age*. Ann Arbor: Society for College and University Planning, 1998.

Norris, Donald M., and Donald Langenberg. "Expeditionary Strategy and Products for the Knowledge Age." *Reinventing the University: Managing and Financing Institutions of Higher Education.* 1998 ed. New York: John Wiley & Sons, forthcoming.

Norris, Donald M., and Theodore Roosevelt Malloch. *Unleashing the Power of Perpetual Learning.* Ann Arbor: Society for College and University Planning, 1998.

Office of the Attorney General. *Letter Opinion No. 97-001*, Austin, TX. 6 Feb. 1997.

O'Neil, Michael J. "The Maricopa Community Colleges: Mission, Culture, Seminal Events and Challenges." *O'Neil Associates, Inc. Study #97-1380.* Oct. 1997.

Organization for Economic Cooperation and Development (OECD). *Reviews of National Policies for Education: Higher Education in California.* Paris, France: OECD, 1990.

Pettit, L. K. "Ambiguities in the Administration of Public University Systems." In L. E. Goodell, ed. *When Colleges Lobby States.* Washington: American Association of State Colleges and Universities, 1987.

———. "Old Problems and New Responsibilities for University System Heads." Normal: Illinois State University [for the National Association of System Heads], 1989.

Pickens, W. "California Perspectives: Three Viewpoints." *Change* 21.5 (Sept./Oct. 1989): 43–51.

Richardson, R. C. "California Case Study Summary." Prepared for the CHEPC, *State Structures for the Governance of Higher Education.* San Jose: The Center, Spring 1997.

Riley, Richard W. *A Back to School Report: The Baby Boom Echo.* Washington, DC: U.S. Department of Education. 21 Aug. 1996.

Robbins, Stephen. *Organizational Behavior.* New Jersey: Prentice Hall, 1988.

Sanchez-Penley, Y., M. C. Martinez, and T. Nodine. "Florida: Protecting Access and Anticipating Growth: 1990–1995." In Patrick Callan and J. E. Finney, eds. *Public and Private Financing of Higher Education: Shaping Public Policy for the Future.* Phoenix: Oryx Press, 1997.

Sanders, K. R. "Report to the Board of Regents On UW System Administration Restructuring." University of Wisconsin System, May 1996.

Sanders, K. R., D. Layzell, and K. Boatright. "University of Wisconsin System's Use of Performance Indicators as Instruments Accountability." In G. H. Gaither, ed. *Performance Indicators in Higher Education: What Works, What Doesn't, and What's Next?* College Station: The Texas A&M University System, 1996.

Schick, E. B. *Shared Visions of Public Higher Education Governance: Structures and Leadership Styles.* Washington, DC: American Association of State Colleges and Universities, 1993.

Schrof, Joannie M. "America's Best Colleges: Community Colleges." *U.S. News & World Report* reprint, 1992.

Sell, K. R. "Linking Budgeting to Planning: The Wisconsin Case." In *Focus on the Budget: Rethinking Current Practice.* Denver: State Higher Education Executive Officers, 1994: 23–39.

Senge, Peter M. *The Fifth Discipline: The Art and Practice of the Learning Organization*. New York: Doubleday-Dell, 1990.

Shevory, K. "Berdahl Leaves Political Conflict of UT Austin Presidency." *The Daily Californian* 11 Jul. 1997.

Stadtman, Verne A. *The University of California: 1868–1968*. New York: MacMillan, 1970.

State Higher Education Executive Officers. "State Survey on Performance Measures." Preliminary results. Denver: State Higher Education Executive Officers, August 1997.

State University of New York. "SUNY 2000: A Vision for The New Century." Albany: State University of New York, 1991.

State University of New York Board of Trustees. "Rethinking SUNY." Albany: State University of New York, 1995.

Stukel, James J. "Urban and Metropolitan Universities: Leaders of the 21st Century." *Metropolitan Universities* 5.2 (1994): 87–92.

Texas Higher Education Coalition. The Competitive Edge: the Economic Future and Higher Education. Austin: The Coalition, 1996.

Texas Higher Education Coordinating Board. *Baccalaureate Graduation Rates: Appendix A*. Austin: THECB, Oct. 1996.

———. *Memorandum on Schedule of Revenue and Expenditure per FTSE*. Austin: THECB, 1996.

———. *Revenue and Expenditures per FTE Student, FY 1995 and FY 1996*. Austin: THECB, 1996.

Technology and Restructuring Roundtable. *Leveraged Learning*. Stanford: Stanford Forum for Higher Education Futures, 1995.

Trombley, William. "Performance-Based Budgeting: South Carolina's New Plan Mired in Detail and Confusion." In *National CrossTalk* [a periodic publication of the Higher Education Policy Institute, now the National Center for Public Policy and Higher Education]. San Jose, CA. Winter 1998.

Twigg, Carol A. *Academic Productivity: The Case for Instructional Software*. A Report from The Broadmoor Roundtable. Washington, DC: Educom, 1996. (Available at http://www.educause.edu/nlii/keydocs/broadmoor.html.)

University of California (UC). "1997–98 Budget for Current Operations." Oakland: Office of the President, Oct. 1996.

University of Houston Office of Planning & Policy Analysis. *Fall 1997 Ethnicity by Student Level and Classification*. Houston: University of Houston Press, 1997.

University of Houston System. *Beyond the Horizon: The Vision for 2015*. Houston: University of Houston Press, 1997.

———. *Working Smarter: A Progress Report*. Houston: University of Houston Press, 1997.

Vines, Diane, Barbara Thorpe, and Robert Threlkeld. "California Higher Education Extends Its Reach." *On the Horizon* (Nov./Dec. 1997): 11–14.

Washington State Higher Education Coordinating Board. *1994–95, 1995–96, 1996–97 Tuition And Fee Rates: A National Comparison.* Olympia: Washington State Higher Education Coordinating Board, 1995, 1996, 1997.

"What Does the Public Want from Higher Education?" *NASULGC Newsline* 4.8 (Oct. 1995): 7.

Womack, Farris W., and Richard S. Podemski. "Criteria for Effective Planning in Multicampus Systems." *Planning for Higher Education* 13.2 (Winter 1985): 1–4.

Zemsky, R., and W. Massy. "Cost Containment." *Change* 22.6 (1990): 16–22.

Gerald (Jerry) H. Gaither is Director of Institutional Effectiveness, Research, and Analysis at the Prairie View A&M University campus of the Texas A&M University System. He has held positions in planning and institutional research in three state systems, and has served as a faculty member. He has also served as a Senior Fulbright Professor of Planning and Management in the Philippines. His many publications focus on planning, institutional research, and financing of higher education. His recent writings on higher education as coauthor, editor, and contributor include *Measuring Up: Promises and Pitfalls of Performance Measures* (1994), *Assessing Performance in an Age of Accountability* (1995), and *Quality Assurance in Higher Education: An International Perspective* (1998). He is currently a member of the editorial board of the *AIR Professional File,* and The Society for College and University Planning's (SCUP) *Journal of Planning.*

He received his B.S. degree from Appalachian State University (1964), and his M.A. (1967) and Ph.D. (1972) from the University of Tennessee, Knoxville. He also has a postdoctoral degree in Business Management from the University of Kentucky, Lexington (1977).

Kevin J. Boatright is assistant vice president for university relations at the University of Wisconsin (UW) System. Prior to joining the System Administration in 1992 as special assistant to the vice president for university relations, he was director of university communications and special projects at UW-Platteville and, previously, assistant publications administrator at the University of Northern Iowa. His academic background includes an M.S. degree (1997) in higher education administration from UW-Madison, an M.A.

degree (1984) in history from the University of Northern Iowa, an M.A. degree (1975) in journalism from the University of Iowa, and a B.A. degree (1974) from Nebraska Wesleyan University. He is currently a doctoral student in higher education administration at UW-Madison.

Frank Bowen is a consultant in higher education governance and administration. He has held positions with the State of California in the Governor's Office and in the State Department of Finance, and, at the University of California at Berkeley, with the Center for Research and Development in Higher Education and the Institute of Governmental Studies. Most recently Bowen was a consultant to the California Higher Education Policy Center, and currently is a consultant to the recently established National Center for Public Policy and Higher Education. He received his B.S. degree from the United States Military Academy and his J.D. degree from the University of Michigan Law School. With Eugene C. Lee, Bowen coauthored *The Multicampus University: A Study of Academic Governance* (1971), *Managing Multicampus Systems: Effective Administration in an Unsteady State* (1975), and *The University of London: An American Perspective* (1989).

Joseph J. Burke is Director of the Public Higher Education Program of the Rockefeller Institute of Government and State University Professor of Higher Education Policy and Management. He combines broad administrative experiences with active research interests. Burke served for nine years as Provost and a year as Interim Chancellor of the State University of New York at Plattsburgh. As SUNY Provost, he initiated a campus-based program of outcomes assessment, a System Performance Report, a major initiative in graduate studies and research, and plans for transforming SUNY's teaching hospitals into public benefit of private corporations. He has written and lectured widely on higher education topics: performance funding and reporting, system governance, autonomy and accountability, and outcomes assessment. Burke is currently conducting a national study of state performance funding for public higher education, supported by the Pew Charitable Trusts. A second national project examines how public higher education in six states responded to the budget problems of the 1990s; it is funded by the Henry Luce Foundation. He received a B.A. (1954) from Bellarmine College in history and philosophy and an M.A. (1958) and a Ph.D. (1965) in history from Indiana University.

J. Kent Caruthers is a Senior Partner with MGT of America, Inc., a national research and management consulting firm that specializes in higher education. He earned his bachelor's, master's, and doctor's degrees from Oklahoma State University in finance and higher education administration.

Much of Dr. Caruthers' consulting practice focuses on planning and funding issues that face state systems of higher education. Since joining MGT in 1980, his engagements have included assignments with 35 systems in 27 states. Dr. Caruthers is active in numerous educational planning and management organizations and is a frequent contributor to the professional literature. His current research interests include performance funding and student access to postsecondary education. He also has collaborated on funding-related projects with the Southern Regional Education Board, the American Association of State Colleges and Universities, and the State Higher Education Executive Officers on several different occasions.

Prior to becoming a full-time consultant, Dr. Caruthers served as director of strategic planning for the National Center for Higher Education Management Systems (NCHEMS), director of planning and budgeting for the State University System of Florida, and coordinator of institutional research and planning at Oklahoma State University.

Laura Helminski is a faculty member at Rio Salado College. She has taught Reading, English, and Communication courses on the community college level for over 20 years and has taught on-line Communication and Reading courses for two years. She is the Faculty Senate President, the Faculty Chair for Reading and Communication, chair of the Student Achievement Committee, a member of the College Leadership council, a TQM Coach and trainer, and is Faculty Development Coordinator. She is currently working on her Ph.D., focusing on changing faculty roles in higher education.

Laura has worked with educators in many states on increasing student achievement. She has completed training and research in Systems Thinking and Learning Organization Theory. Laura has conducted numerous faculty development sessions, and has given presentations across the state and country on organizational change in higher education. She was Rio Salado's Faculty of the Year for 1991–92, and Innovator of the Year in 1988.

Lt. Gov. William P. Hobby is the Radoslav Tsanoff Professor at Rice University and chairman of the Texas Commission on a Representative Student Body. He served as Lieutenant Governor of Texas from 1973 to 1991 and as Chancellor of the University of Houston System from 1995 to 1997. He is former Sid Richardson Professor of Public Affairs at the Lyndon B. Johnson School of Public Affairs, University of Texas at Austin. He was President of the Houston Post for nearly 21 years when the family sold the newspaper in 1982. He then served as Chairman of the Board of H&C Communications until his retirement in 1996. He has been a Naval Intelligence officer, Senate Parliamentarian, Texas Parks and Wildlife Commissioner, member of the Education Commission of the States, the Board of Overseers of the John F. Kennedy School of Government at Harvard University, and the Formula Advisory Committee of the Texas Higher Education Coordinating Board. He is President Emeritus of the Texas Senate, distinguished alumnus of Rice University, and has received the Santa Rita Award from the University of Texas System Board of Regents. Hobby was educated at St. Albans School and received a B.A. degree in American History from Rice University in 1953. He has the following honorary degrees: Doctor of Laws, University of Houston; Doctor of Laws, Austin College; Doctor of Humanities in Medicine, Baylor College of Medicine; and Doctor of Humane Letters, St. Edwards University.

D. Bruce Johnstone is University Professor of Higher and Comparative Education at the State University of New York at Buffalo. His teaching and research interests combine economics, finance, and governance of colleges and universities in both domestic and international contexts. He is director of the Learning Productivity Network, which studies productivity from the vantage of enhancing higher education's outputs, and is currently studying college-level learning in high school. He has studied and written about student finance, particularly tuition policy and student loans, and has been tracking the shift of the higher education cost burden from government to families in other countries, including China, Russia, and other countries that have emerged from the former Soviet Union.

From 1979 to 1988, Johnstone was president of the State University College at Buffalo. From 1988 to 1994, he was chancellor of the State University of New York system, where he continued to research and write about, as well as to practice, the finance, governance, and politics of higher education.

Johnstone received his B.A. (1963) and M.A.T. (1964) degrees from Harvard University and his Ph.D. (1969) from the University of Minnesota.

Donald N. Langenberg is an eminent physicist and a nationally known advocate for higher education. Chancellor Donald N. Langenberg has shaped The University of Maryland System (USM) throughout its formative years—streamlining its academic programs, restructuring its administrative enterprise, and developing measures of productivity and accountability now in use by universities around the nation.

Before coming to Maryland, Dr. Langenberg held both academic and government posts. He was chancellor of the University of Illinois at Chicago, acting director and deputy director of the National Science Foundation, and professor of physics at the University of Pennsylvania. At Penn, where he directed the Laboratory for Research on the Structure of Matter, he also served as Vice Provost for Graduate Studies and Research.

Dr. Langenberg is currently president of the National Association of System Heads and serves on numerous boards, including those of the University of Pennsylvania and the Alfred P. Sloan Foundation. He has been president and chairman of the board of the American Association for the Advancement of Science, chairman of the board of the National Association of State Universities and Land-Grant Colleges, and president of the American Physical Society. He chairs the National Reading Panel.

Dr. Langenberg holds degrees in physics from Iowa State University, UCLA, and University of California, Berkeley. His fields of specialization include materials science and experimental condensed-matter physics. His work on superconductivity led to a new type of voltage standard now in use worldwide.

Daniel T. Layzell is a Principal with MGT of America, a national research and management consulting firm that specializes in higher education. He earned his bachelor's in economics and business administration from Illinois College (1985), his master's in labor and industrial relations from the University of Illinois—Urbana Champaign (1986), and his Ph.D. in higher education administration from The Florida State University (1988).

Dr. Layzell's consulting practice has focused on planning and funding issues pertaining to public institutions and systems of higher education, including statewide master planning, performance-based funding, program needs assessments, and enrollment management. Dr. Layzell is also a frequent contributor to the professional literature.

Prior to becoming a full-time consultant, Dr. Layzell was Director of Policy Analysis and Research for the University of Wisconsin System, research/fiscal analyst with the Arizona Joint Legislative Budget Committee, and Assistant Director for Fiscal Affairs with the Illinois Board of Higher Education.

Eugene C. Lee is a professor of political science emeritus at the University of California at Berkeley, where he served as director of the Institute of Governmental Studies from 1967 to 1988. A former vice president of the university, he had responsibility for managing the reorganization of the systemwide administration, focusing on system-campus relationships, that took place from 1958 to 1966. He was also first chairman of the Commission on California State Government Organization and Economy (the state's "Little Hoover Commission"). Lee received his B.A. degree from UCLA and his M.A. and Ph.D. degrees from Berkeley, while also serving in the campus administration. He has held other university teaching and administrative posts at University College, Dar es Salaam, Tanzania, and at the University of Puerto Rico.

An advisor to state and local governments and to several state university systems, Lee has served as staff consultant to the California Congressional Delegation and to the Special Masters on Redistricting of the California Supreme Court. His research has focused on the fields of state, regional, and local government, and the administration of higher education. His writings on higher education, coauthored with Frank Bowen, include *The Multicampus University: A Study of Academic Governance* (1971), *Managing Multicampus Systems: Effective Administration in an Unsteady State* (1975), and *The University of London: An American Perspective* (1989). Other writings include *The Politics of Nonpartisanship* (1960) and *The Challenge of California* (1976).

Theodore Levitt has served as Project Manager in Miami-Dade Community College's Reengineering Project since its inception in 1995. The project has addressed diverse areas of college functioning including human resource development, planning and budget, maintenance of college facilities, and all aspects of student services. He has also contributed to the college's Education Review, serving on the A.S. taskforce reviewing core curriculum and occupational programs. He is coauthor, with Eduardo J. Padrón, of a chapter on General Education in a 1996 anthology. Prior to the above assignment, he served as Director of Conferences for the Wolfson Campus. His background includes several years of study and work in clinical psychology and group dynamics. He holds a Master's Degree in Psychology from Duquesne University.

Jeffery D. Lukenbill has served as the College Provost of Miami-Dade Community College since May 1997. For the prior 12 years, he served as Dean of Academic Affairs at M-DCC's North Campus. Before going to the North Campus, he was District Dean of Academic Affairs at the District Office. He received his Bachelor's in English from Catholic University, a Master's in Linguistics from the University of Michigan, a Master's in Education from Johns Hopkins University, and his Doctorate in Education from Nova University. His work at M-DCC has included being the Director of a CollegeWide General Education Project and helping to establish the School for Advanced Studies, a dual enrollment program operated with Miami-Dade County Public Schools. He has served on numerous boards of national organizations, including the Southern Region of the College Board, the American Bar Association's Commission on College and University Legal Studies, and the National Council of Institutional Administrators.

Michael F. Middaugh is Assistant Vice President for Institutional Research and Planning and Assistant Professor of Educational Leadership at the University of Delaware, where he also serves as Director of the FIPSE-funded National Study of Instructional Costs and Productivity. He was a member of the NASULGC/AASCU/AACC Joint Commission on Accountability Reporting from 1995–97 and directed their Pilot Study on Faculty Activity Reporting. He has been in the field of institutional research and planning for nearly 20 years. He is a past president of the North East Association for Institutional Research and Planning Officers, a past Board Member and 1997 Forum Chair of the Association for Institutional Research, and is the 1999 Conference Chair for the Society for College and University Planning. He has written extensively on the theory and practice of institutional research and planning, and has for the past several years focused his research interests in the area of instructional costs and productivity.

Donald M. Norris is President of Strategic Initiatives, Inc., a management consulting firm in Herndon, Virginia. Norris has assisted leading-edge corporations, colleges and universities, and associations in realigning to the challenges and opportunities of the Knowledge Age. He is a Senior Fellow at the Institute for Educational Transformation at George Mason University. Norris has over 25 years of experience as a reseacher, administrator, consultant, and author. He has written a Transformation Trilogy for the Society for College and University Planning and dozens of other articles and books on strategic thinking and organizational transformation. He holds a B.S. in Engineering Mechanics (1970), an M.B.A. (1972) from Virginia Tech, and a Ph.D. from The Center for the Study of Higher Education at The University of Michigan (1976).

Eduardo J.Padrón holds a Ph.D. in Economics from the University of Florida. He was appointed President of the Miami-Dade Community College District, including five campuses and several outreach centers, in October 1995. He had served as President of Miami-Dade's Wolfson Campus since 1980.

For over twenty-five years, Dr. Padrón has played key leadership roles both nationally and in the Miami community and is best recognized for his efforts to advance educational opportunity and his innovative approaches to teaching and learning. Student access and retention and the development of new instructional technologies are among his foremost priorities, drawing praise throughout academia. He has served as chairman of the governing board of the Hispanic Association of Colleges and Universities (HACU), as well as holding leadership positions with the American Association of Community Colleges (AACC), the American Council on Education (ACE), and the College Board.

Dr. Padrón has been appointed to posts of national prominence by former President Jimmy Carter and President Bill Clinton, and has served in an advisory capacity to former Secretaries of State Edmund Muskie and Cyrus Vance, and former U.S. Secretary of Education Shirley Hufstedler. More recently, he was appointed to President Clinton's Summit of the Americas Steering Committee and the National Advisory Commission on Educational Excellence for Hispanic Americans. President Clinton has publicly recognized Dr. Padrón as "one of America's outstanding educators."

William H. Pickens is currently the Director of the California citizens' Commission on Higher Education, a blue ribbon group of prominent individuals who are conducting a comprehensive review of higher education in California followed by a set of recommendations.

Pickens has served in senior professional and leadership roles in universities, state agencies, and consulting organizations. He was Deputy Director for Fiscal Analysis and Executive Director of the California Postsecondary Education Commission (1978 to 1988) and Associate Vice President for Administration at California State University (1989 to 1994). Most recently, he was Senior Partner in the nationwide consulting firm, MGT of America, Inc., where his specialty was planning, budgeting, fiscal analysis, strategic planning, and management improvement in colleges and universities (1994 to 1996).

Pickens received a Ph.D. from the University of California at Davis in U. S. Economic History. He has been a Visiting Scholar at the Center for Studies in Higher Education at UC Berkeley and an adjunct professor in the School of Education at UC Berkeley and in the Public Policy Program at CSU Sacramento.

Pickens has published numerous articles and studies on management, planning, and public policy issues in higher education. He is a frequent speaker at national conferences on improving the quality and ethics of higher education administration.

Donna J. Schober is the Director of Employee and Organizational Learning with the Maricopa County Community College District. In that position she and her staff are responsible for employee training and learning opportunities, organizational change initiatives including the people, process, and organizational changes associated with a major technology effort, and work with the Governing Board on board processes. Formerly she served as Executive Assistant to the Chancellor, Dr. Paul Elsner, at the Maricopa district where she was responsible for a variety of special projects and representation on behalf of the Chancellor. She had major responsibilities in facilitating the Quantum Quality Initiative, including development of the District's Vision and Mission Statements and training agenda, and working with the Quantum Quality Executive Council and the Chancellor's Financial Advisory Council. Ms. Schober has worked closely with the Governing Board as they developed and implemented the concepts of Strategic Conversation and Policy Governance. In addition, Ms. Schober served as Maricopa's Project Manager for the Pew Charitable Trusts Restructuring Project for Higher Education and the American Council on Education–Kellogg Project on Leadership and Institutional Transformation. Ms. Schober also serves as an adjunct faculty member for Rio Salado College. In addition, she is a volunteer mediator with the Arizona Attorney General's Office.

Prior to her work with Chancellor Elsner, she served as Executive Director of the Arizona Community College Association, where she had overall responsibility for directing and administering the activities of this statewide, nonprofit association of community college presidents and district governing board members.

Ms. Schober has a law degree from the University of Wisconsin Law School in Madison. She is a member of the State Bar of Arizona and the State Bar of Wisconsin. She has an undergraduate degree from the School of Education, History major, Political Science minor, University of Wisconsin-Oshkosh.

Joseph J. Szutz is Assistant Vice Chancellor for Planning with the Board of Regents, University System of Georgia. He has held positions in higher education planning throughout his career. Before joining the University System of Georgia in 1986, he held positions in facilities, academic, and strategic planning at the Texas Higher Education Coordinating Board, Texas A&I University, and The University System of South Texas. Szutz was awarded his B.A. degree (1965) in history and his MAPA degree (1971) in public administration from the University of Minnesota–Twin Cities, and his M.Ed. degree (1979) and Ph.D. degree (1984) in Foundations of Education from the University of Texas at Austin. He is currently concluding his second two-year term as Secretary of the Society for College and University Planning, where he has served on the board of directors since 1990 and the executive committee since 1992. Since 1997, he also has served the Society as a member of the editorial review board for the journal *Planning for Higher Education*.

Linda M. Thor is President of Rio Salado College, Tempe, Arizona. Rio Salado, which serves some 24,000 credit and 12,000 noncredit students annually, is one of the ten colleges that comprise the Maricopa Community Colleges. Rio Salado is a nontraditional college, which specializes in serving accelerated programs. Prior to joining Rio Salado in 1990, Dr. Thor was President of West Los Angeles College. That appointment in 1986 followed 12 years of service to the Los Angeles Community College District as Senior Director of Occupational and Technical Education, Director of High Technology Programs, and Director of Communications Services. She received a B.A. degree in journalism from Pepperdine University, an M.P.A. degree from California State University, Los Angeles, and an Ed.D. degree from Pepperdine University.

Saralee Tiede, a journalist and public administrator, served as Deputy Chancellor of the University of Houston System during 1996 and 1997, and as project coordinator of the Lyndon B. Johnson School of Public Affairs, University of Texas at Austin, in 1994 and 1995. She is now director of information and education of the Public Utility Commission of Texas. She has also served as Deputy Commissioner of Health and Human Services and Deputy Commissioner of the General Land Office of Texas. She has been Executive Assistant to the Lieutenant Governor of Texas and a reporter on the Dallas Morning News, the Dallas Times Herald, the Houston Chronicle, the Fort Worth Star-Telegram and the Rochester Times-Union. She has been awarded the Outstanding Woman in State Government Award for leadership. Tiede received a B.A. degree in journalism and political science from Pennsylvania State University in 1963.